mber 1577

16 October 1579

26 March 1580

DRAKE

By the same author:

THE MIGHTY HOOD

THE GREAT SIEGE: Malta 1565

ULYSSES FOUND

DRAKE

by

Ernle Bradford

HODDER AND STOUGHTON

First printed 1965

Printed in Great Britain for Hodder and Stoughton Ltd., St. Paul's House,
Warwick Lane, London, E.C.4 by The Camelot Press Ltd.,
London and Southampton

FOR

My Mother

'The wind commands me away. Our ships are under sail. God grant we may so live in His fear as the enemy may have cause to say that God doth fight for Her Majesty as well abroad as at home.

'Haste! From aboard Her Majesty's good ship the Elizabeth Bonaventure, this 2nd April, 1587.'

Sir Francis Drake

Preface

DRAKE long ago passed into the Pantheon of Heroes of the English-speaking world. Like Nelson, he has become a byword for courage, audacity, and the seamanlike qualities of patience and endurance. But, unlike Nelson, he is usually seen as a somewhat shadowy figure. He is not known to have had a romantic private life, something to whet the appetite of biographers, playwrights, or film-makers—those fabricators of modern mythology. He has tended to become one of those legendary figures to whom lip service is paid, but who is rarely thought of as having been a living, breathing, human being—with all the compounded virtues and vices that go to make up a complex and unusual man.

Like certain other heroic figures, Drake has been put aside on that special shelf which is reserved for men who seem a 'little more than human'. Yet, as even a cursory examination of the facts of his life reveals, Drake was much more than a simple Elizabethan 'sea-dog'. If we know little or nothing about his private life, his public life is extremely well documented. He emerges as an extraordinary example of a self-made man, as a navigator of outstanding brilliance, a genius of naval warfare, and as an astonishingly able partisan-leader. He was a legend in his own lifetime.

As his contemporary, the historian John Stow, wrote of him: 'He was also of perfect memory, great observation, eloquent by nature, skilful in artillery . . . In brief, he was as famous in Europe and America, as Tamberlane in Asia and Africa.' If Drake was no more than that, he would still command attention, even though he might seem to have little relevance to inhabitants of the western world in the second half of the 20th century. But he has another and greater claim upon our attention—he was far in advance of his age in his humanity and compassion. His treatment of Spanish prisoners, his conduct towards Negroes and American Indians and his consideration towards his own sailors mark him as exceptional in his own age, and still worthy of emulation in ours. As a seaman he was the first to realise that there could be no distinctions of caste or class aboard ship, but that 'the gentleman must haul and draw with the mariner, and the mariner with the gentleman'. He thus anticipated by some 400 years the democratic navies of today. If England had taken his lesson properly to heart, she would have had a far more efficient fleet in the first half of the 20th century.

Drake, and his life and his times, held a particular fascination for Victorian biographers and historians. They felt that they had inherited an empire which he, more than almost any other, had helped to prepare for them. Sir Julian Corbett—to whom all subsequent students of Drake must always remain grateful—took as the epigraph for his *Drake and the Tudor Navy* Sir Walter Raleigh's saying: 'Whosoever commands the sea commands the trade; whosoever commands the trade of the world commands the riches of the world, and consequently the world itself.'

Such a statement may seem questionable nowadays, when it is apparent that only a giant land-mass can enable a nation to withstand the assault of modern war, as well as to own those natural resources without which an industrial society can hardly flourish. If, for a modern Englishman, Drake means less in terms of his successful exploitation of sea-power, he has a new interest in being one of the first practitioners of 'brinkmanship'. In this, he must inevitably be seen as the instrument of Queen Elizabeth, that remarkable woman who understood better perhaps than any before or since how to handle the conduct of 'a cold war'. The Queen's virginity, or more accurately, her potential marriageability, took the place in 16th-century Europe of the modern 'balance of terror'. Throughout her lifetime she held a Damocles' sword over the head of Philip II, and the thing that made her potential alliance with another European ruler so dangerous to Spain was the English Navy—which Drake, more than any other man, had forged into a terrifying weapon of war.

Drake had few of the courtier's graces which enhanced such royal favourites as Raleigh, Leicester or Essex. Nevertheless, he managed to amass a fortune, endear himself to the Queen, and keep his head. From the moment that he had, as it were, declared a 'personal war' against Philip II, he consciously set himself against the largest empire that the world had ever known. He inflicted more damage upon it than whole nations or large armies ever managed to do. Drake was a living proof that—notwithstanding certain modern theories—one individual can indeed change the course of history.

In the past twenty-five years I have been fortunate enough to sail small boats over many of the seas, and visit many of the places, which Drake knew 'when all the world was young'. A great number of the places—the Canary Islands, the Cape Verde Islands, and the Atlantic seaports of Spain and Portugal—have not greatly changed since Drake first came rolling down towards them in his small square-rigged ships. It is not true that, as Tristan Corbière wrote, '*La mer . . . elle n'est plus* marin!' Seen from the deck of a small sailing boat, the sea is as it ever was—unpredictable and uncorrupted. Perhaps it is no real advantage for the biographer of a naval hero to have a close acquaintanceship with the places and the seas that his subject once knew. Yet I cannot help thinking that all the libraries of the world will not help towards an understanding of the relationship between Drake and Doughty so much as a transatlantic passage in a 20-ton boat.

For assistance and information over the past years, I am particularly indebted to A. A. Cummings, F.M.A., of the City Museum and Art Gallery, Plymouth, and to W. Best Harris, F.L.A., Librarian of the City of Plymouth. I would also like to express my thanks to the authorities of the National Maritime Museum, Greenwich, the British Museum, and the London Library. I am also indebted to the University of California, the California Historical Society, and to the *Mariner's Mirror*—that invaluable publication in which Professor E. G. R. Taylor and others have made so many notable contributions to Drake scholarship. I owe a considerable debt of thanks to Francis Dillon of the B.B.C. for many stimulating conversations about Drake; for his radio play *The World Encompassed*; and for his assistance in the matter of old ballads and songs relating to Sir Francis Drake.

As a Zen Buddhist saying has it, 'Unless at one time the perspiration has streamed down your back, you cannot see the boat sailing before the wind.' Although I can hardly feel that I have made any startling discoveries about Drake, I felt, as I read about him, that I was discovering a man where before, for myself at least, there had only been an impersonal hero. I hope that I may perhaps help others to see him and his ship, alive and vital 'sailing before the wind'.

Contents

Preface   7

1. Voyage into Sunset   17

2. A Child of His Time   25

3. Apprenticeship   32

4. The Dedicated Man   42

5. The Islands and the Main   61

6. The Treasure Trains   80

7. Outward Bound   94

8. Straits of Magellan   105

9. Into the Great South Sea   118

10. New Albion   130

11. Beyond the Spice Islands   140

12. Sailor's Return   146

13. The Glorious Year   156

14. The Enemy   170

15. The Giant Stirs   185

16. The Great Armada sails   192

17. The Narrow Seas   198

18. The Winds of God   216

19. Failure of an Expedition   223

20. Drake Ashore   232

21. The End of a Voyage   239

    Select Bibliography   245

    Index   247

Plates

Facing Page

Sir Francis Drake   96

Sir John Hawkins   97

The *Golden Hind*   112

The Drake coat of arms   112

Buckland Abbey   113

Maps

The Isthmus of Panama   43

Drake's Outward Voyage to Peru and New Albion   107

Drake in the West Indies   157

Cartagena   159

Cadiz   171

The Course of the Armada   199

The route of Drake's circumnavigation   *Endpaper*

CHAPTER ONE

Voyage into Sunset

It was August 1595 and the slopes of Plymouth Hoe were patterned with men, women and children eager to see their first and greatest citizen preparing to set sail. Landsmen, but almost all of them allied in one way or another to the sea, they knew through whose grace it was that their clothes sat snug upon them, that *enseignes* sparkled in the merchants' hats, and enamelled galleons sailed on the breasts of their women. Their children drank the clean water that he had (almost miraculously it seemed) conveyed down from the bare ridges of Dartmoor into their city. But for him there might have been no city standing, and but for him certainly no press of shipping would have been sidling alongside the quays of the Barbican or riding in the lee of St. Nicholas's Island. Soon his ships would be leaving Plymouth.

After years of eclipse and royal disfavour, the Member of Parliament for Plymouth and—appropriately enough—for King Arthur's Tintagel, was about to embark once more for the scene of his youthful triumphs. His destination was the warm Caribbean sea, the islands broomed by the north-easterly trade winds—the golden lifeline of Spain. This was to be no piratical escapade, but an expedition that had the blessing of the Queen, and one from which it was hoped the whole kingdom would reap some benefit. When two such names as Sir Francis Drake and Sir John Hawkins were coupled together in a venture, it was reasonable to expect that any investment would pay ample dividends.

It was true that neither of the men was young: Sir John Hawkins was in his sixties—a good age for those days—while Drake himself was in his middle fifties. Both of the men had been out of favour, and it was surprising perhaps that the Queen should have placed them in joint command of an expedition at such a stage in their lives. But the Queen too was ageing and it is possible that she hoped, like many another gambler, to bring off a coup by backing the names that had proved magical in her youth. Then again, like any ruler or statesman, she could only make use of such talent as was available to her. The disgrace

of Raleigh, and the deaths of Grenville and Frobisher, had removed
some of the brightest stars from her military heaven.

Sir William Monson in his *Naval Tracts* wrote that: 'These two
generals [Sir John Hawkins and Sir Francis Drake], presuming much
upon their own experience and knowledge, used many arguments to
persuade the Queen to undertake this voyage to the West Indies,
assuring her what great services they should perform, and promising to
engage very deeply in the adventure themselves, both with their substance and their persons: and such was the opinion every one had
conceived of these two valiant Commanders, that great were the
expectations of the success of this voyage.' Unusual for those days,
there was no need for pressed men to man the ships. The lure of Drake's
name was so great that volunteers came in their hundreds, and many
of them had to be sent back to their homes.

The Queen herself had put at the disposal of her admirals some of
the finest ships in her Navy. The *Defiance*, Drake's flagship, and the
Garland, Vice-Admiral Hawkins' ship, were both new vessels of the
Revenge class. They were 95 feet on the keel, with a beam of 33 feet,
and a draught of 16 feet. Rated at some 700 tons, their main armament
consisted of sixteen culverins which fired a 17-lb. ball, a secondary
armament of fourteen demi-culverins or 9 pounders, four minions or
4 pounders, and four quick-firing guns. Other Naval vessels were the
Bonaventure, *Hope*, *Foresight* and *Adventure*, the last being commanded
by Captain Thomas Drake, a brother of the admiral. Twelve chartered
merchantmen made up the bulk of the squadron. Sir Thomas Baskerville, whose reputation was at its peak after his success in capturing
Brest, was appointed Commander of the Land Forces. All in all, there
seemed every reason for confidence in the expedition, and the news
that Drake was about to sail for the West Indies caused such a panic
on the continent that the Spanish exchequer declared a moratorium.
Thousands of her soldiers deserted the colours. Lisbon was abandoned
by every citizen who could afford to, and an English spy had reported
to Lord Burghley that in all Spain there was 'no talk of anything but
Drake'.

The expedition had been designed to sail in the spring of that year,
but intrigue at court and the Queen's notorious inability to commit
herself to a decision had delayed it for month after month. Supplies
which should not have been broached until the ships were at sea were
eaten up, and men who had been willing volunteers had already started
to desert. Drake, who had sold the lease of his London house in order
to invest in the expedition, was distraught at the delay, while Sir John
Hawkins was both irritated and dismayed. The idea of a divided

command was the Queen's, and it was unfortunate that, kinsmen though they were, there was no great affection between Drake and his distinguished relative. At one point early in their lives something had happened which seems to have strained their relationship—but that was long ago now. Hawkins, indeed, had over the years invested in some of Drake's projects, but the two men had not sailed together on an expedition since the disaster at San Juan de Ulua in 1567.

While Hawkins was an admirable organiser and could stand the long wait, having amply provisioned and victualled his ships, Drake was the same opportunist that he had always been. As July went by, it was reported that he was being forced to scour the West Country to get provisions for the men in his half of the squadron. Although the two commanders preserved their superficial appearance of friendship and unanimity, sufficient to deceive the citizens of Plymouth or the rank and file of the fleet, those who were in a position to know recognised the friction that existed between them. As one of their captains wrote about their attitude towards each others' subordinates: 'Whom the one loved, the other smally esteemed.'

From the start, the aim of the expedition had been to capture Panama. This was a scheme that had haunted Drake since the first days when he had cruised the Caribbean and landed on the hot shores of the Spanish Main. By capturing the great city of the Spanish Western Empire he would cut the lifeline by which the gold of Peru was channelled to the waiting ships of King Philip II. Had the expedition sailed as Drake had intended in the early spring of the year, the plan would have had a good chance of success. But, as the months went by, more and more time was granted the Spaniards to make their preparations, for the objective of Drake's venture had long been known to King Philip's efficient espionage service. By the beginning of June there was still just time for the expedition to sail and achieve its objective. But already the delay had meant that the English ships would be arriving off the eastern seaboard of America during the hurricane season and, as the old sailors' rhyme has it:

> In July, stand by
> In August, you must,
> In September, remember,
> In October, all over.

September would be a bad time to arrive in those treacherous waters. It was towards the end of July, when it seemed that nothing could any longer delay the sailing of the expedition, that the Spaniards made a daring raid on the Cornish coast. Four galleys disembarked a large

number of troops, who began firing the fishing villages in Mount's
Bay. Mousehole, Newlyn, Penzance, and a number of small villages
were burned or razed to the ground. In the ensuing panic there could
be no question of Drake and Hawkins being allowed to sail. Although
the raid was no more than a gesture, apprehension was naturally felt
that this might be the forerunner of a full-scale invasion. It was well
known that King Philip was preparing a second Armada, designed to
be considerably more formidable than the first, to subdue the Protestant
island.

The two commanders of the English squadron were immediately
ordered to leave Plymouth and cruise the Spanish coast. To this they
rightly replied that their ships, laden with soldiers, were totally un-
suitable for such a purely naval activity, and that the troops would
merely eat up the provisions intended for their long voyage to the West
Indies. Sir Thomas Baskerville, however, the Commander of the
Land Forces, was ordered to make a circuit of the West Country to
inspect the coastal defences and the local militia. In his absence, of
course, the expedition could not sail, and the ships continued idle in
Plymouth Sound and the Barbican. After considerable argument, in
which the two admirals urged upon the Queen yet again the necessity
for their sailing westward at once, while she attempted to keep them at
home (or at the most to send them on a cruise off the Irish coast), it was
finally agreed that they might go. But the condition which she
attached to this was that they must be back in home waters within six
months. It was now the middle of August.

Probably the only thing that finally made up the Queen's mind was
the news that a large treasure ship had been reported as being laid up in
the port of San Juan in Puerto Rico, undergoing repairs. Owing to the
many delays, the annual West Indies treasure fleet had already reached
Spain safely without being attacked. Drake had always hoped to capture it and secure the expedition financially, before crowning it with an
audacious success at Panama. But one treasure ship was better than
nothing at all, and it was as clear to the Queen as to her admirals that
their only chance of storming San Juan and capturing it lay in sailing
at once. Already the rumour was current in Spain that the whole
expedition had been so delayed that there was little or no chance
of its sailing that year. An element of surprise, therefore, was still just
possible.

On the 28th August, 1595, with drums beating and bright with
flags, 27 ships carrying some 2,500 men sailed at last from Plymouth.
Even now, they had not been permitted to make direct for their
destination, but had been ordered, before sailing west, to make a cast

down the coast of Spain. The endless series of setbacks, and the vacil-
lating policy of the Queen, had strained the nerves of both commanders
and men. Morale had sunk, and the old tension between Drake and
Hawkins had come more into the open. Thomas Maynard wrote in
his account of the voyage that Sir John Hawkins was: 'Old and wary,
entering into matters with so leaden a foot, that the other's meat would
be eaten before his spit could come to the fire.'

No more than four days out from Plymouth, Drake approached
Hawkins with the information that he had three hundred more men
in his half of the squadron than he had allowed for, and that his victuals
were already short. His request for assistance from his Vice-Admiral
was met with a somewhat natural refusal, the older man no doubt
feeling a little self-satisfied at the proof of his organisational abilities
when compared with Drake's lack of foresight. A council of war was
held aboard Drake's flagship, *Defiance*, off Cape St. Vincent, and 'the
fire which lay hidden in their stomachs began to break forth, and had
not the Colonel pacified them, it would have grown further'. It was at
this moment that Drake proposed an attack on the Canary Islands,
before proceeding to the West Indies. He was supported in his scheme
by Sir Thomas Baskerville, but Hawkins was very naturally opposed
to the project. He pointed out that they were already late and that, with
every day that passed, their chances of a surprise attack on San Juan
grew less. Drake himself must have been fully aware of this, but owing
to his inefficiency he needed to make a foraging raid in order to get
more supplies, and particularly water, for the troops in his half of the
command. At last, and reluctantly, Hawkins agreed. The ships put St.
Vincent behind them and set a course for the Canaries.

The main object of the expedition was bedevilled from the start.
Drake had never learned the lesson that a squadron of ships could not
be sailed about the ocean as he had done in his youth, with two or three
small vessels of 50 tons or less, and only a handful of young Devonians
to be looked after and victualled. To the end of his life he remained
the opportunist and simple man of action, while Hawkins fore-
shadowed naval admirals of the future, whose concern would be
almost as much with administration and supply as with action. In his
appeal to the popular imagination, Drake might be compared to the
Beatty of Jutland, while Hawkins more nearly resembles the conservative and able Jellicoe.

The attack on the Canaries was a disaster. On arrival off Las Palmas,
the troops were unable to make a landing because of the roughness of
the surf. Furthermore, the beach was dominated by Spanish batteries
and held in strength by their infantry. Baskerville immediately pointed

out the futility of attempting an assault, so the fleet weighed anchor
and coasted round the island to the western side, where they managed
to put watering parties ashore. During these operations some of the
English troops were captured, together with a surgeon from one of the
ships.

It was not long before the Governor of Las Palmas had managed to
extort from these prisoners the secret of their destination. In the lack of
security-precautions that prevailed in those days, the intention of the
English had almost certainly been known to King Philip even before
the ships had sailed from Plymouth. Nevertheless, it is a fact that the
Governor of Las Palmas now despatched a caravel post-haste to Puerto
Rico, to warn his compatriots that Drake and Hawkins intended to
attack San Juan with a view to capturing the treasure ship.

With the trade winds filling their sails, the English squadron now set
off across the Atlantic. They were bound first of all for their rendezvous
off Guadeloupe, a large island in the Leeward group, some 300 miles
south-east of Puerto Rico. Here they intended to make their final
preparations before attacking San Juan. While they were rolling in the
long swell of those blue seas—the soldiers marvelling at the unfamiliar
flying fish and at the snorting dolphins around their bows—five
Spanish frigates, unknown to the English, were coming up hard astern
of them. They had been ordered from Spain with all dispatch to
Puerto Rico, to embark the treasure before 'the pirate Drake' could get
his hands on it.

The ill luck that had dogged the expedition from the start began to
envelop them like a storm cloud. It was October, and in that season of
the year the normally predictable weather of the Caribbean can be
dangerous and capricious. A violent gale, possibly the skirting fringe of
some hurricane moving northward towards America, separated Drake
with one section of the fleet from Hawkins. After three days the two
admirals were finally reunited in their anchorage off Guadeloupe on the
29th October. Two small ships, the *Francis* and the *Delight*, had
unfortunately straggled astern of the main body. They were overhauled
by the Spanish frigates, and the *Francis* was captured. The *Delight* just
managed to escape, and made straightway for the rendezvous; only to
be followed by the Spaniards, who were now able to confirm with their
own eyes the information that they had already got from their
prisoners. Seeing the English men-of-war and the attendant merchantmen at anchor, the Spaniards turned and made all sail northward for
Puerto Rico, to let the Governor know that the enemy was in the
Caribbean.

Now was the moment, if any, when Drake and Hawkins should

have sailed for their destination. But they had just completed an Atlantic crossing and were burdened with troops; they needed to water ship and—most important in those days—to overhaul and clean them. In any event, the fleet could never have overtaken the fast Spanish men-of-war, since the progress of their convoy was necessarily determined by the speed of their slowest merchantmen. Drake, as was to be expected, was in favour of giving chase immediately with the *Defiance* and the other naval vessels. In the discussion that followed, he allowed himself to be overruled by Hawkins. This proved disastrous, for on this occasion Drake's judgement was undoubtedly right. If an attempt was ever to be made upon San Juan and its treasure ship, it should have been done at once. The moral here, as indeed in the abortive attempt on the Canary Islands, is clear. A division of command, in any venture where haste, secrecy, and surprise are all-important, must almost inevitably prove fatal.

In justification of Hawkins' viewpoint it must be remembered that the large guns of the men-of-war were still stowed below, as was the usual custom at that time when ships had to make the Atlantic crossing. Anticipating that these would certainly be needed for any major engagement on bombardment of land fortifications, Hawkins insisted that, before the fleet got under way, the guns must be brought up to their action decks. The Vice-Admiral then fell ill, and the humid wet season of the West Indies was no tonic for an old man's health. It may have been as much out of consideration for his kinsman, as for any other reason, that Drake agreed to wait until all was ready. He was unwise, conditioned perhaps by his late middle age, to adopt the cautious policy of a nature totally remote from his own.

Having assembled the launches that were designed for landing the troops, the ships finally got under way on their fourth day after reaching Guadeloupe. They set course north-westward via Tortola in the Virgin Islands, with the intention of running in towards San Juan with the trade winds favourable over their starboard quarter. Realising that by now there could be no element of surprise in their attack, if they arrived at their objective a few days after the warning carried by the Spanish frigates, Drake decided to attempt a stratagem that had proved successful in the days of his youth. Hoping that the Governor of Puerto Rico would think he had decided to call off the attack and go elsewhere, Drake contrived to make his fleet disappear among the lonely shoals and coral-sand beaches of the Virgin Islands.

They had left Guadeloupe on the 3rd November and it was not until over a week later that the English ships, with Drake sounding his way ahead in their van, nosed their way out into the sea to the east of

Puerto Rico. With a flash of his old brilliance Drake had found a new channel. He had thus avoided the usual route of the Neckar Island Passage, where he knew that enemy scouts would be waiting for them. During these days spent in the Virgin Islands the ships had been enabled to 'top up' with water, and Sir Thomas Baskerville had had time to land his troops and exercise them—an important consideration when soldiers had been long at sea in cramped and unhealthy quarters. It is possible that Drake was also hoping that his slow passage northward would give Hawkins a chance to regain his strength for the hazards that lay ahead. But the old admiral had organised his last expedition.

Sir John Hawkins would sail no more against the enemies of his Faith and his Queen. He was, as Hakluyt tells us, 'extreme sick; which his sickness began upon news of the taking of the *Francis*'. In a last message, dictated to his Queen a few hours before his death, Hawkins said that he 'was old and tired, [and] that he saw no other but danger of ruin likely to ensure of the whole voyage'.

Drake's success in discovering the new passage through the northern-most islands into the sea off Puerto Rico meant that the English ships came sailing steadily in toward their objective—the harbour of San Juan to leeward of them—while the Spanish frigates still vainly backed and filled, guarding the Neckar Island Passage. The sun was setting behind the green mountains of Puerto Rico when, on the 12th November, 1595, Sir John Hawkins died aboard his flagship *Garland*. As the English ships drove in under the last light winds of evening, the old admiral ended what he had sadly called his 'so careful, so miserable, so unfortunate, and so dangerous a life'.

CHAPTER TWO

A Child of His Time

THE man who, with his usual audacity, brought his ships to anchor within range of the guns of San Juan on the evening of the 14th November, 1595, had been born in Devon over half a century before. Of poor parents, and described as of 'middle birth', Francis Drake was to prove himself *par excellence* the 'self-made man' of his own, or indeed any other age. At a time when blood and breeding, or at the very least a prosperous bourgeois background, were essential keys to the doors of power, Drake rose by his own efforts, almost unaided.

His contemporary, the Elizabethan historian Stow, wrote of him: 'He was more skilful in all points of navigation than any that ever was before his time, in his time or since his death. He was also of perfect memory, great observation, eloquent by nature, skilful in artillery, expert and apt to let blood . . . in brief, he was as famous in Europe and America, as Tamberlane in Asia and Africa.' The first Englishman to sail round the world, called 'Pirate' by King Philip II and the 'Terrible Dragon' by the latter's Spanish subjects, he had been hailed as the saviour of his country by his own people, and worshipped with divine honours by the Indians of California.

Of Drake's ancestry we know only that he was born most probably in 1541, in a cottage on the Crowndale estate of Lord Russell, and that his father—who may at one time have been a sailor—was called Edmund Drake. We do not even know his mother's name. English historians, true to their native vice, have often been anxious to find some trace of noble lineage to account for Drake's genius. They have tried to prove a connection between the cottage-dwelling Drakes of Crowndale and the Drakes of Assher. The latter were certainly of gentle blood and entitled to their coat of arms. In the days of Sir Francis Drake's fame they were eager enough to claim kinship with the admiral, and even to call him 'cousin'. It is quite likely that there was some family link, but the matter is of little importance, for the man who was later to be described by the Spanish Ambassador, Mendoza, as 'the master-thief of the unknown world' derived no known benefit from his well-bred relations.

In support of the theory that his father, Edmund, may have been something more than a cottager or small tenant farmer, there is the fact that Francis Russell, eldest son of Lord Russell, stood godfather to Francis Drake at his christening. But the only relations from whom Drake did derive some definite and distinct advantage in his later years were the Hawkins' of Plymouth, a family which had long been established in the great west-country seaport. In the first forty years of the 16th century they had risen by hard work and able trading to be captains, shipowners, and freemen of the city. When Drake was born, the head of the family was the grand old man William Hawkins, who had acted as a naval adviser to Henry VIII when the King was laying the foundations of the new Navy. William Hawkins made several adventurous and profitable voyages to America and the coast of Africa. He was undoubtedly the most prominent citizen of Plymouth, having been Lord Mayor twice, and three times Member of Parliament for the borough. He had two sons who were to play an important part in Drake's life, John and William, both more than ten years older than Francis Drake—whom they were later to call 'cousin' in the somewhat vague way of Elizabethan relationships.

The fact remains that it was Drake's own ability which brought him to the notice of these relatives. He started with no money and little education and was not eased into power in the manner which has so often been the case with other sailors, soldiers and politicians in later generations. Drake's rise to power and fame was almost as unlikely in terms of the mid-20th century as a council school boy marrying into the British Royal family, or an American of Negro descent becoming an Admiral of the United States Navy. What he achieved was clearly not impossible, but the odds against him doing so were almost infinite.

Francis Drake was born into a world divided into two camps—the one consisting of the Lutheran-Protestants who had broken away from the religious beliefs and control of the Papacy; and the other consisting of those countries which still looked for moral and, indeed, political guidance to Rome. At the head of the one camp was England under its excommunicated King, Henry VIII—ultimately to be succeeded in 1558 by his and Anne Boleyn's daughter, Elizabeth. The leadership of the other half of this world rested solidly upon the kingdom of Spain, and upon His Most Catholic Majesty Philip II. Rome might be the theoretical seat of power, but the executive was firmly lodged in Madrid and, later, the Escorial.

An iron curtain of belief and dogma, every whit as rigid as that which separates a die-hard Russian Marxist from a Texan oil-millionaire, divided a Spaniard from a Protestant Englishman. Each side was equally convinced that God was with him, and the other party represented antichrist.

In this atmosphere, spy and counter-spy abounded, and in this atmosphere, too, the techniques which have recently been called 'brain-washing' had been brought to some degree of refinement by the Inquisition. Torture and death were to be expected by stubborn Protestants who fell into the hands of their enemies and refused to be converted. No less a man than St. Thomas Aquinas had written: 'If false coiners or other felons are justly committed to death without delay by worldly princes, much more may heretics, from the moment that they are convicted, be not only excommunicated, but slain justly out of hand.'

Drake's father, whether or not he was ever a sailor, was certainly an ardent lay preacher. It is possible that it was this very fact which brought the family into favour with the Russells. Lord Russell himself had been one of the principal leaders of reform and, associated closely with Thomas Cromwell, he had been one of Henry VIII's right-hand men during the policy of the dissolution of the monasteries. It is probable that he looked with favour upon this tenant farmer because he was a 'Hot Gospeller'. This in itself may well explain why Lord Russell's eldest son stood godfather to Francis Drake. But unfortunately for the Drake family the West Country was one of the strongholds of the Old Faith in England. It is an area which even to this day remains more deeply conservative than any other. It was Edmund Drake's dedication to the reformed church which finally forced him and his family to leave their home near Tavistock.

On Whitsunday 1549, the new Prayer Book of Edward VI was commanded to be read in all churches throughout the land. This was enough to spark off an uprising against the reformers. 'In a week the west country was in a blaze, all favourers of the new book were flying for their lives, the gentry were hiding in woods and caves, and Lord Russell, who was sent down to restore order, found he could not move nearer to his home than Honiton.' It was little wonder that Edmund Drake and his family had to leave an area like Tavistock where the old Abbey had for centuries been the heart and soul of country life.

Along with many other Protestants they probably made their way to Plymouth which, like most seaports, was better disposed towards new and liberal thoughts than the deeply entrenched countryside. Tradition, but no more, says that it was to the Island of St. Nicholas out in Plymouth Sound that the Protestant refugees went for shelter.

Perhaps the story comes a little too conveniently for a place which, after his lifetime, was to be called in his honour, 'Drake's Island'. One thing is certain, the Drake family did not stay long in Plymouth, nor did Francis Drake again know a truly permanent home in the West of England until he came back in the full flush of pride and power to buy Buckland Abbey from the Grenvilles at the age of forty. That act was to be poetic revenge for a young boy who had left Devon penniless—to return in his prime and buy for his private seat one of the once-powerful centres of Catholicism.

Until 1549 the history of Drake is as faint as the crumbling, lichened characters on a gravestone. But from now on the words begin to appear more and more legibly, until in the end we come into the possession of facts and documents a great deal more enduring than 'the gilded monuments of princes'. From the contemporary historian William Camden and from Drake's own nephew we now have confirmation that the family fled to Kent. To make for the east coast of England was a very natural action since the eastern countries were the home of Protestantism. In his work *Sir Francis Drake Revived*, his nephew (who had much of the information from Drake himself) had the following to say about the early family fortunes: '. . . it pleased (God) to raise this man, not only from a low condition, but even from the state of persecution; his father suffered in it, being forced to fly from his house (near South Tavistock in Devon) into Kent, and there to inhabit the hull of a ship, wherein many of his young sons were born: he had twelve in all, and as it pleased God to give most of them a being upon the water, so the greatest part of them died at sea'.

In one of the old naval hulks near Chatham in Kent, Edmund Drake and his wife and children made their home. The vessel lay almost certainly in Gillingham Reach, where paid-off ships were harboured against such a time when they might possibly be required. From the age of about eight onwards—when the child has become a boy and is active on the road to manhood—Francis Drake grew native to the sea. To live aboard a ship, even a hulk that is out of commission, is to experience a totally different life from the landsman's. Daily he heard the tides turn and the waves lap, the shifting groan of the timbers as the old ship settled back upon the mud, the sigh and creak as she lifted off again, and the waterborne sway of her when the flood was up the river. The Devon farmer's son grows up to the smell of damp rich earth, animals steaming after the rain, and the many scents and sounds of the coombes in summer. Such might well have been Drake's childhood memories, but all was changed now to the rhythm of tides, ribbed mudflats, the wind harsh over them when it blew from the east—across the unfriendly banks and cold steep waves of the North Sea. The slop of water in the bilges, the bitter smell of old oak frames and timbers long soaked in salt, the scent of deck-planking drying on a sunny morning when the mist steamed off the estuary and the shapes of other ships rode into view—these became the background to his world.

Where there are ships there are always small sailing and rowing boats, and where there are boys and small boats a love of the sea is often born. He became familiar with the narrow tideways that filled or emptied with a sudden almost miraculous rush, the winding channels through the flat lands, and the banks that stood up like islands at low water—only to hide their treacherous heads when the flood-time came. In later years it was to seem an integral part of his nature that he handled his small ships upon the sea, not with the dogged resolution of Hawkins or Frobisher, but with a happy ease—rather like the acrobat who can afford to appear casual because of his perfect expertise.

'After the death of King Henry,' Camden tells us, 'he [Edmund Drake] got a place among the seamen in the King's Navy, to read prayers to them.' But Henry VIII had died in 1547, before the Drakes left Devon, so it would seem that it was at some time during the brief reign of Edward VI that Francis Drake's father secured his position as a preacher in the Fleet. The sailors of England, and particularly those of the east coast, were a bulwark of Protestantism during these years of religious strife. It seems likely that Lord Russell may have been responsible for securing this respectable position for his old tenant.

One cannot doubt that Francis Drake absorbed from his father an early familiarity with the Bible, and it is most likely that it was from his father also that he received the rudiments of education. As he was to show in later years, he could write a vigorous and simple English, but in one letter a mistake in a simple classical reference shows that though, like all educated Englishmen of the time, he paid a profound respect to the ancient world, he was little familiar with it. If Shakespeare had 'Small Latin and less Greek', it is doubtful whether Drake had any of either. But he will certainly have heard from his earliest years the sonorous English of the *Great Bible*, seven editions of which had issued from the presses between 1539 and 1541. Drake's father, in his capacity as preacher, will have had access to this translation, of which an Act of Parliament had stated that no woman (unless she be noble or gentle-woman), no artificers, apprentices, journeymen, serving men, under the degree of yeoman' might be permitted to read it. In his will, addressing his youngest son, Edmund Drake adjured him to 'make much of the Bible', and one can be sure that this precept was instilled into Francis as well as his other eleven brothers.

Not long after the family had made their home aboard the old ship near Chatham, Edmund Drake was ordained Deacon, and shortly after that he was made Vicar of Upchurch, a small village on the Medway. At what date we do not know, but probably when Francis Drake was about thirteen, his father was compelled 'by reason of his poverty to put his son to the master of a bark, with which he used to coast along the shore, and sometimes to carry merchandise into Zeeland and France.

'The youth, being painful and diligent, so pleased the old man by his industry, that, being a bachelor, at his death he bequeathed his bark unto him by will and testament.'

Edward VI died in 1553, some four years after the Drake family had moved to the east coast, and it was probably during the early years of Mary's reign that Francis Drake went to sea as apprentice in this small coaster. During these years, whenever he returned to the Medway to see his father and his brothers, it was to find a countryside torn by civil and religious strife. The fleet in the Medway supported Wyatt with their artillery—at the time when he held Rochester and called on all patriotic Englishmen to preserve their land and their Faith from Spain and from Rome. Then the Queen married Philip, the man against whom Francis Drake was later to wage an almost personal war. It was to this England, under the shadow of the Spanish alliance and the Inquisition, that he returned from his first ventures on the seas. It is unlikely that he ever forgot the persecution that followed, from the burning of the first Protestant martyrs in 1555, until the end of Queen Mary's reign. Nor, in more personal terms, was he ever likely to forget the years when even the Russells were in disgrace, and his father was penniless.

Meanwhile, against this background of a tragically divided country, he learned the hard trade of the sea on one of the bleakest stretches of water in the world. Even in mid-summer the North Sea is austere, and in winter when the gales pile the short, toppling seas into a thunder over its banks and treacherous shoals, it becomes a killer of ships and men. Had he learned his early sailing out of the deep-water harbours of the west coast, Drake would have become familiar with the long ocean swell, the south-westerlies of the Atlantic, and the ironbound shores of Cornwall. But he would never have gained so deep a knowledge of pilotage as he did working in and out of the harbours of East Anglia and Holland, or finding his way into the awkward Channel Ports of France. There is still no finer area than the Channel and the east coast for learning the pilot's craft, gaining an essential knowledge of log and leadline, or for acquiring an eye that can tell by the oily slick on the water where a bank lies hidden, or by a drift of scum past the bows that the tide is on the point of turning.

An east-coast bark that could be handled by a man and a boy will most likely have been shallow and broad-beamed like a Dutch vessel, setting a simple working area of sail, and able to settle with a sigh of ease into mud-berths round a bend in almost any river.

The name of the old man who taught Drake the trade of the sea is unknown, for, like generations of east-coasters who have followed him over the centuries, he has left no record—only that inherited knowledge which is silently passed on through generations, so that sometimes it seems as if it has been bred in the bone. We know at any rate that Francis Drake inherited the old man's ship, 'a circumstance,' as Dr. Johnson remarked, 'that deserves to be remembered, not only as it may illustrate the private character of this brave man, but as it may hint to all those who may hereafter propose his conduct from their imitation, that virtue is the surest foundation of reputation and fortune, and that the first step to greatness is to be honest.'

Here the Doctor's solemnities may make one pause a moment. Drake was always loved by the men that served with him; he was brave without any shadow of doubt, and brilliant in his capacity as sailor; but it would be hard to maintain that he was invariably 'honest'. The foundation of his reputation and fortune (which can be said to start from that first gift of a small trading ship) was his diligence and ability. Could we hear truthfully from any millionaire, who boasts that he rose to affluence from nothing, just how he acquired his first real working-capital, we should find, more often than not, that Dr. Johnson was a little ingenuous. But, then, Johnson was a poet and a man of letters. Such men rarely comprehend just how sordid is the struggle by which self-made men first hoist themselves out of the cage of poverty that imprisons their fellows.

CHAPTER THREE

Apprenticeship

'SERVE God daily,' wrote John Hawkins in his sailing orders to his fleet. 'Love one another; preserve your victuals; beware of fire; and keep good company.' (By this he meant that the ships should keep close order and not lose sight of one another while on passage.) It was the year 1564, and John Hawkins was aboard the *Jesus of Lubeck*, bound on a slaving expedition to the coast of West Africa, and then onwards with his human cargo to sell them in the Spanish islands of the Caribbean and to the garrison towns on the mainland of America. Old William Hawkins had died in 1555, his eldest son William was managing the family's interests ashore, and John was, as it were, executive manager upon the high seas. In 1559, the year after the accession to the throne of that 'mere English' Queen, Elizabeth I, John Hawkins had married the daughter of Benjamin Gonson, Treasurer to the Navy. This in itself was confirmation of the standing of this Plymouth merchant family.

Francis Drake was now in his early twenties and master of his own craft. But, as Thomas Fuller wrote in his history of *The Worthies of England*, 'he soon grew weary of his bark, which would scarce go alone, but as it crept along the shore.' Drake, in fact, was beginning to grow tired of the exigencies and smallness of local coastal trading at just about the same time that his kinsman, John Hawkins, was pointing the way for all Englishmen of spirit to follow.

On the cold east coast, and in the muddy harbours beyond which lay that sea which seems always stained with mud or abrasive with tide-lifted shingle, Drake heard no doubt of the broad ocean-acres where his Devonian cousins were sailing, and of that New World which the Pope had given to the Kingdom of Spain. There gold ran in the rivers, emeralds came gleaming out of the Peruvian mines, and an Englishman of ability could make more money in one voyage than he could do in years of steady North Sea trading. It is true that Edmund Drake had commended to his sons the Epistle of St. Paul to the Romans, and it is more than likely that he had drawn to their attention verse 18 of chapter 1: 'For the wrath of God is revealed from heaven against all ungodliness and unrighteousness of men, who hold the truth in unrighteousness.' He pointed out, no doubt, that this was clearly intended to indicate to his day and age the false beliefs of the Catholic Church. But it would be absurd to envisage Francis Drake as having left the east coast of England in order to prosecute a crusade against the Pope in the new Spanish empire. He left because he was tired of his present employment, because he was adventurous, and because he had heard that the grass was greener on the other side of the hill.

We know what he looked like when young, for a miniature by Isaac Oliver shows him clean-shaven except for a small moustache, and before his figure had settled into the thickness of middle age. Stow's description of him in later years accords well with the portraits that we have of him. He was 'low of stature, of strong limb, round-headed, brown hair, full-bearded, his eyes round, large and clear, well-favoured face, and of a cheerful countenance'. Other accounts and pictures of him fill in the gaps: his hair grew rather low on this forehead, his hands were strong but shapely, his legs short, and his chest not so much wide as deep-barrelled. Like Odysseus, that archetype of all seamen, he might have equally well been described by Homer as 'Looking nobler when sitting down than standing up.' His eyes were grey, his complexion ruddy, and in later years he wore a full beard, cut to a point and with the tips of the moustaches twirled upward.

To the end of his life he remained a strict disciplinarian, would have no gambling with cards or dice aboard his ship, did not tolerate foul talk, and would not have his crew hanging about bars or brothels when ashore. Such a man might well have been unpopular, but we have it on record (from Spanish prisoners among others) that he was loved by his men. He had an infectious vitality, humour, and a resilient character. He had also that quality which Nelson possessed—an indefinable charm that made men follow him whatever his faults. These were many; for he had a quick and violent temper, and although kind to his inferiors provided they did their work well, he was always difficult with his equals and overbearing to his superiors. Like Nelson again, he was avaricious of fame, loved display and ostentation, and could not be sickened by any amount of flattery.

A simple man in many respects, he nevertheless had his complexities, for, although he never forgot a friend, he never forgave an enemy. Yet, in an age of brutality, when cruelty to prisoners was not considered reprehensible, he always treated captured Spaniards with courtesy and kindness. In his dealings with the native Indians and Negroes of the Caribbean and America he was so far in advance of his time that the

C

Southern States of the U.S.A. have not yet caught up with him. His treatment of women was gentle and respectful. It is probable that, as with many extrovert and masculine men, his respect for women was coupled with a certain, almost timid, incomprehension of their natures. Of his relationship with his two wives we know nothing except that he looked after them well and provided for them to the best of his ability —and left them as soon as there was any opportunity of going to sea. Unlike most sailors he does not seem to have needed the company of women, and unlike so many of his contemporaries he does not appear to have had a homosexual streak. Characters like his were not uncommon, even as late as the 19th century, among the captains of the great ocean-going sailing ships.

Drake never had any children, so one aspect of his nature was never developed. Yet he had a very strong sense of family, and looked after his brothers as best he could, and made sure of his property and name being handed on to them when the time came. He had the gambler's intuitive flair for making the instant decision and acting upon it without delay. So long as his luck held, and while he trusted to this instinctive judgement—like a surf boarder knowing just how, and when to twist his body to make use of the rushing wave—so long he was successful. The moment that he began to age, and tried to repeat earlier successes without feeling in the palms of his hands the necessary instinct to act, he was prone to blunder. Like many another man of action, he probably despised the 'backroom boys', the commissariat, and the staff officers. His, in fact, was the temperament of youth, and it matched the age into which he was born.

In our own century he might have made a brilliant commander of light naval forces, or a special service officer in charge of partisans operating in difficult territory. In the occupied islands of the Pacific, the mountains of Crete, the forests of Burma, or at the head of the commando raid on St. Nazaire during the Second World War, Drake would have been in his element. In the conferences of the great at Yalta or Casablanca he would have felt impatient, despising the politicians and the organisers, and hiding his unease under a display of ill-temper and imperious demands for action. He could never co-operate.

Such was the formed, mature man, but no doubt the characteristics were all there in his youth, only waiting for circumstances and the years to channel them deeply, so that in the end they would stand out like the valleys carved through a landscape by millennia of running water. It was hardly surprising that such a character could not remain content with small-time trading between England and Europe, when a whole new world was opening over the western horizon.

'History is bunk!' Henry Ford is reputed to have remarked, but if so, he only displayed what the Catholic Church has termed 'invincible ignorance'. There would have been no Henry Ford but for Drake, since without the example that he set by his fiery life, the whole of Northern America would almost certainly have become part of the Spanish Empire. Such a northern hybrid would have withered over the centuries, no doubt, and subsequently have been refertilised in different ways by the various European powers. But it is possible that North America could have remained basically little more than a 'bunch of Banana Republics' at loggerheads with one another. Drake did not prevent this but, by stabbing at the Achilles heel of Spanish colonialism, he worked upon a basic weakness. His violence and his gusto showed the Protestant English (and later the Dutch, French, and others) that colonies could be founded and maintained to the north of the Spanish sphere of influence.

Drake always perceived, though not necessarily for the same reasons as a modern observer, that the Panamanian isthmus constituted the artery between two separate continents. By attacking it and its adjacent islands time and time again, he contrived the ultimate containment of Spain within the southern hemisphere of the new world. Drake's effect was, as it were, to establish a *cordon sanitaire* between two ways of life, as much as between two sections of the same continent.

It is only in comparatively recent years that the United States of America, reassured by over a century of progress and prosperity, has felt strong enough to begin a blood transfusion into its cousin continent to the south—debilitated as the latter has been by centuries of misrule, religious intolerance, and an unwillingness to face the facts of the modern world. It can hardly be a coincidence that in modern Europe the most backward areas, in every respect from education to scientific progress and material prosperity, are Spain herself, the Republic of Ireland, Sicily, and Southern Italy. The Church which rejected Galileo has until recently, like the ancient Roman world, always had its eyes turned back towards a supposedly 'Golden Age' in the past. That Golden Age for the Papacy was constituted by the centuries when it had complete dominance over men's lives, in every aspect of their being, from the cradle to the grave.

Drake, that man 'apt to let blood and give physic unto his people according to the climate', was—in his unthinking way—one of the first to bring the benefits of the new humanism, of the reformed church, and of the Renaissance into America. No intellectual, no scholar, and only moderately literate, he nevertheless represented a new type of

man—one who acted not from some inherited dogma, but from self-
interest and expediency, as well as from a hardly-conscious awareness
that the flood-tide was with him. Almost as ignorant of what history
really meant as Henry Ford, he unknowingly represented the wave of
the future. He might have echoed that Epistle of St. Paul to the
Romans which his father Edmund Drake commended to his sons: 'I
reckon that the sufferings of this present time are not worthy to be
compared with the glory which shall be revealed in us.'

One thing that must never be forgotten in any estimate of his later
life is that Francis Drake never outgrew the influence of his father. As
Don Francisco de Zarate was later to record, even during the most
hazardous moments of his voyage round the world, he insisted on
having prayers said twice a day aboard the *Golden Hind*. A practical
man and no mystic, he was to become almost as convinced as St. Paul
himself of the righteousness of his cause: 'If God be for us, who can be
against us?' For this reason, apart from any other, it is true to say that
he was not quite such a simple character as he may at first appear in the
story of his life. He was neither the first, nor the last lay missionary to
have a sword in one hand, the Bible in the other, and a good eye to the
main chance.

It was Prince Henry the Navigator of Portugal who, over a century
before Drake's birth 'had wished to know about the western ocean,
and whether there were islands or continents beyond those that
Ptolemy described. So he sent caravels to search for lands.' Christopher
Columbus was later to marry the daughter of one of Prince Henry's
governors in the new-found islands of the Azores. It was largely
through these Portugese family connections that Columbus acquired
the navigational knowledge and enthusiasm to venture out into the
west. Ever since his discovery of the West Indies in 1492, the Spaniards
had been quietly developing their new empire; first colonising the
main islands of Puerto Rico, Hispaniola (the modern Haiti and
Dominican Republic), Jamaica and Havana. Then, finding that the
islands—despite their first promise of riches—were relatively poor in
mineral wealth and resources, the Spaniards had used them as bases
from which to establish their beach-head on the mainland of America.
Here they were not to be disappointed. From the moment that Hernando Cortes had overthrown the rich civilisation of Mexico, they had
their hands upon the Golden Fleece—the mines of Peru, the emeralds of
Colombia, and the silver of Mexico.

Writing in the prosaic 18th century and echoing Hakluyt, Dr.
Johnson recaptured the enthusiasm and the sense of wonder that fired
men like Drake to make their voyages. (It was as if we should find

within the next decade that the mountains of the moon were inhabited, as well as made of platinum.) 'Nothing was talked of among the mercantile or adventurous part of mankind but the beauty and riches of this new world. Fresh discoveries were frequently made, new countries and nations, never heard of before, were daily described. . . .' Soon enough men would show that they could corrupt and defile a new continent, but for the moment America did indeed seem to justify Miranda's cry, 'O brave New World!'

When Drake was about twenty-three he sold his own boat and enlisted under the patronage of the Hawkins family in their trading fleet. In his first year of deep-sea sailing in large craft, it appears that he went down to the Atlantic coast of Spain as third officer in a merchantman. There was considerable trade between England and Spain at that time, trade which—surprisingly enough perhaps—continued almost throughout the Elizabethan period, even right up to the moments when the 'Cold War' between the two countries was on the point of turning into a 'hot' one. It may have been from this first voyage that Drake picked up a smattering of Spanish, a language in which he was ultimately to become proficient. It was in the following year 1564-5, however, that he first sailed for the land of his destiny, where he was to make his fame and fortune, and where ultimately he was to lie in a lead coffin only a league from its coast.

Of this first voyage we know little except that a Captain John Lovell was in command of his vessel, and that Francis Drake was his second-in-command. Lovell was very probably a Captain in the Hawkins family firm, in which case the trading expedition will have been underwritten by them and no doubt by some 'Merchant Adventurers' in the City of London. Two other ships sailed in company, all bound for the Africa coast to embark Negro slaves. They then seem to have sailed to the Cape Verde Islands where they captured some Portuguese slave ships before setting their course for the West Indies.

Drake, aged twenty-four or -five, was now embarked on a ship for the New World, and beginning to acquire from Captain Lovell the secrets of deep-sea navigation and ocean-sailing. After leaving the barren and volcanic Cape Verde Islands, they will have found the north-east trade winds sitting steadily in their sails. Now for the first time Drake knew, day and night, the sigh of the eternal winds that girdle the earth. With all her canvas spread, and with the wind steady on the starboard quarter, the ship ran down her curving track towards the scattered islands of the Caribbean. At night he watched the Pole Star, his guardian in the harsh waters of Channel and North Sea,

decline towards the horizon. At night the wake boiled with phos-
phorescence, and the water as it ran across the deck was fiery, and warm
to the bare feet of sailors. At dawn he will have seen the sun lift over a
vacant sea astern, and at sunset watched its bearing as it dipped with a
green flash into the sea's curve over their bows. Trade wind sailing!—
And at sunset, too, he will have remarked how the fleecy trade-wind
clouds seemed to bank up all round the horizon while the bowl of sky
overhead, which throughout the day had been busy with their scudding passage, seemed to become empty and clear. Off-watch in his bunk
he will have heard the water slipping past only a few inches away.
Above his head, ropes will have sighed and squealed as the watch on
deck trimmed sails, or freshened 'the nip' where the ropes worked
back and forth through the wooden mouths of the blocks. Then one
day the cry of 'Land-ho!' will have shown him the islands quivering
under the sun, the bursting spray on the windward rocks, and beyond
that the mountain peaks spilling with cloud and the green dance of
tropical trees leaning westward under the prevailing wind.

Whatever he may have felt about his first experience of the Atlantic
ocean and the indulgent climate of the West Indies, all was soon to be
obscured by his first contact with the Spanish colonial régime. At Rio
de la Hacha, a small port on the mainland where the Treasurer of the
Indies resided, Captain Lovell and Drake met with some unknown
disaster. In later years, when he was giving his nephew (Francis) the
material of his early life for *Sir Francis Drake Revised*, Drake never
specified what had happened; only that he and Lovell received some
'wrongs' there. It is not difficult to guess what they were, for something
similar happened to Hawkins in this port, when he tried to do business
with the Treasurer. The fact was, that while most of the merchants
and landowners in the Spanish colonies were only too eager to transact
business with either French or English merchantmen, they were
expressly prohibited from doing so, since the colonies were only
allowed to trade direct with Spain. Such an embargo against free
trading was only natural from Philip II's point of view, for he hoped
that it would assist manufacturers at home and, in general, make for an
economic stability. But Spain was unable either to supply all the
manufactured goods needed by the colonists, or to maintain a sufficient
influx of African slave-labour to maintain the agriculture of the new
territories.

It was over this vexed question of trade with the New World that
so many of the troubles between England and Spain developed in the
next two decades; English merchants claiming the right to trade freely
anywhere, while Philip and his minsters denying it to them, as well as

to other mercantile countries like France. If one may judge by subsequent incidents, what seems to have happened to Captain Lovell and Drake was that they entered Rio de la Hacha at the invitation of some Spanish merchants, only to have their human cargo immediately seized by the Treasurer as contraband. One thing is certain—Drake never forgot his first introduction to Spanish methods, nor to the double code of honour that was allowed to exist for a Spanish Catholic when he was dealing with a Protestant heretic. He had been used to the ordinary harsh conditions of a coastal merchant skipper's life, but not to the outright confiscation of a cargo—justified by a Spanish law that seemed to contravene the trading agreements between the two countries. Drake never forgot or forgave, and the disaster of his next expedition to the West Indies only reinforced an unconquerable hatred.

It was indeed sometimes possible for foreign merchants to obtain licences from the Spanish government to trade with their overseas colonies, but such licences were rarely granted, and most 'merchant adventurers' were willing to take the risk that they would be able to dispose of their cargoes without them. John Hawkins was certainly no exception, for he had entered the West Indian slave trade as early as 1562 and had done very well for himself, without the benefit of any official licence to trade. Aware that the colonists needed all the labour that they could get—and that not enough was provided by the licensed Spanish ships coming over from West Africa—Hawkins had run two successful slave-trading expeditions to the West Indies, one in 1562-3 and another in 1564-5. As Dr. J. A. Williamson wrote: 'He behaved as an honest trader, paid for all goods he had, and avoided the piratical plundering which the French adventurers were carrying on in the Caribbean. He hoped to obtain by this conduct the license of the Spanish Government. But King Philip II was determined not to allow English Protestants in his colonies and sent orders that Hawkins was to be expelled as a pirate.'

The morality of the slave trade is something which seems to have totally engrossed modern historians (preoccupied as they are with the current emergence of African and Asian peoples into the status of full and equal citizens in the world), and this to the exclusion of any historical sense. The history of slavery is as old as the human race, the less efficient and the weaker having always become the slaves of the strong. Physically, Africans were of course just as strong as Europeans, but intellectually they had remained so far inferior as to invite conquest. There has never been an African civilisation or culture that has made any significant contribution to the history of the world. Slavery was endemic in Africa itself, and a victorious raiding tribe would automatically enslave the defeated. The sentimental idea, sometimes put out by modern propagandists—both African and European—that slavery was introduced into Africa by cynical European capitalists has no substance whatever in fact.

In the ancient world, slavery had provided the necessary manpower to keep industry and agriculture turning over. Slaves or serfs existed in Russia, to take another example, until the late 19th century—only because Russia had not become industrialised, and converted her slaves into 'artificers' and 'working men'. Slavery still existed in 16th-century Europe, and any European who ventured as a sailor into the eastern Mediterranean knew that, if the ship in which he sailed was captured by a Moslem galley, he might expect to find himself a slave at the oar-benches within a matter of minutes. Similarly, the galleys of the Knights of Malta were crewed almost exclusively by Moslem slaves—Turks and Arabs captured by those 'Most Christian Knights' on their forays into the Aegean or the waters off North Africa.

An English seaman, for instance, who fell into the hands of the Spaniards—if he were not so recalcitrant against the Catholic Faith as to merit death by burning at the stake—was almost certain to end up as a slave in a Spanish mine or galley. This was a chance that every sailor took. Just as, in every age, sailors and fishermen risk their lives to enable landsmen to eat, so no one thought of protesting at what was considered no more than an 'industrial hazard'. 'We live not as we would wish to, but as we must', as a classical saying has it, was an outlook that was generally accepted in the 16th century.

To begin with, the African slave trade as practised by Europeans had had a curiously sanctimonious atmosphere about it. When it had started in the 15th century as a result of the expeditions organised by the Portuguese Prince, Henry the Navigator, the latter had been able to believe quite sincerely that these Africans were being saved from Limbo by being Christianised. 'Prince Henry's own attitude to the slave trade is made abundantly clear. . . . He knew that there was little hope of converting the Moors from the religion of Mahomet, but he saw every heathen Negro as a potential Christian. His aim was to create a Christian Kingdom in Africa. . . . When the first Portuguese ships return with Negro prisoners aboard them, there was rejoicing in their conversion and acceptance of the Christian faith. There was no conception of 'colour bar'. The Africans were freely permitted to intermarry with the Portuguese, always provided that such marriages were Christian ones. It was not until much later that a cynical approach to the slave trade infected nearly all Europe.'

It would be absurd to believe that this mediaeval Christian outlook had any influence upon John Hawkins or his 'merchant adventurers.' They did not even have the justification that Henry the Navigator had had, a century or so before, of believing they were saving souls. Nor was this believed by Spanish Catholics at this period, although (once a commercial advantage is apparent) men are capable of convincing themselves of almost anything.

Drake, as far as we know, only twice engaged in the slave trade, the second occasion being the Hawkins expedition of 1567. It will become apparent from his later life that, for an Englishman of his time, Drake was exceptional in his sympathetic treatment of peoples of other races. The Spaniards' native cruelty, and their determination to enslave all those who would not accept their faith and way of life, was quite alien to him—this despite the fact that he and his own family had suffered under Catholic intolerance in England. Perhaps this should not be laid entirely as credit at his door, but should be attributed to that essentially practical and mercantile sense which was to make Napoleon many centuries later call the English scornfully, 'a nation of shopkeepers'. Shopkeepers may not be idealists, but they are compelled by the nature of their lives to make a compromise to accept customers as they are, and to try and give a fair return for money spent.

As another Frenchman, Baudelaire, was later to write: '*Qui n'accepte les conditions de la vie, vend son ame.*' Drake was no intellectual and never sold his soul. He accepted the harsh fact that, as Hemingway was to put it in our own time: 'The world breaks everyone and afterward many are strong at the broken places. But those that will not break it kills. It kills the very good and the very gentle and the very brave impartially. If you are none of these you can be sure that it will kill you too, but there will be no special hurry'. It is doubtful whether Drake saw life in quite such conscious terms: he was a seaman with his way to make in the world, and not an artist. The expedition on which he set off with John Hawkins, on the 2nd October, 1567, seemed likely to present a fine return both in experience and money to a poor young man. Drake had little to commend him but his relationship with this one powerful family, and an already established competence as a sailor in small ships. His life had never been easy, and he was to continue to learn things the hard way. By the time that he came back from the sorrowful voyage to San Juan de Ulua in 1568 he would have learned two invaluable lessons. The first was, never trust an enemy, and the second was summarised centuries later by a dying Italian bandit:— 'Thumb on the blade, strike upwards, and strike first!'

CHAPTER FOUR

The Dedicated Man

DRAKE reached Plymouth in Captain Lovell's ship in August 1567. Within two months he was away again, bound once more for Africa and the West Indies. But this time he was engaged in an important venture, for John Hawkins himself was putting to sea with a fleet of six ships, and two of them had been provided by the Queen, a sure sign that Her Majesty had a private interest in the expedition— whatever she may have said to the Spanish ambassador.

Don Diego Guzman de Silva, the Spanish Ambassador in London, had had his eye on the expedition ever since he had first heard about some of the ships refitting at Rochester in the May of that year. Upon his voicing a certain uneasiness about the destination of these ships, the Queen had hastened to assure him that the expedition was not bound for the West Indies. Sir William Cecil, the Lord High Treasurer, had even given him his oath that the ships were only destined for Guinea and the West Coast of Africa—an area which fell within the Portuguese sphere of influence. Both the Queen and her minister were lying. Hawkins, when he came to London—and asked the ambassador to convey his respects to the King of Spain—was combining the lie direct with a certain kind of jovial insolence.

On both sides of the diplomatic fence it was recognised that little short of open hostilities between England and Spain could render the relationship between the two countries any worse. The English, for their part, knew that the Spanish ambassador was at the bottom of every plot against the life of their Queen, and therefore of their country's freedom. De Silva was equally aware that the English would do all they could to disrupt Spanish colonial trade and even—if it were possible—capture the gold-bearing ships of the West Indies fleet upon which the economy of Spain so largely depended. With charm of word, with elegance of gesture, and with pomanders held in their white hands (to ward off the stench of the common people), they veiled their Billingsgate brawl in a manner of which Machiavelli himself would have approved.

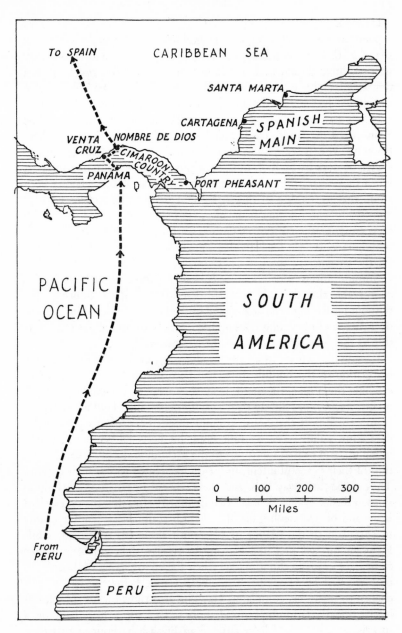

The Isthmus of Panama

Hawkins was ever a pessimist and, in later years, he described this expedition in the following terms: 'If all the miseries and troublesome affairs of this sorrowful voyage should be perfectly and thoroughly written, there should need a painful man with his pen and as great a time as he had that wrote the lives and deaths of the Martyrs.' The trouble had started even before the ships had left their rendevzous at Plymouth.

It was late in August when a squadron of seven ships from the Spanish Netherlands Fleet sailed into Plymouth Sound, where Hawkins' vessels were lying at anchor at the mouth of the cat-water. Called on deck by his look-outs, Hawkins saw the foreign men-of-war, when they were still to seaward of St. Nicholas' Island. Having been afraid that something of this sort might happen, he had kept all his guns ready, and his men at the alert. The ships came on, failed to dip their ensigns—the customary gesture to show that they came in peace —and made straight for Hawkins' squadron. They were clearly headed for the entrance to the inner harbour, and Hawkins did not hesitate. Communications were necessarily bad in those days, and it was conceivable that the cold war had deteriorated into a shooting war, without his having been acquainted of the fact. He ordered his ships to open fire, and his young cousin Drake was with him aboard the flag-ship as the guns rumbled across the narrow waters.

It seems likely that this squadron, advised by De Silva of the suspected destination of the English ships, had been despatched in the hope of catching them off their guard. If so, they were sadly disappointed, for no one sleeps more lightly than a guilty man—and Hawkins had good reason to suspect that some attempt might be made to prevent his fleet from sailing. The Spanish ships, hit between wind and water, luffed up, and retired swiftly from the harbour entrance. As an indica-tion of their peaceful intent, they now consented to dip their ensigns. They made their way back and anchored out of range of the English ships in the lee of St. Nicholas' Island. Shortly after this, the despatch of boats and of protests began—the Flemish commander sending ashore to complain to the Mayor of Plymouth about his treatment, while Hawkins himself prepared his ship to receive their emissary. Drake must have enjoyed the moment when the envoy came on board—to be castigated by Hawkins in no mean terms, before he had even a chance to make his complaint. Hawkins had right on his side, for as international relationships stood, only a fool (or a man bent on a surprise attack) would have entered an English harbour at that time without making the customary acknowledgement that he came in peace. The incident was smoothed over, apologies accepted on both sides, and the usual formal exchange of gifts took place.

Unknown to Hawkins, however, the Flemish admiral, De Wachen, an old enemy of the English, had reported the whole matter posthaste to the Spanish Ambassador in London. His despatch arrived before Hawkins' own, with the result that 'These reports prejudiced the reception of Hawkins' own account of the incident which arrived later, and caused Cecil to write, on the Queen's authority, a rebuke to her subject, forbidding him to take such presumptuous action in her name again.'

The Queen was hardly ever prepared to stand behind her seamen when it came to a showdown—a fact which Philip II was often able to trade upon. Elizabeth could hardly be blamed for this reluctance of hers, since her country's role was then—as almost ever since—to maintain an equipoise of power in the world. Confronted at that time by the greatest empire since the Roman, England could only balance and prevaricate, or use her seapower for raids that weakened the enemy. She never had the strength to administer the *coup de grâce*.

Elizabeth has often been unfairly blamed by historians for a 'feminine inability' to come to a decision, and this is something that every biographer of Drake or of the Elizabethan seamen must feel bitterly. But she was no more able to force a final decision than is the banderillero in the bull-ring, whose duty it is to administer the darts that confuse and weaken the immense animal. He has to depend on the brute strength of horse and picador to break down its shoulder muscles efficiently, and in the final event, he must always rely upon the matador to administer the death-blow. Such, in the language of Spain's own national 'sport', was the role of England during the 16th century, and Elizabeth realised it. So too did Drake, more by instinct than by reasoning.

After this abortive raid by De Wachen's squadron, and the troubles that ensued, the ships under Hawkins did not manage to get under way until the 2nd October. Hawkins with his young kinsman Drake aboard his flagship, sailed in the great ship *Jesus of Lubeck*, belonging to the Queen. With him went another of the Queen's ships, the *Minion*, an old fourmaster of about 300 tons. The Hawkins brothers had contributed the rest of the squadron, the *William and John*, called after the two brothers, of 150 tons; the *Swallow*, a new ship of 100 tons; and the *Judith* and the *Angel*, both small craft of 50 tons and 33 tons respectively. The flagship, the *Jesus of Lubeck*, so-called because she had originally been built in that Baltic port of merchants of the Hanseatic League, was an old vessel. She had been sold as long ago as 1545 to Henry VIII, and she belonged both in rig and design to another age. With her enormous forecastle and aftercastle, she had been built for the days when a great ship was a land-fort. In the Baltic, the North Sea, or on the Mediterranean run, the *Jesus* in her time would have been a most formidable ship, but beyond a certain age—however much she may have been refitted, repaired, and recaulked—any wooden vessel reaches a 'point of no return'. The *Jesus* had been recaulked during that year and had been armed with new cannon, but in Bay of Biscay weather, or the long swell of trade wind seas, she was certain to leak badly, for her high superstructures imposed an immense strain on the planking and ribs of her main body. Hawkins had sailed in her before, knew her defects, and perhaps with these in mind had made sure that she was fitted with the new type of chain pumps, which could shift a large volume of water efficiently. The Queen's other ship, the *Minion*, was equally old and had an unhappy record.

Although Elizabeth invested two ships in the expedition, she was only venturing vessels that were almost due for the breakers' yard—and both of them had had to be refitted at the other investors' expense. Hawkins, however, was not intending to engage in naval action against other warships, and the *Jesus* with her imposing appearance and her ample accommodation looked as if she would suit him well for a trading expedition. To the Governors of the Spanish ports, where he hoped to dispose of his cargo of slaves, the *Jesus* would present an air of dignity, and convey to them that they were not just dealing with a small-time merchant. Furthermore, by having induced the Queen to invest in the enterprise, Hawkins knew that—as far as was possible—he had her backing should he run into any trouble.

They immediately found trouble in terms of weather. It was late in the year, and not surprising therefore that in the region of Cape Finisterre they ran into a typical winter gale, which lasted for four days and scattered the ships over the ocean. In those awkward piled-up seas, where the full sweep of the Atlantic breaks on the continental shelf of Europe, even the most efficient ships of the period were liable to suffer damage. The *Jesus of Lubeck*, old, strained, and top-heavy, spewed her caulking and leaked like a sieve. Night and day the pumps were manned, and carpenters worked until they dropped exhausted, reinforcing the strained seams or putting tingles of lead and baize over the worst places where the vast superstructure threatened to tear itself away from the hull. On the fourth day, almost convinced that their last hour had come, John Hawkins led the ship's company in prayer. When the wind did finally ease, the *Jesus* was wallowing drunkenly in the long pewter-coloured rollers, still afloat but only, so it seemed, by a miracle.

Hawkins, who at one moment had thought of abandoning the whole expedition, was encouraged by the reports from his carpenters

and shipwrights that they had the damage under control. Aware that
with every mile he made further to the south, and into the clement
weather, the better his chances of success, he decided to carry on to the
previously-arranged rendezvous at the Canary Islands. When they
sighted the high peak of Mount Teide lifting out of the sea, the flagship
and the two small vessels *Angel* and *Judith*, who had come up with her
after the storm, altered course for the roadstead of Santa Cruz in Teneriffe. This was a recognised port of assembly for ships bound for Africa,
or westward across the Atlantic.

It was while they were lying here at anchor, making good the
damage suffered during the past few days, that something akin to a
mutiny broke out. This arose through a quarrel between Edward
Dudley, captain of the land soldiers, and George Fitzwilliam, one of
Hawkins' officers. The way in which Hawkins dealt swiftly and
efficiently with the affair is irrelevant to the story of the voyage. The
only thing that is very relevant is that the young Francis Drake for the
first time was brought face to face with a problem of this type—something always liable to beset a captain in charge of a squadron far from
home, and headed for dangerous waters.

Having revictualled and watered, and having made good all the
storm-damage, Hawkins led his squadron south from the Canary
Islands towards the African coast. Sighting the barren, featureless land,
with its shifting off-shore sandbanks and its tricky currents, they
pursued their course until they reached Cape Blanco. Once the outermost point of the known world, Cape Blanco had been rounded by
Nuno Tristão, one of Henry the Navigator's great captains, in 1441.
For over a hundred years the Portuguese had been sailing down to this
part of the coast in their shallow-draught caravels, lured by the slave
trade, and by the plentiful fishing to be had off these banks, where a
cold current from the Atlantic swirls in towards the African shore.

It was in this area that the fleet came across a caravel, which appears to
have been abandoned by its crew. Francis Drake was now given his
first command in the Hawkins fleet, and was put in charge of this small
vessel, which was re-named *The Grace of God*. Later, Hawkins appears
to have annexed or bought another caravel, whilst two French privateers also joined his flag (possibly under duress), bringing the number of
his ships up to ten. Since, in his own account, Hawkins necessarily
glosses over anything prejudicial to his conduct, it must remain in
doubt how much the acquisition of these small ships was just plain
piracy, or how much luck or honest dealing. Some small boats which
the squadron had been towing behind them had been lost in the storm
in the Bay of Biscay. Shallow-draught boats were always needed on

the African coast for landing troops and embarking slaves, since the
waters were too shallow to permit ocean-going ships to close the shore.
It seems a more than fortunate coincidence that, having lost his own
small craft, Hawkins should just have 'chanced upon' the very vessels
that he needed.

Arriving off the Guinea coast, Hawkins put 150 men ashore to
capture his cargo. But a hundred years of the slave trade had naturally
made the Africans wary of European ships, and Hawkins' men managed
to capture only a very few Negroes. They suffered a number of losses
themselves, for the natives in this part of the world used poisoned
arrows—something that had been found out by Henry the Navigator's
sailors a century before. Hawkins tells us that these arrow wounds 'although in the beginning they seemed to be but small hurts, yet there
hardly escaped any, that had blood drawn of them, but died in strange
sort, with their mouths shut some ten days before they died, and after
their wounds were whole; when I myself had one of the greatest
wounds, yet, thanks be to God, escaped.' Hawkins himself would
appear to have recovered through the application of a dose of garlic to
his wound. From the description of the symptons, the venom used on
the arrows was most probably a vegetable poison similar to aconitine.

The fleet rounded Cape Verde and sailed south to Cape Roxo in the
region of the Gambia Delta where, in collaboration with one of the
native kings, Hawkins' men raided the principal town of another tribe
and took some 250 prisoners. Their ally captured 600 but, refusing to
share his booty with the English, made off with them overnight,
causing Hawkins to remark that this race is 'habitually void of truth'.
As E. F. Benson commented: 'This regret for their low moral standard
comes oddly from a man who was stealing human beings to sell them
beyond the sea. . . .' In the event, they only had 500 slaves when
Hawkins decided that it was time to sail.

On the 7th February, 1568 the ships weighed anchor and stood out
from the African coast, bound on what later came to be called, in the
horrifying history of the slave trade, 'the Middle Passage'. Drake was
transferred from the Portuguese caravel and put in command of the
50-ton *Judith*, thus for the first time taking on the responsibility of
ship's captain on an Atlantic crossing. For 52 days the ten ships were at
sea; a slow crossing, perhaps due to the fact that Hawkins insisted on
good station-keeping, which meant that the speed of the slowest
regulated that of the whole fleet, and perhaps also to the fact that they
had now been four months afloat. Delayed by the difficulties of
capturing enough slaves, Hawkins had not been willing to waste any
time in careening his vessels before they left Africa.

On the 27th March the look-outs called down from the mast-tops, and the sailors cheered as they raised their first sight of the new western world. This was the precipitous, tree-clad island of Dominica—one of the few places where the native Caribs held out against the Europeans (and where the last remaining Caribs still live to this day). The ships altered course, and sailed with the full press of the trade winds behind them through the Dominica-Martinique Channel. They made their way south to the Spanish island of Margarita, lying just off the mainland of modern Venezuela.

Here, for eight days, Hawkins carried on a friendly and profitable trade with the Governor and the other inhabitants. The English ships, apart from their captured Africans, were well-laden with manufactured goods. At first it seemed likely that the expedition was going to be most lucrative, and Hawkins' own account gives the impression that everything proceeded reasonably well: 'From thence [Margarita] we coasted from place to place making our traffic with the Spaniards as we might; somewhat hardly because the King had straightly commanded all his Governors in those parts by no means to suffer any trade to be made with us. Notwithstanding we had reasonable trade and entertainment, from the Isle of Margarita unto Cartegena without anything greatly worth the noting, save at Cape de la Vela in a town called Rio de la Hacha.'

One thing that must be remembered is that Hawkins' report was designed for the eyes of his Queen and her advisers, so he carefully omits, as far as possible, any suggestion that he or his men ever conducted themselves other than as honest traders. An account written years later by Job Hartop, a gunner in the *Jesus of Lubeck*, suggests that things went far from smoothly, and that the English attitude to the Spaniards on several occasions was like that of a modern operator in the 'protection racket', who says to his potential customer: 'Trade with me or else . . .'

However much the English in later centuries may have resented it, it must always be remembered that the sobriquet 'Perfidious Albion' did not stem from nothing. Nations grow old, like men, and in the process they grow—as we so kindly say—'more tolerant', meaning 'less aggressive'. Sir Osbert Sitwell, nostalgic for past grandeur but not without a certain justification, described the English nation as it emerged at the end of the Second World War: 'Their former vigour and robustness had succumbed before a cult of timid, pallid suffering, alternating with paltry rewards. Issuing victorious from a long war waged with stubborn heroism by the whole people, they now dingily begged—*out of an Empire which their buccaneering forefathers had smashed entire nations to build, salvaging it from the ensuing chaos*—only to retain a few dehydrated or reconstituted eggs, a once-a-week dusting of tea, and a banana for the children. . . .' (My italics.)

After two months of more-or-less trouble-free trading at Borburata on the mainland, the ships moved on to Rio de la Hacha, where Captain Lovell and Drake had previously suffered a rebuff. It was not so surprising that the Treasurer (who appears to have been a good Governor, and one who conformed to the regulations laid down by his King), was unwilling to receive the English. Hawkins' account naturally suggests that all the blame was to be laid on the Spaniard. 'He had fortified his town with divers bulwarks, and furnished himself with 100 arquibusiers, so that he thought by famine to have forced us to put a-land our negroes, of which purpose he had not greatly failed unless we had not by force entered the town, which (after we could by no means obtain his favour) we were enforced to do.'

In advance of the main body of the fleet, the *Angel* and *Judith* were sent ahead to announce that an English squadron under John Hawkins had come to trade. Remembering Drake's previous experiences with Miguel de Castellanos, Job Hartop's account of the episode is probably more reliable than that of John Hawkins. Drake had not forgotten his earlier lesson, and was ready enough to act. Hartop says that, as the two small vessels sailed up to the town and dropped anchor, 'The Spaniards shot three pieces at us, which we requited with two of ours and shot through the Governor's house. . . .' This has the authentic fire, the 'Drake touch', and is quite unlike the circumspect Hawkins.

The two ships now weighed but, far from standing out to sea until the main body of the fleet had come up with them, they insolently dropped anchor again within gun-shot of the town. Drake's character is so apparent in this action, and indeed it was similar to one of the last of his life in 1595, off the port of San Juan, in Puerto Rico. No one knew better than he the demoralising effect upon civilians and towns-people of seeing a hostile man-of-war—however small she might be—lying within range of their homes.

Such an action spoke more clearly than words of a supreme arro-gance, and of a confidence that sea-power was more effective than land-forts. While the two ships were riding there, a Spanish despatch boat arrived, and at this point (whatever the protestations of Hawkins and later historians) one must freely admit that Drake acted like a pirate, for 'we chased and drove [the boat] to the shore: we fetched him from thence in spite of 200 Spaniards' arquebus shot, and anchored again before the town, and rode there with them, till our general's coming, who anchored, landed his men, and valiently took the town.

We landed and planted on the shore for our safeties our field-ordinance: we drove the Spaniards up into the country above 2 leagues, whereby they were inforced to trade with our general, to whom he sold most part of his negroes.'

Even Sir Julian Corbett, writing in the 19th century, when Drake was held up to the English youth as a model hero whose deeds ought to be emulated, was forced to admit: 'It was the act of a pirate, lawless, indefensible, and probably in excess of his instructions—the first of the long series of reckless exploits with which Drake was to display his scepticism of the Spanish power and to preach his new creed of the way in which their monopoly was to be broken down.'

It is not hard to sympathise with the inhabitants of these distant Spanish colonies, and it is understandable that they should write to Philip II: 'We entreat Your Majesty to remedy the grievous conditions prevailing today in Indies. For every two ships that come hither from Spain, twenty corsairs appear. . . . They go so far as to boast that they are Lords of the Sea and of the Land—Unless Your Majesty deign to favour all this coast by remedying the situation, all these settlements must necessarily be abandoned.'

Having completed their trading at Rio de la Hacha—trading to which Castellanos was forced to submit not only by the English, but by a revolt of his own townspeople who were eager to buy slaves— the squadron moved on westwards up the coast. Soon they had in sight the high spiny ridges of the Sierra Nevada. Capped by snow, they signalled like a beacon that, at the point where the land swung south-ward towards the Gulf of Darien, lay the township of Santa Marta. Here the trading was more in the style that Hawkins liked to expect. The Governor made an official protest, stating that he was not allowed to deal with any other than ships holding a licence from the King of Spain, while Hawkins made a mock assault on the city (so that the Governor could report officially that he had had no option but to trade with these heretic merchants). This was all part of the accepted and normal custom. At Santa Marta there was no trouble between traders and colonists, for 'the Spanish inhabitants were glad of us, and traded willingly'.

It was not until they reached Cartagena, the capital city of the 'Spanish Main' (that section of the mainland of South America occupied and developed by the Spaniards, and in its usual references meaning the Panamanian isthmus), that Hawkins found the laws regarding trade with foreigners could really be preserved. Drake had a good chance to take stock of Cartagena; it was strong and well defended, built, like many cities of the ancient world, on an arm of land almost entirely surrounded by sea. In many respects it resembled one of the great harbours of antiquity (Syracuse in Sicily, for example) being an 'island-peninsula' that enclosed a great bay in which a whole fleet might happily take shelter. Hawkins only had about sixty slaves left to sell—and presumably little left of his English merchandise—so he hoped that in his important city he might easily clear off his 'remaining stock'. He was to be sadly disillusioned, for the Governor was an honest servant of his King, and—unlike Castellanos—had the strength to back up his rejection of the Englishman's demands. Not only did he forbid these foreigners to trade, but he also denied them any port facilities, such as watering or storing ship.

Hawkins had counted on getting rid of the last of his cargo here, and the season was far advanced. The hurricane-centres were raising their towering anvil-heads out of the hot Caribbean, to blow Englishman or Spaniard to destruction. They managed to anchor their ships in the outer harbour, and even to re-water—without permission—from a nearby island. Now, for a whole week, the winds turned against them and blew onshore, so that they were forced to wait. While the ships sat there port-bound, their small boats must undoubtedly have crossed the bay now and again. It is more than likely that in one of them sat the man who was destined to storm this city 18 years later, for it is almost certain that Drake made use of these days of enforced idleness to study the weaknesses of proud Cartagena.

There was just enough food aboard the ships to make the passage back to England, and Hawkins would have been glad to weigh anchor, and leave as soon as the unfriendly winds allowed him. All the ships were badly in need of a refit and, above all, of cleaning and tarring after the many months in tropical waters—especially the *Jesus of Lubeck*, old and more prone, through her soft planking, to the attacks of teredo worm than any other. He left Cartagena as soon as he could, though not before he had carried off a fair amount of wine and oil from a storage place whose whereabouts had been revealed to them by a Negro caretaker. In return for these unlooked-for stores, Hawkins left behind as much English woollen and linen cloth as he estimated that they were worth. In later days his young relative Drake would not bother with such niceties.

Putting Cartagena behind them, the ships did their best to get clear of the Caribbean before the hot winds and hurricanes of autumn caught up with them. They made their way north-westward, intending to pass round Cape St. Antonio at the extreme western tip of Cuba. Then, with the Gulf Stream favouring them, they would have beat out against the trade winds into the Atlantic, before making as much

northing as possible in order to pick up the favourable westerlies in the
area of Bermuda. As it turned out, the squadron was struck by a violent
storm—probably the fringe of a hurricane—while beating up towards
Cape St. Antonio. In the ensuing whirl of wind and water, the ships
had immense difficulty in keeping in sight of one another.

The ships were now in the Florida Channel, that strange area where
the Gulf Stream streams through the opening to the ocean—where the
marlin and the great sailfish leap, and where the Gulf weed spreads out,
to drift in yellow folds all the way across the Atlantic to Ireland, and
the fringes of the English Channel. The Gulf Stream produces more
awkward seas, tumbled churned waters, humid weather, and sinister
patches of steamy fog than any comparable area in the world. It was no
place for Hawkins' old flagship to be. Her caulking had been patched up
many months ago in the Canaries, and only such temporary repairs
had been made to her as were possible after this long ocean voyage, and
her steady trading and sailing in the Caribbean.

There was nothing for the ships to do but run before the wind and
weather. They could not keep station in the entrance to the Florida
Channel, for the storm, pursuing a usual course for the Caribbean
area, was blasting its way northwards towards the coast of America.
Battered by the wind and blinded by the blown spume, the English
ships ran before it towards the coastline of Florida. At dawn they were
in soundings, and for two days they staggered desperately along the
gap-toothed reefs, clawing off to safety as best they could, and managing by luck as much as seamanship to avoid grounding. Then at last
the storm took off but, as its coat-tails flickered overhead, so the wind
suddenly backed, and a strong northerly began to blow. Ravaged by
the weather, with the exhausted men toiling to the clank-clank-clank
of the chain-pumps, the ships fled again—this time blown into the
open mouth of the Gulf of Mexico.

At least they were swept clear of the dangerous Florida shore, but
their situation was still desperate. All of them had suffered severe storm-
damage, and the *Jesus of Lubeck*, which had hardly been in a condition
to face the autumn Atlantic beforehand, now had to find sheltered
water. But only one suitable port lay to leeward, and this was San Juan
de Ulua, deep in the Gulf of Mexico, and the principal landing-place
for the city of Mexico itself. It was also vitally important to the
Spaniards, because it was the port where the annual treasure fleet
embarked the gold and silver from Vera Cruz for shipment to Spain.

Hawkins took aboard the passengers from some small vessels he
encountered—to act as hostages for his safe-conduct—and shaped his
course for San Juan de Ulua. Unfortunately, unknown to him, the

inhabitants of San Juan were hourly expecting the arrival of the escort
for the treasure fleet. Seeing a number of ships under sail, and making
their way towards their harbour, the authorities and citizens of San
Juan naturally concluded that it was the expected escort. They did not
know, nor had they any reason to suspect, that another fleet was at that
time in the Gulf of Mexico. So Hawkins' ships drove up towards the
land and, on the evening of the 15th September, dropped anchor just
clear of the reefs which fringed the port.

San Juan in itself was little more than a roadstead, protected from the
prevailing northerlies by a low island. On the following morning the
English ships were just rounding this island, preparatory to coming up
into the wind and dropping anchor in the harbour, when a number of
Spanish boats came out to greet them. The battery at the south-eastern
end of the island sprang into life as Hawkins' flagship rolled slowly past,
and all five guns fired—but to his great relief, only blank shot! They
were firing a courtesy salute, having assumed that this great ship
carried aboard her Don Martin Enriquez, the Viceroy of New Spain.
It was only a few minutes before panic broke loose. Francisco de
Bustamente, Treasurer of Vera Cruz, was already going aboard, when
he saw that it was the Royal Standard of England that flew above the
leading ship. At almost the same moment the watchers on the island
realised their mistake. A panic-stricken cry went up 'The heretics are
upon us!' Men jumped into the sea and began to swim for the shore,
while those who could, piled into launches and small boats, and rowed
as if the devil was at their heels for the mainland.

It cannot have taken Hawkins more than a few minutes to realise
that whoever held the low island-reef which protected the anchorage,
held the whole port of San Juan de Ulua in his grasp. If he had been
intending to capture the treasure fleet of New Spain he could not have
arrived at a better moment. But it is perfectly clear that such an undertaking was never in Hawkins' mind. It would probably have led to
war in any case—something he dared not risk—and his ships and men
were in no condition to fight even a minor, let alone a major, engagement. He hastened to assure the Treasurer, and the Captain of the
battery, that the English ships came in peace, and that their only
intention was to make good their storm-damage before departing. He
went on to make it clear that he would pay like a peaceable and honest
trader for any stores or supplies that he might need. Indeed, he did
everything that he could to reassure all those in authority that they had
nothing to fear from him. For Hawkins now learned that the ships
which were to form the treasure fleet were hourly expected, and that he
had been mistaken for them. He realised at once into what a lion's den

he had put his head, and there can be little doubt that he would have sailed immediately if it had been possible. But the damage to the *Jesus* alone meant that he could not leave. He must stay and make good his ships—and pray that the treasure fleet was delayed, so that he could sail without ever setting eyes on it.

But on the very next morning, as Hawkins himself tells the story, 'We saw open of the haven thirteen great ships, and understanding them to be the fleet of Spain, I sent immediately to advertise the General of the fleet of my being there, giving him to understand, that before I would suffer them to enter the port, there should be some order of conditions pass between us, for our safe-being there, and maintenance of peace.' The new Viceroy of Mexico, Don Martin Enriquez, very naturally felt the humiliation of his position. Here he was, arriving to take over his all-important post, with a powerful fleet and a large military force—only to find an English squadron in possession of the island that commanded the gateway to the province of New Spain.

Protesting that he was the Viceroy, and had a thousand men with him, and would enter his own port without any conditions being imposed or accepted, Don Martin in turn received Hawkins' reply: 'I represent my Queen's person and I am Viceroy as well: and if you have a thousand men, my powder and shot will take the better place.' This arrogant tone was somewhat necessary—for Hawkins realised only too well how desperate was his position, and that the only possible remedy was, in the phrase of the day, 'to put a brag countenance' upon it.

For four days negotiations went on, and boats sped back and forth between the English and Spanish ships. Then, on Tuesday, the 21st September, 1568, the Spanish ships weighed anchor and entered their own harbour. The two parties had finally reached an agreement. The English might repair their ships in peace and buy what stores and victuals they needed ashore. Hawkins, as a guarantee of his safety, might also retain control of the island as well as keeping the guns that he had landed from his ships mounted upon it. Finally, the Spaniards agreed that no armed members of their crew would land on the island, and that each party to this pact should exchange ten hostages. On the surface, it would seem that for a man with a few almost disabled ships—though tactically well placed—Hawkins had managed to get very good terms. But he knew from his previous experience in trading and dealing with Spaniards, that what really mattered was whether they would keep to their side of the bargain. He had good reason to fear that they would attempt to crush his weak force with their superior arms and men. This, in fact, was what Don Martin had clearly determined upon from the beginning.

At first it might have appeared to an onlooker that, in a situation so awkward for both sides, all was going reasonably well. As Rayner Unwin points out in *The Defeat of John Hawkins*: 'The courtesies of the sea were scrupulously observed. Salutes were exchanged, and when the preliminary mooring [of the Spanish ships] had taken place, trumpets were sounded and the text of the agreement was read aloud to men of both nations. Visits were exchanged, and despite the barriers of language and religion both sides were at pains to show their friendliness and their determination to give no reason for offence. . . .' The two groups of ships were finally lying at anchor with no more than 20 yards between their nearest vessels—their bows secured by warps inshore, and their sterns held off by anchors.

John Hawkins had been right to anticipate trouble, and on the night of Wednesday, the 22nd September his suspicions were confirmed. The Spanish Viceroy quietly and secretively started to move a large body of armed men by rowing boats from the mainland into his ships. Hawkins had been awake throughout the night and, in company with other observers—among whom one must certainly include Francis Drake—they heard all the sounds (chink of arms and muffled orders) which indicated some treachery afoot.

In the morning Hawkins was not slow to send Robert Barnett, the Spanish-speaking master of the *Jesus of Lubeck*, over to the Viceroy, to voice his suspicions. Unknown to Hawkins, Barnett was immediately seized. He himself—just as he was sitting down to dine—was nearly the victim of a treacherous attack by one of his hostages, a Spanish gentleman by the name of Agustin de Villanueva, who had come to the table with a dagger concealed in his sleeve. No doubt the murder of Hawkins was to have been the signal for the concerted attack on the English. As it turned out, the dagger fell from Villanueva's sleeve who was immediately seized by Hawkins' cabin steward.

It was too late, however, to prevent the general massacre which the Spaniards had been so carefully preparing. Hawkins and the other officers with him had hardly reached the upper deck of the *Jesus*, to make their protest, when a trumpet-call rang out. Immediately the Spanish sailors and soliders ashore (who up till then had been fraternising apparently cheerfully with the English) all drew concealed weapons, and fell upon them. The soldiers who had been smuggled aboard the ships overnight showed themselves as they leapt ashore to take possession of the battery.

Fortunately the noises in the night, together with Hawkins' permanent suspicion of a Spaniard's assurances (not for nothing do Spaniards, when they wish to convey that something is really true, say 'On the word of an Englishman') had already alerted the ships. Most of the sailors, therefore, were near to their action stations and the guns were ready. While the scene ashore was one of desperate confusion, a Spanish ship laden with soldiers began to close the *Minion*, hauled over towards her by a line already made fast to her stern. As the two vessels touched, and the soldiers began to jump aboard with the battle cry of Spain, 'Santiago!', Hawkins rallied his men with a shout of 'God and St. George!' The guns now began to thunder between the closely-packed ships.

While the English cut the head-ropes that secured them to the shore, and the sailors manned the capstans to haul the ships out towards their anchors, the gunners opened fire. Perhaps because the attack had been precipitated, the Spaniards were not as ready as they should have been, and the sudden fire of the English guns at close range wrought havoc amongst them. The Spanish *Almirante*, hit by a broadside which set off part of her magazine, blew up with a shattering explosion and became a smoking wreck. Not long afterwards Don Martin's flagship, hit time and time again, began to settle down in the water. The superior weight of the English fire power proved on this occasion—as it was to do so often during Drake's furious life—that it is not the size of a ship that counts.

On shore the Spanish attack had been entirely successful. All the Englishmen in the battery but three were massacred, and the guns were soon in Spanish hands. These were now turned upon Hawkins' ships and but for this, as the official Spanish account admits, all would have been lost. Hawkins, a silver tankard of beer in his hand, stood on the upper deck encouraging his crew, 'Stand by your ordnance lustily like men!' It is said that, as he put down his tankard, a shot knocked it over, at which he called out: 'Fear not, for God who hath delivered me from the shot will also deliver us from these traitors and villains!'

Meanwhile, the *Angel* had been sunk by the fire of the shore batteries, the *Swallow* had been so damaged as to be unserviceable, and one of the caravels was lost. Indeed, the only ship out of the original expedition ever to reach England without damage was the *William and John*—and this was only because she had never entered San Juan de Ulua, but had parted company in the gale and made her own way home. The *Jesus of Lubeck*, almost a ruin before the action began, had to be abandoned and, although Hawkins managed to save much of the profits from the season's trading, this meant a severe loss to the Queen.

When he abandoned the *Jesus*, Hawkins, taking all the men with him that he could muster, transhipped to the *Minion*. At the same time he signalled Drake in the *Judith* to embark all whom he could. In the end only these two ships, out of the ten with which he had entered San Juan, fought their way clear. They left behind them many dead, and many who were soon to die at the hands of the Inquisition. They left also the proud squadron of the Spanish Viceroy so hard-hit and battered that, much though they would have like to seal their victory, the Spaniards were in no condition to pursue the two small English ships. Five hundred of their men had been killed and four of their ships were a total loss.

Drake, in obedience to Hawkins' orders, had already got the 50-ton *Judith* clear of the harbour. The *Minion*, however, with Hawkins aboard, was compelled to shelter overnight in the lee of a small island, for the weather now turned against him. For two days he was forced to take refuge, as one of the harsh northerlies that sweep over the Gulf of Mexico blew dead in his teeth. When he finally got clear (to the bitter disappointment of the Viceroy, who had been expecting to capture the ship as well as Hawkins himself), he found that the *Judith* was nowhere to be seen. From this incident, and from Hawkins' account of it, there has arisen a story that Drake deliberately abandoned his kinsman, and all the other men with him, in order to seek his own safety. This has largely stemmed from Hawkins' words that the '*Judith* forsook us in our great misery. . . .' Another account, however, has it merely that 'the *Judith* lost us'.

Since on no occasion in his life can Drake have been accused of a lack of courage, it is worth examining the situation in more detail. Drake, obeying his orders, had fought his way clear of the harbour. He had as many men aboard the *Judith* as he could carry and now, with night coming on, he dropped anchor and waited. But the violent northerly which blew up, and which caused Hawkins to stay at anchor under the lee of an islet, meant that Drake—who was clear of the harbour and the reefs—was on a lee shore. There can be no doubt that, like any sensible mariner, he at once stood out to sea. On the following day, having failed to sight the *Minion*, which was still concealed behind the islet, he made his own way home. If Hawkins had truly believed that his young cousin had callously abandoned him to his fate, it is hardly conceivable that he would have worked together with him on other ventures in the course of his life. It is not the first time in warfare that men have complained of an ally, only to forget their complaint as soon as they have learned the true facts of the case.

The defeat of John Hawkins at San Juan de Ulua, a defeat which Spanish historians have frankly admitted was based upon an act of treachery by Don Martin Enriquez, was to prove a most costly victory. When, after many weeks at sea, the two surviving ships finally limped

into Plymouth—Drake in January, and Hawkins in February, 1569—
the fury of the English knew no bounds. The perfidy of Don Martin
was on every man's lips. Many years later, when two or three of the
survivors struggled back to England, the stories of the brutality to
which they had been subjected reinforced an implacable hatred. As one
of the survivors, Miles Philips, recounted in 1582: 'All such of our men
as were not in them [the *Judith* and the *Minion*] were inforced to abide
the tyrannous cruelty of the Spaniards. For it is a certain truth, that
whereas they had taken certain of our men ashore, they took and hung
them up by the arms, upon high posts, until the blood burst out of
their fingers' ends. . . .' Others were ordered to suffer two or three
hundred lashes before being sent to the galleys for sentences of up to
ten years.

Even if England and Spain had been at war, there could have been no
justification for such treatment of prisoners. Hawkins himself had
behaved with dignity and restraint, for the ten Spanish hostages aboard
the *Jesus* were later found by their compatriots without a hair of their
heads having been touched. Yet Hawkins had had every right to have
them killed the moment that the attack was launched upon his ships
and men.

But, over and above the deep bitterness which was aroused in
England by the tragic affair at San Juan de Ulua, the Spaniards had
unwittingly created a deadly enemy. No doubt when the small *Judith*
beat her way out of the harbour Don Martin Enriquez did not feel that
he had lost much by so unimportant a prize gaining the safety of the
sea. But in the *Judith* went one man with a long memory. Drake had
seen with his own eyes the massacre of his friends and countrymen. He
saw that a Spaniard's word meant less than the air which voiced it, or
the paper upon which it was written. Whatever his father may earlier
have taught him about that Antichrist who supposedly dwelled in
Rome—but whose principal servant was the king of Spain—it would
seem that from now on Drake equated Spain with the Devil. His
hatred was implacable, and he was a man who under no circumstance
was prepared to forgive an injury. His outlook was Old Testament, not
Christian: 'An eye for an eye, and a tooth for a tooth!'

On his long and lone voyage back to England, having lost, as he no
doubt thought, Hawkins as well as all the others who had sailed on the
expedition, it is doubtful whether Drake had much cause to smile. Yet
it was remarked by Spaniards who were later to be his prisoners that
he had a cheerful character. It is from this time, perhaps, that one may
date a Spanish proverb: 'Three things in the world to beware of—horn
of a bull, hoof of a horse, and smile of a Saxon!'

The young man who had gone out to learn the ways of the Atlantic, and the methods of trade in the New World, returned dedicated to revenge. From the moment that the Spanish soldiers drew their concealed weapons and began to massacre the English sailors on that narrow sea-stained island off San Juan de Ulua, Drake was engaged in a personal war. Until the end of his life he was dedicated to the destruction of Spain, her ships, her empire, her religion, and her king.

CHAPTER FIVE

The Islands and the Main

FRANCIS DRAKE found himself, for the first time, a person commanding attention, and the circumstances of it cannot have been to his liking. He had arrived in Plymouth, with the few half-starved survivors of the expedition, on the 20th January, 1569. He had to report to William Hawkins that, as far as he knew, his brother John was either dead or captured, that the whole expedition was a failure, and that there were no survivors except the men aboard the small *Judith*.

There is no record of what William Hawkins felt, but one must remember that Drake suffered nearly all his life from the story that he had 'forsaken' John Hawkins and his ship in the moment of danger. Men like Frobisher and Grenville never forgot this early 'stain'— although they held Drake's common blood against him almost as much as any supposed deficiences in his character. We shall never know the truth now, but sinister stories were certainly current about him. The contemporary Spanish historian, Antonio de Herrera, who like all Spaniards had good reason to dislike Drake, maintained that he was guilty of cowardice and worse. Sir Julian Corbett summarised Herrera's evidence by saying that he embellished the story: 'accusing Drake not only of disobeying Hawkins' orders, but of embezzling the gold that was saved from the *Jesus*, "And this," Herrera said, "was his beginning. For this offence the Queen imprisoned him for three months, but on intercession being made on his behalf he was pardoned, and so the matter rested." These assertions are supported by no English authorities, and may safely be rejected together with so many other Spanish stories, as an invention to Drake's discredit.'

It is impossible that Drake 'embezzled' the gold from the *Jesus*, for Hawkins arrived only a short time after him in Plymouth, and would never have let his young relative get away with such a monstrous act— nor would the Queen herself. We know, furthermore, that Hawkins brought back aboard the *Minion* most of the trading profits that he had been able to salvage from the venture, and that it took four pack-horses to carry the gold, silver and pearls to London. Herrera, an honest historian in many respects (he was prepared to admit that the affair at San Juan de Ulua was initiated by the treachery of his own countrymen), was somewhat naturally blinded by hatred of Drake. He was prepared to promulgate any story that could show that 'the Dragon' was not only the enemy of God, but of mankind—of any man, indeed, even his own cousin and countryman. Drake, as his later history reveals quite clearly, was ruthless. He was unscrupulous in many ways, he was certainly a pirate, and he was the deadly enemy of Spain. Yet there is no occasion on record when he broke his word, for instance, to any prisoners he took. Despite the fact that he knew what the fate of his countrymen was when they fell into Spanish hands, he always treated prisoners with scrupulous fairness, nor did any of his companions ever have complaints to make against him in his subsequent sharing of booty from captured ships.

Only one thought unpleasantly suggests itself. Did Drake take a certain amount of the trading profits aboard the *Judith* in San Juan de Ulua? And did the two cousins later proceed to split these 'undeclared' proceeds—Hawkins on the understanding that he would say no more about his cousin having deserted him? It is not entirely impossible. A certain element of mystery hangs over the next few months of Drake's life. He disappears from view, only to re-emerge in charge of two small vessels, the *Dragon* and the *Swan*, bound once again for the scene of the recent disaster. Now, either Hawkins financed him on this next expedition, or Drake financed himself. If Hawkins was behind him, then one can discredit all rumours that there was any bitterness between the two over the affair at San Juan de Ulua. If Drake financed himself, then with what did he do it? He had never owned anything except his old trading boat, and it is reasonable to assume that any profit he had made out of the sale of her had been ploughed into the recent venture to the West Indies. In this case, a third possibility suggests itself—that Drake did indeed invest his small capital in the venture to San Juan, and that the dividend from it was enough to pay for his next expedition. As with so many self-made men, a deep and obscuring fog hangs over the means whereby Drake acquired his first working capital.

It has been suggested, though on slight evidence, that during these 'missing' months Drake took service in the Navy. One thing is certain, that Drake was not present when the official inquiry was held into the affair at San Juan de Ulua—nor did Hawkins during the course of the inquiry ever accuse Drake of having abandoned him. The simple solution of the case is probably the right one: that, when both men met, and Drake explained how he could not stay at anchor on a lee shore, Hawkins understood what the other's situation had been and accepted his account. Some of the commentators who have been unable to understand why Drake did not wait for Hawkins, or how he came to miss him—if he did stand off the land and wait for him—have clearly had little experience of the difficulties of handling small ships under sail. Both Drake and Hawkins had been in bad weather, in ill-chartered waters that were unfamiliar to them, and in small, primitive vessels. The really astounding thing is that either of them ever got home at all.

While they had been away, an unusual political situation had arisen, and one which was to have considerable bearing upon Drake's future. Towards the close of 1568, Philip II had despatched a number of bullion ships from Spain, destined for Antwerp. The greater part of the money aboard them was designed to pay the troops of the Duke of Alva, the Spanish Governor in the Netherlands, and the prime harrier of Protestantism in Europe. While these ships were on their way up Channel, they were chased by French privateers operating out of La Rochelle. Flying before the 'lawless' Frenchman, the Spaniards took refuge in peaceful Plymouth, harbour of that law-abiding monarch Queen Elizabeth.

To begin with, the Queen was prepared to give safe custody to the treasure, even to have it convoyed to the Netherlands under the protection of her own ships. Then something happened that altered things considerably. A rumour reached England about the affair at San Juan de Ulua, to the effect that not only had all the English ships been seized, but that there were no survivors. A safe conduct for the transportation of the treasure had actually been signed when Elizabeth decided to impound it. She was driven to this action largely, one may assume, by her realisation that the money (which totalled some £100,000) was destined for Spanish troops in the Netherlands whose ultimate even if unspoken aim was the invasion of England.

The Spanish reaction was swift and violent. An embargo was laid on all English property in the Netherlands, the English ambassador at Madrid was asked to withdraw from the court, and all trade between the two countries came to a standstill. The Queen who had merely impounded the money, promising to repay at a later date (which, in fact, she did), was now given some justification for seizing all the Spanish property in England, while the Spanish ambassador was placed under house arrest.

Of the relations between Elizabeth and Philip at this moment, John Barrow wrote: 'The two sovereigns were to each other in a state of peaceable antipathy, each "willing to wound", but each "afraid to strike".' Sir Julian Corbett, writing in the calm atmosphere of the late 19th century, commented with some surprise: 'The feature of international relations which most sharply distinguishes the sixteenth century from our own time is the length to which hostilities could be pushed without leading to an open rupture. Continually we encounter the phenomenon of two powers standing with regard to each other in a position that was neither peace nor war. . . .' Such a situation is familiar enough to citizens of the mid-20th century who, like the Elizabethans, have grown inured to living in a climate of 'cold war'. But whereas in our own century it is the 'balance of terror' that has avoided the precipitation of open conflict, in the 16th century it was the inability of the two enemies to get to grips with one another. Spain was a land colossus, with an Achilles' heel in her treasure route from South America. England, although her fleet was being slowly improved, was as yet no Leviathan that could confidently assert for herself the ruler-ship of the seas. Drake, with that astonishing perspicuity of his (which was a form of genius), had detected where the weakness of the Spanish adversary lay. When he and Hawkins arrived back in England with their tale of disaster, the relationship between the two countries was as bad as it could be. The story of San Juan de Ulua deepened the crisis, and from 1569 for several years onwards nothing short of open warfare could have worsened it.

It was during the summer of 1569 that Drake married Mary New-man, a Cornish girl from the parish of St. Budeaux near Plymouth. She may well have been the sister of one of Drake's companions, Harry Newman, who had taken part in the recent expedition. The marriage took place on the 4th July, and it is Mary Newman's one brief incursion into history. Although she was destined to become the first Lady Drake, we have no portrait of her, and know no more about her than that she died in January 1583 and was buried in her home parish. The marriage was childless, and Mary Newman saw little of her husband during all the fourteen years of their marriage. Without golden ring or symbolic gesture her husband, like the Doges of Venice, had long ago wedded the sea. There was to be little room in his violent life for the content-ment of domesticity.

Within less than a year of his marriage, he had sailed again for that continent which still bears the impress of his fiery individualism. He was a man who could not endure to be beaten, and he was aware that so far he had been beaten twice. The narrative of *Drake Revived* puts it: 'As there is a general vengeance which secretly pursueth the doers of wrong, and suffereth them not to prosper, albeit no man of purpose impeach them: So there is a particular indignation engrafted in the bosom of all that are wronged, which ceaseth not seeking by all means possible to redress or remedy the wrong received. . . .' This is how he described (or allowed to be described) the mission upon which he was now engaged—and which was to engage him to the end of his life. There were, as he saw it, two people involved in a personal quarrel: 'The one being (in his own conceit) the mightiest Monarch of all the world; the other an English Captain, a mean subject of Her Majesty's, who, (besides the wrongs received at Rio de la Hacha with Captain John Lovell in the years '65 and '66) having been grieveously en-damaged at San Juan de Ulua with Captain John Hawkins in the years '67 and '68—not only in the loss of goods of some value, but also of his kinsmen and friends, and that by the falsehood of Don Martin Enriquez then the Vice-Roy of Mexico, and finding that no recom-pence could be recovered out of Spain by any of his own means or by Her Majesty's letters: he used such help as he might by two several voyages into the West Indies; the first with two ships, the one called the *Dragon*, the other the *Swan*, in the year '70: the other in the *Swan* alone, in the year '71—*to gain such intelligence as might further him to get some amend for his loss. . . .'*

It is the last sentence which commands attention, for it states quite clearly the object of the next two voyages made by Drake. Impetuous he certainly was, but he was not foolhardy, and he did not dash—as some older commentators suggested—like an enraged bulldog straight at the throat of Spain. Far from it: he very carefully carried out two reconnaissance expeditions to examine the situation in the Spanish colonies of the New World. He wished to see for himself where the point of weakness lay, and how he could take advantage of it. Like many another man of action he liked to make a careful assessment of the enemy before committing himself to a blow. Drake, in the language of the boxing ring, was 'a counter-puncher' and, as the late Ernest Hemingway remarked: 'You never saw a counter-puncher who was punchy. Never lead against a hitter unless you can out-hit him. . . .' It was not until his powers were failing, and he 'had gone into the ring' too often, that Drake ever made that mistake. It is not absurd to see him in such simple and personal terms, for that was exactly how Drake saw himself: 'an English Captain' in a contest with 'the mightiest Monarch of all the world'.

While the Spanish intelligence service and their fifth-column in England concerned themselves with the doings of John Hawkins in the last months of 1569 and the spring of 1570—suspecting that, with the Queen's approval, Hawkins was fitting out a fleet to take his revenge, they scarcely noticed the departure from Devon of two small ships under a young and unknown captain. There was no reason why they should, for both vessels were under 50 tons, and similar to scores of

E

others which were trading in the Channel. Few people could have suspected that with such diminutive craft there was to be undertaken a 'reconnaissance flight' over the Spanish Empire, which would reveal the routes and sources of her treasure and the places where it might most easily be tapped.

It was upon the isthmus of Panama that Drake had set his sights. There, he was soon to realise, lay the narrow neck which a small raiding party might seize and strangle. All the treasure of Peru which had been shipped up the west coast of South America to Panama was transferred at this point to pack animals, and carried overland to the port of Nombre de Dios in the Caribbean, where it was embarked in the treasure fleet for Spain. Some of the heavier treasure such as gold and silver bullion was also ferried down the River Chagres, which came out into the Atlantic quite close to Nombre de Dios.

These were the main facts that Drake was to learn in his two voyages in the years 1570 and 1571. Whoever financed his two small ships, there can be little doubt that they had the unspoken blessing of those in authority—for anything that could lead to the injury of Spanish power must have commanded sympathy in the English Court. It was an added convenience that the expeditions were both so small, and so essentially private. It enabled the Queen and her ministers to disclaim any knowledge of, or responsibility for them. We know from a *Draft Answer to the complaints of Spain* (1580) that this was exactly the tone which was adopted about so many of the 'piracies' practised by Drake and his compatriots during those years. It was an attitude very similar to that adopted by the great powers in later centuries when, to any suggestion that some businessman has been engaged in espionage, there comes a bland disclaimer of any knowledge of the person concerned or of his activities.

The tricks and stratagems that are still practised in modern diplomacy were very familiar to Queen Elizabeth I of England and to her enemy Philip II of Spain. Nicholas Machiavelli of Florence had first codified, as it were, in his *Il Principe* the means whereby a man may rise to power. What modern Senators in America, or Members of Parliament in England may like to call Machiavelli's cynicism (although practising it themselves), was openly accepted by 16th-century monarchs and statesmen as being the most intelligent guide to the game of power that had ever been framed. Although Drake was familiar with Spanish, it is unlikely that he could read Italian. He was not a man who learned much from books, but he knew by instinct the things that an intellectual like Machiavelli had elaborated in his *Discorsi, Arte della Guerra* and *Il Principe*. The English seaman was now to put into practice against the Spaniards, those confirmed believers in 'double-think' and double talk, a policy of action so daring that it still seems to belong to the realm of fiction. It is important to remember, though, that Drake—as he himself admitted—was concerned only with a private action, a personal war. He had lost money, and his friends had lost both their money and their lives, and he intended to square the balance sheet. It is highly unlikely that he saw himself as a representative of England and her policy. That would come later.

We have no records of Drake's first voyage, except that one must assume it was successful for, in the following year, he went back again, alone this time, in the 25-ton *Swan*. Passing through the circling outriders of New Spain, the Spanish-occupied islands of the Caribbean, he dropped down (more like a hawk than a swan) into the steamy Gulf of Darien. Here on this almost virgin coast, where the isthmus of Panama connects with the South American mainland, he found a hideaway—a small natural harbour which he called Port Pheasant after the wild pheasants of the forest. A narrow entrance, screened by thick vegetation and protected by two small headlands, made it an ideal secret anchorage —invisible from the sea, where the ships and coastal trade of the Spanish Empire went driving before the winds 'upon their lawful occasions'. There was fruit and good fish, and all that was needed for security was to build a stockade in case of discovery and attack.

It was not long before Drake began to take his toll. A later Spanish account of his activities is entitled *A summary relation of the harms and robberies done by Fr. Drake an Englishman, with the assistance and help of other Englishmen*. From this we learn that 'upon the coast of Nombre de Dios they did rob divers barks in the river Chagres that were transporting merchandise of 40,000 ducats of velvets, and taffetas, besides other merchandise, besides gold and silver in other barks, and with the same came to Plymouth where it was divided amongst his partners. . . .' The damage was probably exaggerated, since this is a Spanish account; even so the small venture was clearly paying ample dividends. The *Swan* had a crew of less than thirty men, and they were self-supporting from the moment that they reached their operational area. It was piracy—such as the Bretons amongst others had been practising in the Caribbean for some time.

To understand just what Drake achieved in these early ventures one must imagine oneself in a small boat of 25 tons—about the same size as many a modern sailing yacht—thousands of miles from home, operating from a concealed base, and in the very heart of a foreign power hostile to one's own country. Drake and his men had no official backing. They would have been disowned if they had been caught; and all of them would have died on the scaffold as pirates, or have been burned at the stake as heretics.

He came to the conclusion that the first place to attack must be the city and harbour of Nombre de Dios, where the treasure was stored until its shipment to Spain. He had gained some useful information from the native Indians, and particularly from the Cimaroons. These were Negro slaves who had escaped from Spanish plantations, inter-married with the Indians, and who now lived in the wild hinterland and preyed upon the Spaniards. The Cimaroons' natural hatred of slavery had been reinforced by the inhumanity with which the Spani-ards used them. Drake, with his usual kindness in his dealings with his fellow-men, soon established a happy relationship with them. He even managed to get a plan of Nombre de Dios, as well as other detailed information, so that before he returned to England at the close of 1571, he knew where the batteries were sighted, how the streets ran, and even where the bulk of the treasure awaiting shipment was stored. From captured Spaniards he acquired further useful knowledge about the trade and treasure routes, and the general management of the Spanish colonies.

Before he sailed for England he set his Spanish prisoners free, even though this meant that his future security was compromised. If the Spaniards had understood and practised Drake's qualities of tolerance and mercy, their empire would have cohered for many more centuries than it did. Their influence might even now be predominant over North as well as South America.

Drake spent that winter at home in Devon with his wife. But Mary Drake was to see no more of him once the Channel gales had lifted, and the wild flowers had begun to shine along the Devon lanes. On Whit-sun Eve, the 24th May, 1572, Francis Drake sailed on the third of his private expeditions to the West Indies and the Spanish Main. One of the most authentic and greatest adventure books in history (already quoted from in this biography), published in 1626 and edited by Drake's nephew, tells the story of his ancestor's next venture. It was a tale that would ring in history for centuries to come, giving substance to novelists, and providing the fuel for a thousand young men's rocket-like flights into the world of hardship and adventure. *Sir Francis Drake Revived* was compiled from the reports of sailors who took part in the voyage, and it was revised and annotated by Drake himself, who also wrote the dedication to Queen Elizabeth. If it is suspect, therefore, it is only in so far as it may show Drake's actions in a more favourable light than that of other sources, but the truth of his assertions is generally borne out by Spanish records.

As E. F. Benson wrote: 'No book of sky-larking schoolboy adventure comes anywhere near, in the matter of romance, of escapes and escapades, of buccaneering failures and achievements, to this authentic history.' From the moment that one opens the narrative an extraordinary spell—like youth remembered—has one in its grasp. 'He accordingly prepared his ships and company, and then taking the first opportunity of a good wind had such success in his proceedings, as now follows further to be declared . . . Captain Drake in the *Pascha* of Plymouth of 70 tons, his Admiral, with the *Swan* of the same port of 25 tons, his Vice-Admiral, in which his brother John Drake was Captain, having in both of them, in men, and boys, 73: all voluntarily assembled, of which the eldest man was 50: all the rest under 30: so divided that there were 47 in one ship and 26 in the other, both richly furnished with victuals and apparel for a whole year: and no less heedfully provided of all manner of munition, artillery, stuff and tools that were requisite for such a man of war, in such an attempt, but especially having three dainty pinnaces made in Plymouth, taken asunder in all pieces, and stowed aboard, to be set up (as occasion served), set sail from out of the Sound of Plymouth with intent to land at Nombre de Dios. . . .'

So, with seventy-three young men in two small sailing ships, Francis Drake left the Channel and sailed for America, his intention being to capture a town as large as Plymouth and to carry off its treasure. Nombre de Dios was at that time, as Prince describes it in his *Worthies of Devon*, 'the Granary of the West Indies, wherein the golden harvest brought from Peru and Mexico to Panama was hoarded up till it could be conveyed to Spain'. The sheer audacity of the venture still retains its power to move, amaze, and astound.

The two ships made an excellent run across the Atlantic, reaching Guadeloupe and the flying-fish weather only twenty-five days out from Plymouth. Such a quick passage is proof in itself of the good condition of the ships, and of the accuracy of the 'Admiral's' navigation. Guadeloupe, as it remained to the end of Drake's life, when he and Hawkins watered here on his last voyage, was still an independent island, unconquered by the Spaniards, and an ideal place therefore for sea-rovers to water, careen, and repair their ships. Under the blue skies, broken only by the flying trade-wind clouds, they could idle for a brief spell, run on the white sand beaches, and bathe in the warm-silk waters and feel—for the first time in many cases—the sun of the tropics on their pale English skins.

It was not for long, and three days later the *Swan* and the *Pascha* dropped the point of Basse Terre at the southern end of Guadeloupe behind them. Taking the north-easterly trades over their sterns, they set course through the Spanish-dominated Caribbean for the Gulf of Darien.

It was on the 12th July, 1572, that Drake and his brother dived through the knife-gash in the green land and brought their ships to anchor in Port Pheasant. Here an unwelcome surprise awaited them. 'On a plate of leade, fastened to a very great tree' they found the following message inscribed:

'Captain Drake, if you fortune to come into this port make haste away; for the Spaniards which you had with you here last year have betrayed this place, and taken away all that you left here. I departed hence this present 7th July 1572.

Your very loving friend,
JOHN GARRET.'

Garret was another Devon man, who had been an officer in one of Hawkins' ships, and had been with Drake the previous year. Rather than return home, however, he had stayed out in the Caribbean as captain of a small trading vessel. He had obviously put into Port Pheasant for much the same reasons as Drake, only to find evidence that the Spaniards had been there before, and had rifled Drake's cache of stores. But the latter was not to be deterred for he reckoned that, so narrow was the entrance to Port Pheasant, he could easily prevent any enemy from sailing in and attacking his ships. The position of the little natural harbour—so well sheltered and so near his objective, Nombre de Dios—made it too good to be abandoned in favour of some other anchorage which might be even better known to the Spaniards. At once he set his men to work on building a log stockade, 'raised with trees and boughs thirty foot in height round about, leaving only one gate to issue at, near the water side, which every night was shut up, with a great tree drawn athwart it.'

Work had hardly begun when another English ship was sighted on her way into Port Pheasant. (The harbour had clearly become a hideout for all the British 'merchants', legal or illegal, on this part of the coastline.) The vessel was commanded by James Rance, another one of Hawkins' officers who, after two years working in conjunction with Huguenot privateers in the Channel, had decided to extend the range of his 'piracy' to the Caribbean. Rance had thirty men with him, and Drake probably reckoned that he and his ship would be a useful addition to his small force. Rance was accordingly made a formal partner in the enterprise against Nombre de Dios.

Having completed the stockade, and constructed the pinnaces from the parts which he had brought out from Plymouth, Drake and his three ships slipped out of their hiding place. They made their way up the coast to a small group of islands known as the Isles of Pines. His intention was to anchor the ships here, leaving only a small guard aboard them, and then drop down on Nombre de Dios in the pinnaces. He found some Negroes on the islands—Spanish slaves who had rowed across to cut wood for their masters on the mainland. The presence of these slaves turned out to be a stroke of luck for, with their usual dislike of their masters, they willingly gave Drake all the latest information about affairs on the mainland. Drake learned that Nombre de Dios had only recently been attacked by the Cimaroons and, in consequence of this, reinforcements were being sent from Panama. This meant that not only would the town soon be strongly defended, but that it was already on the alert. Drake decided that the sooner the attempt was made, the better. If he delayed, the reinforcements from Panama would have had time to reach the city.

Leaving Rance in charge of the ships with thirty men, he took fifty-three of his own men and twenty of Rance's, and set off after dark in the pinnaces from his island. The whole point of his using the small boats was that they could be rowed, and this meant that they could make a co-ordinated attack on Nombre de Dios. This would not have been the case had he used the sailing ships, for they would almost certainly have been becalmed when the wind dropped after sunset—as it tends to do in this area. Here, as always behind Drake's apparent impetuosity, one finds a clever calculation of risks. One sees also that his reasons for taking with him a young crew (all, save one man, under thirty) was not merely that he knew the young are more inclined to hold their lives cheaply, but that they have the physical strength to cope with long hours of rowing. If he had projected any sea-engagements, or the bombardment of a well-defended and fortified port, he would no doubt have been happy to have had veteran gunners and seamen among his crew.

As they approached the town, Drake realised that the morale of his small force was declining (they had heard too much from the Negro slaves about the strength of Nombre de Dios). With his usual quick understanding of men's natures, he decided that the attack should be carried through at once, rather than hold back—as he had originally intended—until the first light of dawn. 'We arrived there,' as he said, 'by three of the clock after midnight. . . .' There was a good hour to wait before the first light began to lift over the Caribbean to the east of them but, taking advantage of a fitful moon in its last quarter, he urged his men on to immediate action. It was just as they were nearing the town that a 60-ton Spanish ship, with a cargo of Canary wine aboard, arrived in the roadstead. Seeing the four strange rowing boats, she lowered a boat of her own, and sent her at once to warn the guard of Nombre de Dios that something was afoot. Drake did not hesitate, but dashed forward in the pinnace he was commanding, cut off the Spanish boat, and drove her ashore. His other three pinnaces followed, and the men all landed at the same point, capturing and tying up the Spaniards to prevent them getting into Nombre de Dios and giving the alarm.

Despite the fact that the town had only recently been attacked by the Cimaroons, it is evidence of the Spaniards' complacency that they were not keeping a proper watch. They had no idea as yet of the dangers they were up against, now that a man like Drake was active on their sea-board. The English landed without being discovered and raced for the gun-platform which was designed to guard Nombre de Dios from the sea. They found only one man on watch, but there were guns designed to repel just such sea-raiders as themselves, 'six great pieces of brass ordinance mounted upon their carriages, some demi-, and some whole culverins; we presently dismounted them, the gunner fled, the town took alarm (being very ready thereto by reason of their often disquieting by their near neighbours, the Cimaroons), as we perceived not only by the noise and cries of the people, but by the bell ringing out, and drums running up and down the town. Our Captain sent some of our men to stay the ringing of the Alarum Bell, which had continued all this while, but the Church being very strongly built, and fast shut, they could not without firing (which our Captain forbad) get into the steeple where the bell hung. . . .' Once again one notices the strict discipline which Drake imposed even in these early days upon the men who served with him, as well as—somewhat rare for him—a consideration for a Catholic church.

Leaving twelve men to guard the pinnaces and the landing place, he pressed on to the far side of the town, where he had heard that a further battery was being constructed. He found new earth- and stone-works, but no guns had yet been mounted, and there was no guard on the position. Sending his brother, together with John Oxenham and a body of men, to make an attack from the other direction, Drake led the main party of his young volunteers down the main street towards the market square—the heart of the city.

Nombre de Dios was by now in a state of panic. Some citizens, and their wives and families, were running out of the town, others were hiding in their cellars, the guards were confused, and no one knew whether this was yet another attack by the Cimaroons, or whether some sea-rovers had landed. Drake's tactics added to the general confusion, for he had ordered his small band of men to have burning

tow attached to their arrows, a trumpeter to 'blow lustily', and drums
to be beaten. In the darkness, none of the defenders could be quite sure
whether they had been attacked by a large body of men, or could even
tell from which direction the main assault was being launched. Again
Drake showed his quick grasp of a situation, for, by dividing his own
forces, he had even further divided the pathetic and piecemeal resistance
that was offered him. His surprise attack on Nombre de Dios contains
all the elements of his genius,

Not all of the Spaniards were daunted by the irruption of this
extraordinary invading force. Then as now, many brave men were to
be found among their nation. In the south-east corner of the main
square a group of Spanish soldiers formed up and loosed off a volley as
the English under Drake burst in from the other end. Drake's boy
trumpeter was killed by one of the shots, and Drake himself—although
he concealed it at the time—was wounded in the leg. The raiders
replied to this volley by that 'best of ancient English compliments,' a
shower of arrows, and the defenders were momentarily driven off.

The English were now in possession of the square. Two captured
Spaniards were compelled to show Drake the way to the Governor's
house. It was here, as he had learned the year before, that the bulk of
the treasure was stored before shipment to Spain. As John Barrow told
the story, 'Drake and his party went to the house, and found the door
open, a candle lighted on the stairs, and a fine Spanish horse ready
saddled; by means of this light they saw a vast heap of silver in the
lower room, consisting of bars of silver, piled up against the wall, (as
nearly as they could guess) seventy feet in length, ten in breadth, and
twelve in height, each bar between thirty-five and forty pounds'
weight. If the eye-measurement of silver be nearly the truth, the heap
must have been about the value of a million sterling. He next proceeded to the King's Treasure House, telling his people, "That he had
now brought them to the mouth of the Treasury of the World; which
if they did not gain, none but themselves were to be blamed."'

So far Drake's surprise plan had worked well, the only setback being
his unlooked-for wound—something that no man can allow for in his
calculations—but destined, like so many accidents, to prove fatal to
the whole success of the expedition. While some of his men were trying
to break open the main Treasure House, where Drake had guessed that
better things than simple bars of silver lay in wait for them, a tropical
thunderstorm broke over the town. For half an hour the rain fell so
heavily that neither attackers nor defenders could do much, or anything, about their respective positions. (It is worth noting that Drake
was not being old-fashioned or conservative when he had insisted on

most of his men being armed with bows and arrows. In the humid conditions of the West Indies and South America the simple bow and arrow was far more reliable than the arquebus, which had to be ignited by a slow-match.)

As the last trailing edges of the rain-clouds flickered away overhead, Drake called on the men to follow him, and at the same time sent his brother and John Oxenham with a few others to break down the door of the Treasure House. It was his greed for gold, pearls, and emeralds that undid him, for he had had within his grasp, less than an hour before, what would seem to have amounted to about 360 tons of silver —far more than he could ever have carried away in the pinnaces. But perhaps it was the very fact of its weight which made him stay, in order to get his hands on more easily transportable treasure.

While John Drake and Oxenham were trying to break down the door, Drake himself led out his men from the shed where they had taken shelter, to give covering fire—if need be—to the others. As he was stepping briskly forward over the rough and sandy ground of the square, he suddenly threw up his arms and fell down in a faint. It was now, for the first time, that those with him realised that he had been wounded. He had lost so much blood 'that it soon filled the very prints which our footsteps made, to the great dismay of all our company, who thought it not credible that one should be able to lose so much blood and live'.

Thus, in effect, ended Drake's great and almost unbelievable raid on this principal city of the Spanish Empire. Despite his protestations that his men should get on with the real work—looting, not to put too brave a word on it—his young Devonians were more concerned with their equally young commander. For the first time in his life Drake was faced with a resolute and successful mutiny. His friends bound up his leg, gave him a drop of rum, and insisted on carrying him back to the pinnaces. Some of them, it is true, were wounded themselves, but it was the inability of their leader to carry on that took the fight out of them. Without Drake they had no head to command them, and no heart to give them endurance.

The raid was not a total failure as far as the English seamen were concerned, for 'many of them,' we learn, 'got good booty before they left the place'. Quite apart from which, as soon as they were out in the bay again, they boarded and took the Spanish ship whose rowing boat they had captured earlier. This is how we know that the ship was laden with Canary wines, for 'they took them along with them, for the relief of their Captain and themselves'.

Not content, as it were, with the ferocious daring of their raid,

Drake's men now proceeded—not to their chosen anchorage at the Isles of Pines, as might have been expected—but to a small islet right off the mouth of Nombre de Dios itself. It is possible that they went there mainly in order to get Drake and the other wounded into some degree of comfort as soon as possible. In any event, it soon proved that Drake's wound was not serious, and his immense vitality and courage soon had him on his feet again. The English must have been dispirited, though, for they had come so near to complete success. The careful work of months and even years had come to nothing. All Drake's meticulous planning, and all the dash and execution of his attempt on Nombre de Dios had been foiled. But, as is clear enough already, every failure only sharpened his iron determination to exact his pound of flesh.

It was while the English were still somewhat insolently inhabiting the island off Nombre de Dios that a courteous Spanish gentleman came out to them under a flag of truce. His action, theoretically, was to pay his compliments to the bravery of his enemies but in fact (somewhat naturally) to discover who they were, how many, and in what kind of spirit. If he expected to find a disillusioned band of pirates ready to submit, or eager to be off from the coast of the New World, he was to be sadly mistaken. Despatched by the Governor of Nombre de Dios, one of the other objectives of this officer was to find 'whether the captain was the same Drake who had been the last two years on their coast. And because many of the Spaniards were wounded with arrows, he desired to know "Whether the English poisoned them, and how they might be cured?" To whom the Captain returned answers: "That he was the same Drake they meant; that it was never his custom to poison arrows; that their wounds might be cured with ordinary remedies; and that he wanted only some of that excellent commodity, gold and silver (which that country yielded), for himself and his company; and that he was resolved, by the help of God, to reap some of the golden harvest which they had got out of the earth, *and then sent into Spain to trouble the earth.*' Drake, of course, revised and annotated this account a good many years after the events which he describes. It is possible that he had by then acquired a somewhat apocalyptic idea of his mission in the world, yet this is the first time that one has the feeling that Drake is not merely making an excuse for his actions, but is even justifying them.

The Spanish officer returned to Nombre de Dios with a report that must have given the Governor cause to reflect upon his adversary, for he learned how his emissary had been treated 'with great favour and courteous entertainment besides such gifts from the Captain as most

contented him, after dinner he was in such sort dismissed to make
report of that he had seen, that he protested he was never honoured so
much of any of his life'. It was as if Drake wished to establish, early in
his life and long before he held any official commission, that he was not
one of the barbarous 'Brethren of the Coast' but an 'English Captain,
a mean subject of Her Majesty's' resolved to do no more than exact
from the Spaniards a fair return for the losses he had suffered in the past.
It is important to realise that Drake never considered himself as having
'gone on the account'—the phrase for turning pirate. As soon as he did
indeed have a formal commission from the Queen, no one was quicker
than he to assume the dignity of his office, and even to assume a coat-of-
arms some time before he was entitled to one.

Despite the protestations of the Spanish officer, and the flag of truce
under which he came, Drake realised that now the secret of his lack of
numbers was out, it would only be a matter of time before the Spaniards attempted something against him like their action at San Juan
de Ulua. (And in this case he could never say that he had not thoroughly
provoked them.) Accordingly he and his men got the pinnaces launched
and made their way back to the rendezvous at the Isles of Pines. On
reaching their ships, the partnership with James Rance was dissolved.
The latter pointed out, that the whole coast would now be on the alert,
and that they would not be able to achieve anything without the
necessary element of surprise. Rance was a man inured to hardship,
but he was cautious. He did not understand Drake who, now that his
blood was up, was determined to keep stinging the harbours of the
Spanish main like a gadfly.

Rance sailed away on the 7th July, and within a week Drake and his
ships and pinnaces had impertinently entered the harbour of Cartagena,
the capital of the Spanish Main. Sweeping in, as sudden and implacable
as a tropical storm, Drake captured a frigate which he found at anchor,
without a shot being fired. Only one old man had been left aboard
the ship as watchman, the others, as he told Drake (whose Spanish by
now must have been fluent), having gone ashore 'to fight about a
mistress'. Not for the first time, over the centuries that were to follow,
does one detect a certain Anglo-Saxon smugness over the weaknesses
of the flesh to which Latins appear particularly subject. All the other
ships and small craft, he said, were at anchor under the guns of the
castle of Cartagena but he admitted that there was one large ship,
ready-laden and destined for Seville, at anchor round the next point.
This was enough for Drake. He immediately set off in the three pinnaces, ran alongside the merchantman, boarded her, and catching her
crew asleep, imprisoned them all below.

'Having cut their cables, with the three pinnaces they towed her without the island into the sound, right afore the town, without danger of their great shot. . . .' So, in his three open rowing boats, Drake and some young Devon seamen almost casually sailed into the heart of the Spanish Empire and, right in view of the city and the castle, cut out a large merchantman. Then, with almost unbelievable arrogance, he proceeded to tow her away, with all her crew locked below decks. The ship was about 200 tons, more than twice the size of Drake's largest vessel. He then lay impudently at anchor off the port, while his men transferred the bulk of the vessel's cargo to the *Swan* and the *Pascha*. 'Meanwhile the town, having intelligence hereof by their watch, took the alarum; rang out their bells, shot off about thirty pieces of great ordnance; put all their men in a readiness, horse and foot, came down on the very point of the wood, and discharged their culverins. . . .' It was all to no avail. Not content with having captured this large merchantman, Drake proceeded to intercept two small sailing craft from Nombre de Dios, which were headed for Cartagena. Aboard them were two Government officials who, ironically enough, had despatches for the Governor of Cartegena. These warned him that 'Captain Drake had been at Nombre de Dios, had taken it, and had it not been that he was hurt with some blessed shot, by all likelihood he had sacked it; that he was yet still upon the coast; and that they should therefore carefully prepare for him.'

Having questioned his prisoners and put them all safely ashore, Drake retired to his anchorage at the Isles of Pines. It was a disappearing act that must have baffled the Spaniards for after questioning the prisoners, he had left them with the impression that he was about to quit the scene of his recent activities. Far from it: he now planned to make a further excursion against the Isthmus of Panama. Once again he realised that the pinnaces would prove invaluable for what he had in mind. These light open craft, which would sail well, row easily, and operate in shallow water where no ship was able to follow them, were the most brilliant of Drake's provisions for his expedition. But he was troubled by the fact that he was very short-handed. He really needed only one ship to act as a store-ship and main base, while using all his men aboard the pinnaces. Despite his apparently open nature, he was a man of considerable subtlety and he knew 'the affection of his company, how loath they were to leave either of their ships (being both so good sailors and so well furnished), [so] he purposed in himself, by some policy, to make them most willing to effect that which he intended'.

He deliberately arranged for the *Swan*, his brother's ship, to be sunk. She was smaller than the *Pascha* and, although a good new vessel, was clearly the one which had to go. Accordingly, 'he sent for one Thomas Moone (who was carpenter of the *Swan*), and taking him into his cabin, charged him to conceal for a time a piece of service which he must in any case consent to do aboard his own ship—that was, in the middle of the second watch, to go down secretly into the well of the ship, and with a great spike gimlet to bore three holes as near to the keel as he could, and lay something against it, that the force of the water entering might make no great noise nor be discovered by boiling up.

'Thomas Moone, at the hearing hereof, being utterly dismayed, desired to know "What cause there might be to move him to sink so goodly a bark of his own, new and strong, and that by his means, who had been in two such rich and gainful voyages in her with himself heretofore. If his brother, the Master, and the rest of the company should know of such his fact, he thought verily they would kill him." But when the Captain had imparted to him his cause, and persuaded him with promises that it should not be known, till all of them should be glad of it, he undertook it, and did it accordingly. . . .'

Early next morning, on the 15th August, Drake blandly sailed over to his brother's ship in his pinnace, bound for a fishing expedition. He called up to John Drake and asked him to come along with him. Then —while his boat was bobbing about alongside—he roused himself, took a careful look, and shouted up to his brother: 'Why is your ship so deep in the water?' John Drake immediately sent his steward to see whether there was any water in the hold. The latter, stepping smartly below, at once found himself up to the waist in water. John Drake very naturally could not understand what had happened. While his men rushed to the pumps, he excused himself from going fishing, exclaiming with amazement that: 'they had not pumped in six weeks before, [yet] they now had six feet of water in the hold.' His brother at once offered his assistance, but John motioned him away, saying he had enough men aboard and, 'let Francis carry on with his fishing'.

When Drake came back, he found the men still at the pumps, but making no impression on the water. All of them, including Drake himself, gave a hand at the pumps. But, by three in the afternoon, it was clear that there was no hope of saving the *Swan*. Sadly and reluctantly her captain and crew prepared to abandon her, and—on Drake's advice—set her afire, so that she should not fall into Spanish hands and be used against them. John Drake was broken-hearted at the loss of his stout little ship, but his brother quickly cheered him up by giving him command of the *Pascha*. Drake himself, although he was in command of the whole expedition, willingly transferred to one of the pinnaces.

The whole manœuvre had worked out exactly as he had planned, and so 'our Captain had his desire and men enough for his pinnaces'. He was all ready for his great stroke against the Spanish treasure route, but, first of all, he meant to give his men a rest, as well as lying low for a few weeks while the Spaniards relapsed into their customary torpor and complacency.

With brother John in charge of the *Pascha*, and himself living and sleeping rough in one of the open boats, Drake ordered his minute squadron to set course for the Gulf of Darien. If any Spanish frigates, sent out to get news of the English, were to come to the Isles of Pines, all that they would find would be the charred wreckage on the beach. There was nothing left of the marauders but the indication that one of them had, somehow or other, caught fire. It would be only natural for the Spaniards to conclude that Drake and his men, after such a serious loss, had quitted the Caribbean and set sail for England.

CHAPTER SIX

The Treasure Trains

SOME years after his death, Francis Drake was described in a ballad as:

The Dragon that on our seas did raise his crest
And brought back heaps of gold unto his nest,
Unto his Foes more terrible than Thunder . . .

This extraordinary, and almost supernatural, reputation which Drake earned notably among the Spaniards, but also among his own people, dated from these early years. It was now that, as a young and almost unknown captain of small ships, he plunged into the Spanish Empire, lodged himself there like a virus, and extracted a tribute of blood and gold. His was a world where violence, quick thinking and the philosophy of 'every man for himself' were recognised as not only natural, but right.

As he brought his one ship and his three open boats into the Gulf of Darien, Drake was preparing to engage the enemy on two chosen fronts. First of all, he intended to keep up his waspish attacks along their coast; and secondly, he intended to make contact with the Cimaroons, and to organise an overland raid on the treasure route. He hoped that a continuance of his provocative, but not vitally damaging, attacks on the Spanish coastal shipping, would distract the authorities from any suspicion of a land attack on the treasure trains.

Port Pheasant was getting a little too well known, so Drake looked for, and found, another safe and secret anchorage. This was similar to Port Pheasant, for the wild land swarmed with game, and the warm sea was electric with fish. In this new hideout he gave his young crew a fortnight's 'shore-leave', as it were, but he also saw to it that they were kept fit and active. He encouraged them to construct a small hamlet ashore, modelled on the villages built by the Cimaroons. They were helped in this by a Negro called Diego, who had deserted his Spanish masters at Nombre de Dios, and who had attached himself to Drake, following him everywhere with an almost dog-like devotion. It was Diego who confirmed Drake's idea of getting in touch with the

Cimaroons by saying that Drake's name was already held in honour among them because of his activities against the Spaniards in previous years. Diego offered to open communications with them, for he was sure that they would collaborate in any attacks on the treasure trains.

In this pleasant hideout on the mainland of South America the young Devon seamen cleared a section of the jungle, and, while half the crew worked, the other half took the Englishman's usual relaxation—sport. They played bowls, quoits and ninepins, and set up butts so that they could practise their archery. Those who had been wounded had time to recover, and all of them ate and slept well in their cool, leafy huts under the indulgent sky. Soon enough it would be time for further action.

'Having continued here fifteen days to silence the noise of their discovery, Drake, leaving his ship with his brother, went with two pinnaces for the River Grande . . . Passing by Cartegena, out of sight, and coming within two leagues of the river, they landed on the mainland westward.' Here they bought some cattle from the native Indians, and then sailed back by way of Cartagena, capturing several small trading vessels on their passage. Forced to take shelter from a storm which blew up out of the steamy Caribbean, Drake entered Cartagena harbour with his two pinnaces. There he impudently rode out the storm, defying the Spaniards, as it were, to come and take him. Incensed at last, they brought up against him 'a great shallop, a fine gundaloe (or ship's boat) and a great canoe', which were manned by Spanish musketeers and Indian archers. Far from retreating, Drake attacked them, drove them off, and even forced them to abandon their boats. In this skirmish he had one man slightly wounded, but the Spanish boats were shot through and through, and one of them blown up.

This was one incident alone among the many raids that he now made up and down the coast. On one occasion he even returned to Cartagena, while on another he captured a coastal trader, recording the event in these simple words. '. . . In short time we had taken her; finding her laden with victual well powdered and dry; which at that present we received as sent of God's mercy.'

His custom in all these actions was to take whatever he needed from the ships, and then send them and their crews safely on their way again. He had no need of further vessels for his own use, and the stores which he seized from the Spaniards were hidden in various places up and down the coast. If one or more of these hiding-places was discovered, there would still remain others where they could revictual, if at any time they were running short of powder, food, ship's gear, or other materials.

F

On one occasion the Spaniards baited a trap for him, sending out two empty coastal frigates to tempt the English, while keeping out of sight over the horizon two well armed ships, designed to appear the moment that they heard the sound of gun- and musket-fire. Drake promptly sank one of the coasters, burned the other, and then—before the enemy warships could catch him—ran his two shoal-draught pinnaces ashore. Here he held off the Spanish troops who were waiting for him with culverin and musket shot, while he himself leapt ashore, as if to dare the enemy to come and take him.

Dr. Johnson ponderously commented upon this exploit that: 'To leap upon an enemy's coast, only to show how little they were feared, was an act that would in these times meet with little applause; nor can the general be seriously commended, or rationally vindicated, who exposes his person to destruction, and, by consequence, his expedition to miscarriage, only for the pleasure of an idle insult, and insignificant bravado. . . .' But he goes on to say, 'Perhaps the Spaniards, whose notions of courage are sufficiently romantic, might look upon him as a more formidable enemy, and yield more easily to a hero, of whose fortitude they had so high an idea.' This was just the effect that Drake's conduct did have upon his enemies. Furthermore, it induced in his young followers a wholehearted and almost blind devotion to their leader. His character and his actions inspired in them a contempt for their enemies, and led to the feeling that was to linger in their native land for many centuries: 'One Englishman is worth half-a-dozen foreigners.'

One of the obvious reasons why Drake was so active along the seaboard of the Spanish Main was that he wanted to draw the authorities' attention away from his projected mainland expedition. Another was that—as he had learned from the Cimaroons—there would be no movement of the treasure trains until the rainy season was over. This would not be until towards the end of January, so it meant that he had about three months in which to occupy his time, as well as that of the Spanish authorities.

It was not until the first week of the New Year 1573 that Drake came sailing back to the quiet anchorage where he had left his brother John with the *Pascha* and the other pinnaces. His men may well have been exuberant at their recent successes when they first rounded into the small bay, and rowed across to their depot-ship. But bitter news awaited them. John Drake had been killed in a foolhardy attempt to capture a trading vessel in the pinnace. There had been no arms in the pinnace except one broken rapier, and a rusty old musket. But such self-confidence had these young Devonians acquired that the boat's crew had urged John Drake—against his better inclination—to make the attempt. Unfortunately for them, the Spanish ship had been manned by a number of well armed troops, and John Drake and another sailor had been killed before the pinnace could break off the engagement. His last recorded words, as they went in to attack, had been: 'If ye will needs adventure, it shall never be said that I will be hindmost, neither shall you report to my brother that you lost your voyage by any cowardice you found in me.'

Far worse was to follow for, on the 3rd January, 'Six of the company fell sick and died within two or three days, yea, they had thirty at a time sick of a calenture [fever] occasioned by a sudden change from cold to heat, or from salt or brackish water, taken in at the mouth of the river, by the sloth of these seamen who would not go further up. . . . This was very probably the dreaded *Vomito negro*, or yellow fever, which for the next three centuries would continue in the West Indies and Mexico to claim more than a fifty-per-cent mortality among its victims. It was not of course the 'brackish water' but the mosquitoes that bred on the river that afflicted Drake's young seamen. Among those who caught the disease and never recovered from it was yet another of his brothers, Joseph Drake, who 'died in our Captain's arms'.

Drake had wisely brought a surgeon in his small company, but he of course had no knowledge of tropical diseases. He decided that they must try and find out what the disease was that was laying his men low. He was well aware, however, that most men at that time regarded the dissection of a body as sacrilege, so he could not order the surgeon to conduct an autopsy on any stranger. He spared himself nothing, but had his own brother's body dissected—an action which none of the other men could possibly prevent. Among other things, they found that the liver was swollen: a further indication that it was probably yellow fever, a disease in which the organs usually become congested. But even for the rational Drake, this primitive autopsy was perhaps a little hard to bear. The narrative concludes in its unemotional but nonetheless moving way: 'This was the first and last experiment that our Captain made of anatomy in this voyage.'

The surgeon then mixed up a powerful drug which he hoped might cure the fever. True to his calling and to the scientific spirit, he tried it first upon himself, and died from its effects, while his assistant—who also tried it—did not recover for many months. During these few weeks towards the close of the deadly rainy season, when the mosquitoes must have risen like steam off the swampy river-mouth, Drake lost nearly thirty men out of his small force. He was thus left with little more than thirty men with whom to attack the golden heart of Spain.

Lesser men, or men with a less unconquerable faith in themselves and their star, would surely have given up and sailed back to England. Drake became even more granite-like in his determination. He could not suffer that these tragic losses, along with all the others, should be only vain and useless.

The end of January came, and slowly the health of the survivors improved. The Cimaroons, with whom John Drake had been in contact before his death, brought the news that the treasure was beginning to move. The ships from Peru had begun to arrive in Panama and the mule-trains laden with gold and silver were starting to make their way through the forest paths and along the rough dirt roads. The Spanish fleet had arrived to transport the treasure across the Atlantic, and was lying at anchor in Nombre de Dios. No doubt their officers and men had heard about the daring raid made on the city by a troublesome Englishman, Francis Drake, during the previous summer. They may well have hoped that he would have the audacity to try again—only to find the warships of Spain ready to receive him. They could never have guessed that, less than two hundred miles away, the man concerned was making his preparations to snatch the treasure before it even reached them.

Drake's plans were all ready to put into operation. Taking with him the redoubtable John Oxenham as his lieutenant, and seventeen of his crew, he left the others behind to guard the *Pascha*, the pinnaces and the stores, and set off. In company with his men went thirty Cimaroons: a grand total of forty-eight men for an attempt on the treasure route of the Spanish Empire. The date was Shrove Tuesday, the 3rd February.

After two days' march they were nearing the region of Venta Cruz, that half-way house between Panama and Nombre de Dios where the treasure was transhipped to barges waiting on the river Chagres, now navigable at the end of the rainy season. It was all-important that the small force should not be seen, and the Spaniards alerted to their presence in the area, so they kept to the forest and the jungle paths. Soon they were making their way up the pine-clad slopes of the Cordilleras—the air sweet and crisp after the humid scents of the jungle, and the stars acid-sharp in the clear night above the tree-tops.

Between the English and their Cimaroon helpers a deep affection grew up—a friendship strengthened by their shared dangers. The English admired the local knowledge and the woodcraft of these men to whom the wild hinterland was home, while the Cimaroons, for their part, felt an increasing respect for these bearded, light-skinned men who treated them as equals, and who seemed to hate the Spaniards as much as they did. Pedro, the leader of the Cimaroons, promised

Drake that he would lead him to a place where he might see, at one and the same time, the ocean which he had left behind him, and the blue expanse of the Pacific, the secret ocean of Spain.

It was on the 11th February, 1573 that perhaps the most dramatic moment in Drake's life occurred. The party had at last reached the watershed of the Cordilleras and there, near a small clearing where the Cimaroons had built one of their villages, Pedro pointed to a 'goodly and great high tree'. There were steps cut in its trunk, and high up in the branches the natives had built a look-out platform, big enough to hold a dozen men. Pedro took Drake by the hand, and English sea-captain and Cimaroon chief climbed up the giant tree. To the north and south of it the Cimaroons had felled other trees to open up the view, and when Drake saw it, he fell on his knees in prayer. Behind him shone the Caribbean, the blue island-studded arm on the Atlantic, and ahead of him lay the misty vastness of the Pacific, that 'Great South Sea' of which Englishmen until that moment had only dreamed. Here, or somewhere near here, in 1513, Balboa, too, had offered up a prayer at the sight of the fabled ocean. Later the great Spanish explorer had waded into its waters, and taken symbolic possession of the Pacific in the name of the King of Castile and Leon. Keats, with poetic licence, attributed this incident to 'stout Cortez', but he might equally well have written of Drake that:

> *With eagle eyes*
> *He stared at the Pacific—and all his men*
> *Look'd at each other with a wild surmise—*
> *Silent, upon a peak in Darien.*

As Camden tells the story, Drake 'was so vehemently transported with desire to navigate that sea, that falling down there upon his knees, he implored the Divine assistance that he might, at some time or other, sail thither and make a perfect discovery of the same; and here-unto he bound himself with a vow. From that time forward, his mind was pricked on continually night and day to perform this vow.' John Oxenham joined his captain and the other men in viewing the Pacific from the tree-top platform. Oxenham echoed Drake's prayer, and vowed that 'unless our Captain did beat him from his company, he would follow him by God's grace'.

From the high peaks of the Cordilleras the party proceeded to make their way down towards the plains and Panama. After two days they were out of the cover of the tree-clad mountains and had reached the most dangerous part of their expedition—the open pampas. Unless they moved with the greatest care, taking advantage of every piece of cover, it would be all too easy for the Spaniards to see them. They drew nearer and nearer to their goal, haunted by the sight—every now and again, as they made their way over the crest of some hillock—of the golden city of Panama, its towers and spires gleaming in the distance. Beyond it they could see the harbour, dense with shipping, where the treasure ships were disembarking their gold for transportation to Nombre de Dios.

One of the Cimaroons who had once worked in Panama bravely volunteered to go into the city to find out the latest news about the treasure and the mule trains. He came back with the information that two mule trains were starting out that very night—one laden with stores, and the other with silver. He had even better news than that: the Treasurer of Lima, together with his daughter, was to be in the convoy, and the Treasurer had a private mule-train laden with gold and precious stones.

The mule trains always travelled at night, in order to cross the scorched plains during the cool hours. A surprise attack under cover of darkness should not be too difficult. Drake ordered his party to withdraw in the direction of Venta Cruz, planning to lay his ambush halfway between the two cities. En route they captured a lone Spanish soldier, who confirmed everything they had heard.

Reaching a suitable place for the ambush, Drake divided his men into two groups, stationing one on either side of the highway. He ordered the men to wear their shirts outside their other clothes, so that they could easily distinguish friend from foe in the inevitable confusion of a night encounter. Then they lay down to wait in the long dry grasses, listening intently for the sound of the mule bells that would tell them when the convoy was approaching.

The night came down, the pampas-grass rustled, the dew fell, and then far off they heard what they had been waiting for—the soursweet sound of the mule bells. It was just then, when it seemed as if success was theirs at last, that disaster struck. The clip-clop of horse's hooves told of a solitary traveller coming down from Venta Cruz towards Panama. This was a possibility that Drake had foreseen, and it was for this reason that he had given orders for everyone to stay in their place until he blew his whistle—the signal for the general attack. But one of his men who was further up the road towards Venta Cruz, Robert Pike by name, 'had drunk too much *aqua vitae* without water,' and excitedly started up from his hiding place in the grass, thinking that this was the mule-train. Immediately, the Cimaroons who were with him knocked him down, and held him struggling on the ground. It was too late—the horseman had seen the flutter of a white-shirted man rising from the tall grass beside the highway. He put spurs to his horse and clattered off down the road for Panama. He had not gone very far when he ran into the two mule-trains. Reining up, he told the escort that he thought something was afoot, Drake himself knew nothing of what happened—only that a solitary horseman had cantered past, headed for the coast. As the sound of the mule-train began to draw near, he thought no more about it. At last, when the whole line of pack animals was abreast the place where his men lay concealed, he blew his whistle.

The English and Cimaroons rushed out from either side and, with almost surprising ease, overpowered the muleteers. There was no fighting, no one was hurt, and for a few minutes it must have seemed the easiest operation in the whole course of their time on the Spanish Main. But then, as man after man ripped open the pack-saddles and bags with their knives, there were murmurs of dismay and cries of disappointment. All that had fallen into their hands were stores and provisions. There was nothing but a handful of silver and no sign at all of the Treasurer, his gold and his gems. It was now that one of the muleteers explained to Drake that they had been warned by the horseman, and—just in case some Cimaroon attack was in the offing—the second and relatively unimportant provision-train had been sent on ahead.

Once again, as at Nombre de Dios, Drake had been within an inch of success, only to be mocked by total failure. The situation was far worse now, for the whole countryside would be on the lookout for him. There seemed to be no alternative but a swift retreat, back the way they had come, over the mountains, and into the safety of the jungle on the Caribbean seaboard. Drake was renowned for his insistence on discipline, as well as for his fiery temper, and Robert Pike must have wished he had never been born. It was at this moment that Pedro, the Cimaroon chief, suggested that instead of retracing their route they should make direct for Venta Cruz. If they went fast enough, rumour of their presence in the area would not have time to reach the citizens, and their expedition might still be justified. Drake agreed, commandeered the mules and their drivers, and headed back for the city.

Arriving off Venta Cruz, they ran into guards who were stationed there on the look-out for marauding bands of Cimaroons—but totally unprepared for Cimaroons led by English sailors. There was little trouble in routing them. The Cimaroons, indeed, were so inflamed at the sight of their Spanish tormentors that they could not be held back but, with war-cries and war-dances, hurled themselves on the enemy. The guards, beaten back, were swept through the gate of the small city.

They took refuge in the monastery, while the victors—disappointed of their real intention—took their revenge by looting Venta Cruz. Even in the midst of this confusion, Drake's will prevailed, and all women and unarmed men were allowed to go unmolested. It was on this occasion that Drake distinguished himself by one of those acts of gallantry and panache which made him a legend in his lifetime, even among his enemies. Hearing that Venta Cruz was used by the ladies of Nombre de Dios as a hospital when it was their time to be confined, he hastened to assure them personally that no harm would befall them so long as he, Captain Drake, was in the town. 'Surely never was a pirate so tender. . . .'

By the time that the soldiers from Panama had arrived at Venta Cruz in pursuit, Drake and his men had left the town. They made their way by forced marches through that forest where no Spaniard would ever follow, for this was the domain of the Cimaroons, and known only to these strange natives of the interior. Reaching the coast he found to his relief that their hideout was still undiscovered, the men who had stayed behind were in good health and heart, and the *Pascha*, and her invaluable pinnaces were sound, and ready for new work. It was a moment, though, when all but the foolhardy or the invincibly stubborn might have counted their losses and gone. Behind him the whole land was roused, and aware that the Englishman Drake was on the Isthmus. At sea, the injuries the Spaniards had suffered meant that every ship, port, and even small trading station was on the alert.

Drake acted in much the same way as he had done before—changed his ground slightly but continued his harassing tactics, determined that the enemy should never know from which direction the next blow might fall. Having seen Panama and the mule-trains, he was more than ever aware that his real chances of success lay on the land. This being so, the obvious thing, as he saw it, was to alert the Spaniards along all the shores of the Caribbean. It was all-important that they should once more begin to relax on land, and regard the treasure trains as secure from any further interference.

Drake sent John Oxenham in a pinnace to cruise eastwards and capture a supply ship. Meanwhile he himself set off westwards in another pinnace and captured a Spanish frigate, which had a certain amount of gold aboard her. Returning to his base, he found that Oxenham had also been successful, and that he had brought in a fine new coastal vessel with a good supply of stores aboard. Without wasting a moment, Drake put to sea again in a pinnace, and took the captured Spanish ship to act as escort and storeship.

Sighting a sail on the horizon he made for it, only to find that this was a fellow privateer, captained by a Huguenot called Guillaume le Testu. He and his crew were without water and nearly starving. Le Testu was a navigator and pilot of some distinction, and a confirmed enemy of Spain and her Church. It was from him that Drake heard for the first time of the massacre of the French Huguenots by the Catholics, on St. Bartholomew's Day during the previous August. It has been estimated that, on that tragic and bloody day, 50,000 Huguenots were killed throughout the whole of France. Some commentators have perhaps made too much of the effect that this news had upon Drake. He was so deeply committed already to an implacable war against Spain and her religion, that nothing further was needed to reinforce his feelings of antipathy. At the same time it must have proved an added confirmation of the fact that he, his country, and his young Devonians, were fighting against intolerance, oppression and evil. His feelings would indeed have been further outraged, if he had known that Pope Gregory XIII had congratulated the French Queen-Mother on her action, that he had ordered bonfires to be lighted in celebration throughout Europe, and had even had a special medal struck to commemorate the deaths of so many heretics.

It was understandable that for both practical and emotional reasons Drake should have been willing to take the Frenchmen into partnership. The practical reasons possibly predominated, for Drake's shortage of manpower was acute, and Captain Le Testu had 70 men aboard his ship. Having introduced these new allies to his hideout, Drake allowed them a few days to rest and recuperate, and then outlined his new plan. This was astonishing in its audacity, for he intended to land on the coast near Nombre de Dios, march overland, and cut off the treasure trains after they had left Venta Cruz, and when they were almost in reach of Nombre de Dios itself. He calculated that it was no good going back and making a further attempt against the route between Panama and Venta Cruz. He would lay this next ambush within a mile of the western gate of Nombre de Dios, so 'close to home', in fact, that the guards would almost certainly have relaxed their vigilance. He would, furthermore, be striking at the route out of virgin forest, and from a place where no one could possibly have any reason to expect danger.

Twenty Frenchmen, and fifteen Englishmen, with Pedro and his Cimaroons, were chosen for the treasure, with the captured Spanish frigate, and the rest of the men in two pinnaces. His destination was the Rio Francisco, a small river which enters the sea a few miles to the east of Nombre de Dios. Arriving here unseen by the Spaniards, Drake left the ship concealed, and made up river in the two shoal-draught pinnaces. Having gone as far upstream as possible, he left a few men in the boats—ordering them to keep out of sight, but to be sure to be back at the same place after four days.

He and his party struck inland, making a detour through the jungle to avoid any outposts from Nombre de Dios, and came round to the west at the point where the treasure route led down to the city. They were so close to Nombre de Dios that they could hear the noise and bustle of the dockyard, the clunk! of caulking hammers, and the growl of saws as carpenters worked on the treasure fleet. After so many losses, disappointments and failures, their fortune turned at last. On a still morning when the first light was just beginning to silver the sea, the Cimaroon scouts came running back with the news that a large mule-train—nearly 200 animals in all—was making its way towards their ambush. There was no mistake this time, and at Drake's signal they swarmed out of their hiding place and fell on the frightened muleteers and their escort of dumbfounded soldiers. A flight of arrows, a few volleys of musketry—and the treasure train was in their hands. The Spanish guards fled for Nombre de Dios, while Drake and his combined band of English and French threw open the saddle bags, and slashed at the heavy sacks and bales. They realised that at last they had even more on their hands than they could carry. One sad accident marred their triumph, for Captain Le Testu had been severely wounded in the stomach, but other than him there were only three wounded, and one Cimaroon killed.

Having cached the main bulk of the silver which they could not take with them at various points in the forest, each man loaded himself with as much gold as he could carry. They were still at work burying the residue of the treasure when the sound of foot-soldiers and horsemen coming out from the city forced them to leave in a hurry. Captain le Testu, at his own request, was carried into the forest and left there with two Frenchmen to look after him. The rest, staggering under the weight of their plunder, made their way back to the rendezvous point on the Rio Francisco where they expected to find the pinnaces waiting for them. Drake's intention was to load up the pinnaces, go back again for the treasure buried in the forest, and collect Le Testu and his two men.

Two things disrupted the perfect execution of the plan. One Frenchman—unnoticed at the time—had lost the party and had subsequently been captured. Then, when they reached the river, they were confronted with the sight of seven Spanish open boats in the bay. There was no sign of their own pinnaces or the frigate. There had been a westerly gale during the night and Drake, paying no attention to the despair of his followers—who maintained that their own boats must certainly have been captured—came to the conclusion that the pinnaces had merely been delayed by the weather while the frigate, for the same reason, must have stood out to sea. He proposed that he and a few others should go down the river immediately, find the pinnaces, and then return to collect the main party. It was one of those moments when one sees Drake at his indomitable best, walking the tight-wire between success and total failure, and yet with no visible sign of nerves to indicate that, even for a second, he felt any doubts as to his ability.

There were a good many logs and uprooted trees bowling down the river in the brown floodwater after the storm, so he and his seamen hauled them ashore and, working with desperate haste, started building a raft. With a piece of sacking for a sail, and with one other Englishman and two Frenchmen aboard, Francis Drake embarked on the most extraordinary voyage of his life. Just before they set out on the swollen river he shouted to the men who were staying behind: 'If it please God that I shall ever set foot aboard my frigate in safety, I will, God willing, by one means or another get you all aboard in despite of all the Spaniards in the Indies.' Then leaping on to his log craft, he and the other three shot out of sight downstream.

Drake's estimate had been right: the pinnaces had only been held back by the storm, not captured by the Spaniards. After leaving the mouth of the river, Drake and his companions, parched, spray-drenched and burnt by the sun, worked their raft slowly eastward. Then, just past a headland, they sighted the two pinnaces beating up towards them. Drake immediately turned the raft towards the beach, and drove it on to the shingle. The four of them had been six hours aboard the raft, after all their exertions of the previous days, yet it is recorded that Drake ran across the rocky land urging his companions to make haste and follow him.

When the men in the pinnaces looked up and saw their captain bounding down the shore towards them—ragged, dishevelled and alt-stained—and with him only three men out of all those who had gone on the venture against the treasure train, their hearts fell. Drake's wry humour did not fail him. He acted as if he was downcast, and, when taken aboard one of the pinnaces and asked how things had gone, replied laconically: 'Well.' The crew knew that this was his stoic way of accepting every disaster. And then, fishing his hand inside his torn jacket, he drew out a large gold ring. 'Our voyage is made,' he said.

After so many desperate adventures and misadventures, their voyage was indeed 'made'. It only remained to collect the rest of the party who had been left up the river, which they managed to do without any further losses or difficulties. The only bitterness attaching to the whole expedition was that Le Testu and the Frenchman who had been captured earlier were never seen again. The two who had stayed behind with Le Testu were brought off along with the main party, for Le Testu had begged them to leave him and rejoin the others by the river bank. Drake, however, had no intention of abandoning his comrade-in-arms. Having seen the treasure safely lodged at their base, he came back, yet a third time, to the Rio Francisco. Here his crew did another of their affectionate mutinies and would not allow him to go ashore, so Oxenham landed and went with a party to look for Le Testu and to recover the silver buried in the forest. Le Testu was gone and nearly all the silver bars had been dug up. The Spaniards must have found Le Testu and the other Frenchman, and tortured them until they revealed the places where the silver bars had been hidden.

Drake at least had tried and done his best to recover his ally—even at the risk of returning again to the scene of his recent raid, an area which must have been almost as dangerous for an Englishman by now as the market place of Nombre de Dios. As a sign of his friendship and agreement with Drake, Le Testu had earlier given him a scimitar of great value, that had formerly been given to him by the famous Huguenot, Admiral Coligny. Drake, in his turn, now gave this scimitar to Pedro the Cimaroon chief as a mark of his affection.

It was time for the expedition to be disbanded. The Frenchmen received, as had been agreed, half of the plunder from the raid on the treasure train and sailed off into the Caribbean. The Cimaroons were rewarded and Drake broke up the pinnaces which had served him so well, giving his allies all the iron and nails from them to use as arrowheads—gold in their unsophisticated world having little or no value. The *Pascha* was too old and small for his return to England. It is quite possible also that she had grown soft from worm after her year in tropic waters, so she too was broken up. Drake was left with the new Spanish 'frigate', the fast-sailing coaster that Oxenham had captured, and she was adequate for transporting the bulk of the treasure, stores, and men. He still needed another vessel, however, to act as a tender and storeship. So—as if to rub salt into the Spanish wounds—he proceeded to sail boldly up the coast to Cartagena. Despite the fact that the galleons of the Treasure Guard and a great number of other Spanish ships were lying in the harbour, he would have no truck with standing out to sea for safety's sake. Quite deliberately he closed the town and passed 'hard by Cartagena, in the sight of all the fleet, with a flag of St. George in the maintop of our frigate, with silken streamers and ancients down to the water, sailing forward with a large wind'. The whole of his nature sounds like trumpets in the words.

Off the mouth of the Magdalena river he fell in with a frigate of about the size he was looking for and, after a short but fierce engagement, captured her. She proved to be laden with fresh victuals, 'hens, hogs and honey', just what he needed for his ocean passage. Sailing back again to his anchorage to careen and refit his two ships for their voyage, he completed his arrangements, said goodbye to the Cimaroons who took leave of him with tears, and saw to it that he had left nothing behind that could be of service to his enemies.

It was time to go. 'Being now resolved for England and fully prepared for sea, they sailed, steered a direct course for home and proceeded with so prosperous a gale, that in twenty-three days they passed from Cape Florida to the Isles of Scilly.' Behind them there was hardly a city in all the Spanish Main that was not on the verge of panic, and hardly a coastal vessel that had not been captured once (some two or even three times). With the bilge water slopping over the gold and silver ingots that had been destined to be 'sent into Spain to trouble the earth', Francis Drake came back once more into the grey waters of the English Channel. After the orchid scents of the jungle and the languid airs of South America, he smelled once more the tide-twisted sea of England and the winds of summer off his native Devon. It was in the second week of August 1573 that he and his two captured Spanish ships left the fanged Bishop's Rock to port, stood over toward the Lizard, and then came in on their last tack home, to Plymouth.

CHAPTER SEVEN

Outward Bound

IT was on the 9th August, 1573 that Francis Drake and the remaining sailors from the *Pascha* and the *Swan* slipped past the green mound of Plymouth Hoe. They came alongside in the narrow, sheltered waters of the harbour where the tall wooden houses stooped over their re-flections, and the merchantmen and fishing boats were sidling against the quays. It was a Sunday and nearly all the people of the town were in church. But there are always some in a port whose inclination or business keeps them near the quay. It was not long—probably before the ropes were even ashore—that the news went round that Francis Drake and his men were back. They were no longer in the *Pascha* and the *Swan*, but in two strange foreign craft, and each man had made his fortune. . . . Soon the word reached St. Andrew's, and 'The news of our Captain's return . . . did so speedily pass over all the church, and surpass their minds with desire and delight to see him that very few or none remained with the preacher, all hastening to see the evidence of God's love and blessing towards our Gracious Queen and country, by the fruit of our Captain's labour and success.'

His success was borne out by the treasure in his two ships. Spanish records show that the value of the gold and silver captured by Drake outside Nombre de Dios was about 150,000 *pesos*, and that about 100,000 *pesos* of this was in gold. Since the gold *peso* was worth about nine English shillings of the period, this amounted to about £45,000— an enormous sum at that time. This of course, had been divided equally with the Frenchmen from Captain Le Testu's vessel, which still meant that Drake had brought back over £20,000, to be shared between himself, his investors, if any, and the survivors. This was far from the total haul, for there is no record of the other amounts of gold, silver, jewels, and other cargo, that Drake and his men had lifted off passing Spanish merchantmen during their months off the Spanish Main. Nor do we know on what basis the prize money was shared out, only that Drake as the senior officer, and leader of the expedition, must have received the lion's share.

When he returned to Plymouth he was, if not a millionaire, certainly one of the richest men in the West Country. In those days, when there was little industry, a man's financial position was very largely judged by his land, his rents, and his farming turnover. Drake's share of the plunder from his raid on the treasure train must have been more than even the largest local landowner could make in a lifetime. For a man in his early thirties, son of a tenant-farmer who had been driven almost penniless away from Plymouth, Drake would have been more —or less—than human, if he had not relished this triumphant return to his adopted city and to the land of his birth.

One thing he could never have reckoned upon, nor known about in the communications of those days, was that the whole political pattern had changed during his absence. The Queen and Philip of Spain, neither able to hurt the other mortally, had decided that things must be patched up—at least on the surface—so that trade and relations between their two countries could resume something like a normal pattern. There had been, as we would say nowadays, a 'thaw' in the cold war. This was of course no more than a matter of mutual convenience, and Philip's intention was still to 'bury' Protestant England as soon as it could be managed. But he hoped this could be effected by a change of sovereign, rather than by the risky and vastly expensive project of an invasion. Quite apart from this, the situation in the Netherlands was such that he certainly could not spare the men, nor the money, to make war on England, for the heretics of his own empire were in open rebellion. From Queen Elizabeth's point of view, sovereign of a small country dependent then as ever on trade, and without any access to the blood-transfusion of specie that kept Spain alive, it was essential that normal relations with the continent should be resumed as soon as possible.

Such being the changed political climate, Drake happened to return to Plymouth, laden with plunder from the Spanish Main, at a most unfortunate moment. In London and Madrid, ambassadors were mutually toasting one another, and pretending that all was forgotten and forgiven—or that there had never been anything to forgive. Suddenly two pirate ships arrived in Plymouth laden with stolen goods, captained by a man who had spent the best part of the previous year harassing the Spanish Empire.

The Queen must secretly have approved, and secretly also earmarked Drake for future ventures, but officially she could not acknowledge his existence. It was, in any case, most fortunate that she did not have to admit to any knowledge of this hitherto unknown Devonian sea-captain. It made it so much easier to have word conveyed to him that his absence from the kingdom would be the better for all concerned. No doubt such advice reached Drake via Hawkins and his connections, who had access to news at court and official navy circles. In any case it left the Queen free to deny any knowledge of this Englishman who had been behaving in such an unfriendly way in her royal brother's papally-assigned preserves.

Just as he had done after his return from San Juan de Ulua, and just as he had done so often during the past months, when Spanish troops and ships had been looking for him—Drake disappeared from sight. Certainly on this occasion one would not look for him as holding a commission in the Navy, at least not in home waters. As Dr. J. A. Williamson commented: 'He disappeared so effectively that to this day no one knows where he was in the next two years, which are an absolute blank in his record. In 1575 he turns up in Ireland, serving in the forces with which the Earl of Essex was striving to put down a rebellion. He may perhaps have been in Ireland all the time. . . .'

It seems very likely that this was where he had been concealed. In those days 'to take to Ireland' was the simplest solution for men of whatever rank who were in trouble or out of favour—rather like wanted men in other countries taking to the *maquis*, or making for the hills. Ireland, unhappy Ireland, was a home from home for English rogues, freebooters and undesirables—a situation which has been mildly reversed in recent years.

It is known that John Hawkins, quite apart from his ventures in the Caribbean, also invested ships and money in the Earl of Essex's campaign in Ireland. Drake, maybe, was once again acting in collaboration with his relative. Ireland, after the seaboard of South America, is wet and rainy, but its sheltered coves, inlets and harbours were not so dissimilar. Drake may well have played much the same game here as he had recently been playing in the Caribbean. Turbulent Ireland, with its Catholic propensities, was ever an Achilles' heel to England, and Drake's special talents will have been useful for raiding Irish ports and for cutting out Spanish supply ships.

In any case, the fact that his disappearance over this period is so complete argues some official connivance, for Drake was no longer an unknown young man. He had already become a legend in the West Country. His whispered exploits (known well enough to Spanish agents in England) had made him something of a hero in every port and section of the coast. It is just possible that for a time, like his former companion Captain Rance, he may have worked with the Breton sea-rovers in the Channel. But there seems no real reason for disbelieving Stow's statement that he 'furnished, at his own expense,

Sir Francis Drake: from an oil painting by an unknown artist
(*By permission of the Trustees of the National Maritime Museum*)

Sir John Hawkins: by Federigo Zuccaro
(*Modern Portraits Ltd., Plymouth*)

three frigates with men and munitions, and served voluntary in Ireland under Walter, Earl of Essex; where he did excellent service both by sea and land, at the winning of divers strong forts'.

These missing months have little bearing on his life story, although— as with all gaps in one's information about an unusual man—it would be pleasant to be able to cast some light upon them. What is important is the moment when Drake reappears, for he is now on the brink of his greatest achievement. He emerges suddenly from the darkness, and with him steps the strange figure of Thomas Doughty.

Captain Thomas Doughty was as unlike Drake as it was possible for a man to be, and perhaps it was this very fact which attracted Drake to him. He was, first of all, a gentleman by birth, a scholar with 'a good gift for the Greek tongue and a reasonable taste of Hebrew,' an orator, and to all outward intents and purposes a man of high religious principles. Doughty was totally remote from the men with whom Drake had passed his years at sea, but he was far from unique in his period. He represented a comparatively new type, the 'Renaissance Englishman', who delighted in subtlety and intrigue, and who gave rise to the Italian proverb *Inglese italianato é diavolo incarnato*'. As is often the case when men ape the customs, manners and habits of a country other than their own, they seem to lose the virtues of both sides.

There can be no doubt that Doughty had charm and ability, for Essex had taken to him and had used the captain for a time as confidant and a messenger. Doughty did not long remain in Essex's good graces, for he was revealed as a restless intriguer. Essex had felt that he was being thwarted by some influence against him at Court, and sent Doughty back from Ireland to try and find out whom this might be. Doughty returned in due course with the tale that Leicester was the man aligned against Essex, and the latter at once wrote a hasty letter home based on this assumption. The result was an open row between him and Leicester, which was only resolved through the good offices of Lord Burghley. After the quarrel had been patched up, an explanation was provided by Leicester and an apology given by Essex. It became clear to both parties that it was Doughty who had provoked the whole affair for some reason best known to himself.

It is worth looking at the conclusion that Essex came to about Doughty. In his letter to Leicester, he wrote: '. . . I see how perilous it is to believe in any servant's speech. And yet I was rather induced to give him [Doughty] credit because he had before that time spoken as much as any other of his devotion to me and my cause. . . . And as I mean not to use the man any more in that trust or any way in soliciting my cause, so if I have been over-earnest in my later letters, I pray you to impute it to my plain and open nature.'

If Essex had for a time been deceived by Thomas Doughty, it is hardly surprising that Francis Drake, whose nature was even more 'plain and open', was completely taken in by this smooth-tongued Iago. Doughty probably knew how to prey on Drake's weaknesses: his love of flattery, and his desire to be well thought of by those who had been born gentlemen. Soon, where he had formerly been Essex's confidant, Doughty became Drake's. The latter poured out all his dreams and ambitions to him—and in particular that dream, and that vow he had made, one day to sail an English ship into the Pacific.

In 1576 Drake and Doughty were both back in England. The latter had become secretary to Christopher Hatton, Captain of the Guard, and the Queen's new favourite. Doughty may possibly have been acting to further Drake's interests at Court and in other high circles. Although his godfather Lord Russell was now the Earl of Bedford, and might well put in a good word for him, Drake needed as many influential backers for the project he had in mind as possible. It was true that Essex had given him an introduction to Walsingham, the Secretary of State, but he no doubt felt that Doughty, with his many and varied connections, would prove invaluable.

The Devon seaman who had won an immense reputation for his daring and success was soon 'adopted', as it were, by the war party in England. In 1577 a syndicate was formed in London which comprised some of the most important men in the kingdom: Privy Councillors Leicester, Walsingham and Lincoln (the Lord Admiral), together with Sir Christopher Hatton (he had recently been knighted), and Sir William Winter, Surveyor of the Navy, his brother George Winter, and John Hawkins. Hawkins at this time was acting as Treasurer of the Navy, an office he assumed before the end of the year. Numbered among these august personages, in what almost amounted to an official State undertaking, was Francis Drake, who had been chosen leader of the projected expedition. Richard Grenville had earlier proposed a somewhat similar expedition, and he had naturally been considered for the command of the present one. The fact that Drake, of low birth and little education or gentlemanly graces, was given the command would rankle with Grenville for years to come.

We know what the object of this expedition was, at any rate as officially stated, for a draft of the instructions is in the British Museum. Drake was ordered to pass round South America through the Straits of Magellan, and explore the coast that lay beyond. There, in a territory which was described as not being 'under the obedience of any Christian prince', he was instructed to make friends with the rulers of the land, and to arrange for the sale of English goods, and to conclude trading treaties. Clearly what the authors of these instructions had in mind was, not that Drake should sail up the west coast of South America, but that he should open up to English interests the country then called *Terra Australis Incognita*. This was the unknown land that was believed to lie to the south of the Magellan Straits.

It was well known to the men who framed these instructions that the Spaniards had been active for years on the coast of Chile, and all along the western seaboard of South America. They could never have described this area as not being under the authority of any Christian princes. What the English syndicate was proposing, in fact, was to open up for their own interests and trade a new land which was presumed to lie south of the sphere of Spanish influence.

Drake's subsequent conduct, when he found no exploitable territory to the south of the Straits, becomes immediately explicable. As we only have the draft plan of the instructions, we cannot be sure what alternatives Drake was allowed in the event of his failure to locate *Terra Australis*. But, on his own evidence, the Queen herself had a secret interest in the venture, and she allowed him a latitude which had no part in his official instructions. Quite apart from the Queen's own devious nature, it was absolutely essential that to all outward appearances she should seem to be totally ignorant of a 'private' venture that might well lead to bad relations with Philip II.

Drake's interview with Elizabeth was arranged by Walsingham, who told him at the same time that the Queen was eager to have some revenge on the King of Spain. Walsingham then showed him a chart, and asked Drake: 'to set my hand and to note down where I thought he [Philip II] might be most annoyed; but I told him some part of my mind, but refused to set my hand to anything, affirming that Her Majesty was mortal, and that if it should please God to take Her Majesty away it might be that some prince might reign that might be in league with the King of Spain, and then will my own hand be a witness against myself.'

Drake may have been taken in by Captain Doughty, but he was never any man's fool, and his action here is only too comprehensible. He knew that the state of England hung by the tenuous thread of the Queen's life, and that plots were being contrived almost hourly against her. For him to put his own hand to a document which might later incriminate him—if there were a change of ruler and of policy—would be equivalent to signing his own death-warrant. When, in fact, he did return from his voyage round the world, his first action on reaching

Plymouth was to inquire whether the Queen was alive and in good health. Had she not been he would, without doubt, have done another of his famous disappearing acts.

Having failed to get Drake to commit himself in writing, Walsingham finally took him for his interview with the Queen.

This meeting between the brilliant, subtle Elizabeth and the Devonian sea-captain still shines out from the pages of history like one of those gems in which the Queen herself delighted. She looked perhaps somewhat as a later visitor to the court described her: 'The Queen had in her ears two pearls with very rich drops. . . . Upon her head she had a small crown; her bosom was uncovered, and she had on a necklace of exceeding fine jewels. She was dressed in white silk, bordered with pearls of the size of beans, and over it a mantle of black silk shot with silver threads.'

The Queen was forty-four, several years older than Drake, feminine to her long ring-encrusted fingers, but a woman who, for her own reasons and for her country's sake, was determined never to take any man as master. Drake undoubtedly appealed to her, not in the same way as the elegant, handsome and well-bred men who became her favourites, but for that air of good-humoured courage which shone off him, like salt in a sailor's hair. For Drake, with his background of obscurity, poverty and hardship, this meeting with the Queen must have been one of the most important events in his life. He knew from his own experience the loneliness of command, and he can hardly have failed to be impressed by this woman of whom her enemy, Pope Sixtus V, was later to say: 'She is a great woman; and were she only a Catholic she would be without her match. . . . Look how well she governs; she is only a woman, only mistress of half an island, and yet she makes herself feared by Spain, by France, by the Emperor, by all.' Elizabeth recognised the nature of the man who stood before her and did not waste time on subtleties. She came straight to the point, and said: 'I would gladly be revenged on the King of Spain for divers injuries that I have received.'

Drake, who perhaps doubted the existence of a land to the south of Cape Horn, or who had always had an eye to those treasure-laden, unprotected ships he had seen idling in the warm waters off Panama, immediately proposed something quite different from his written instructions. This was that he should pass through the Straits of Magellan, and then turn north, sail into the private sea of Spain, and make a raid on the treasure ships. It seems that the Queen agreed wholeheartedly to this piratical suggestion. It was at this point that the official written instructions came in so handy, and it was here that Drake and the Queen came to a verbal agreement. Officially he was bound on the expedition that was sanctioned by his orders, but unofficially he was to make sure of a lucrative voyage by raiding the unprotected coastline of the New World.

It is probable that only Walsingham among the promoters of the venture had any knowledge of Drake's real intentions. Hawkins may possibly have done, for he was to provide the ships, and he and Drake always had a bond of interest that linked them together. One thing that the Queen stressed was that 'of all men my Lord Treasurer should not know it.'' She added that, if anyone should pass on the information, 'They should lose their heads therefor.' Burghley must certainly have no inkling of Drake's real intentions, for he was the leader of the party which desired, rationally enough, to preserve the peace with Spain. Intimate though Doughty and Drake had become, it seems unlikely that Drake would ever have disregarded Her Majesty's strict instructions and told him of the plan.

It was impossible of course to keep an expedition of this nature totally secret—one that involved so many prominent men in the country—so it was announced that Captain Francis Drake was preparing to sail on a voyage for Alexandria, where he intended to negotiate a trading agreement for spices with the Ottoman empire. This was the story that was current among the general public, and the one under which the sailors were recruited for the ships. These were the *Pelican* (later renamed *The Golden Hind*) of a little over 100 tons, and carrying eighteen guns; the *Elizabeth* of 80 tons; the *Marigold* of 30 tons; the *Swan* of 50 tons, designed to act as a storeship; and the 15-ton *Benedict*. In addition, and bearing in mind how invaluable they had proved on his previous expedition, Drake had four unassembled pinnaces carried aboard the ships. John Winter, son of George Winter, Clerk of the Queen's ships, commanded the *Elizabeth*; John Thomas, one of Hatton's men, the *Marigold*; John Chester, the *Swan*; and Thomas Moone (Drake's former carpenter who had served him so slyly in the matter of the old *Swan*), was in command of the small *Benedict*.

But if it was enough to let the sailors believe they were going on a voyage to the Levant—once away from England they would have no opportunity to desert—the officers had to be given some better tale. The marine officers and the gentlemen-adventures were told that the purpose of the expedition was the one laid down in the official instructions—to make contact with the rulers of *Terra Australis*.

From a remark that Thomas Doughty let slip later, it seems more than likely that Burghley used this 'Italianate' Englishman to try and worm out of Drake the real object of the voyage. At any rate, there is every indication that once Doughty guessed what Drake's intentions were, he did all he could to sabotage the expedition. It is unlikely at this late date that anything will turn up to prove or disprove the assertion, but it seems probable that Doughty was Burghley's man from the very beginning. Not that the great Burghley had an ounce of treachery in his nature, but he was absolutely determined, by almost any means, to prevent the Queen from risking open war with Spain.

One hundred and sixty-four men and boys sailed on the expedition. Among them were Thomas Doughty and his brother, John; William Hawkins, a nephew of John Hawkins; Francis Fletcher, a chaplain; and a brother and a nephew of the commander, Thomas and John Drake. The description of the equipment carried shows that this was no simple privateering venture. The vessels were all well armed, and provided with a good store of pistols, arquebuses, chain-shot (for cutting down an enemy's masts and rigging) and wild-fire. This was a kind of incendiary mixture that could be discharged either from special flame-throwers, known as trumps, or hurled in thin pots which were fused and ignited on impact. Drake, true to his character, and also no doubt because he had realised that foreign visitors, whether Cimaroons or Spanish prisoners, were impressed by a certain amount of display, had seen to it that his flagship was as far removed as possible from the typical down-at-heel trader-privateer that worked the Caribbean. He had not omitted, 'to make provision also for ornament and delight, carrying to this purpose with him expert musicians, rich furniture (all the vessels for his table, yea many belonging even to the cook-room, being of pure silver), and divers shows of all sorts of curious workmanship whereby the civility and magnificence of his native country might amongst all nations whithersoever he should be come, be the more admired.' It was a far cry from the *Pascha* and the *Swan* of five years before, yet even so it must be remarked that his largest ship was, at the maximum reckoning, only 120 tons.

The voyage started badly. Leaving Plymouth in November the small fleet ran straight into a south-wester booming up from the Atlantic, and the *Pelican* was so badly damaged that they had to put back to have her repaired. It was not until the 13th December, 1577 that Francis Drake made his real start on what was to prove one of the epic voyages in history. Once clear of the Channel mouth, and out into the long rollers of the winter Atlantic, Drake broke the news to the men that they were bound on no simple voyage to Alexandria, but were destined for the Pacific Ocean. In view of the trouble that later broke out, it is worth bearing in mind what effect this may have had upon the seamen. They now realised that they were on passage to the ill-omened Magellan

Straits, which according to Monson in his *Naval Tracts* 'were counted so terrible in those days that the very thought of attempting it were accounted dreadful'.

The great Magellan had first made the passage in 1520, sailing on to meet his death the following year in the Philippines. Sebastian Cabot had tried the passage and failed, the redoubtable Genoese seamen had met with disaster in two attempts, while Amerigo Vespucci had failed even to locate the Straits. Other explorers had been turned back through mutinies, and the last Spaniard to attempt the passage had been murdered by his own men. Since then the Spaniards had given up trying to use the Straits, transporting the goods and treasure from their empire, as we have seen, across the isthmus of Panama and shipping it home from the Caribbean. Drake must certainly have been familiar with these previous attempts at the passage of the Straits. He must have known well enough that mutiny was a bigger danger than any failure of seamanship or navigation. In those realms he rightly possessed supreme self-confidence, but he could by no means feel so secure about the disposition of his company.

Taking the normal southern route down towards the Moroccan coast, they fell in with a Portuguese ship which they found at anchor in the lee of Cape Blanco. Drake had no hesitation in seizing her when he saw that she was in good condition, of about 40 tons burden, and would make a welcome addition to his command. 'Fair exchange is no robbery', so he gave the Portuguese sailors the 15-ton *Benedict* (if it can be called a fair exchange) and sailed on south to the lonely Cape Verde Islands. This was the last place where he could water or revictual before making the Atlantic crossing, and he intended to use the victualling depot at Maio for this purpose. Doughty, who seems still to have enjoyed Drake's confidence, was put in charge of a shore expedition to capture the depot, but the raid was a failure.

Fortunately Drake came across two Portuguese ships bound for Brazil, and managed to capture one of them. She proved to be a sound vessel, and was laden with wine, food and other stores. Appropriating her in his usual fashion, he decided to take her pilot, Nuño da Silva, along with him. At the same time, and surely an indication that as yet he had no suspicions of Doughty, Drake put him in command of the new ship, which was re-christened the *Mary*. Along with the prize crew went twenty-two-year-old Thomas Drake, and Drake's trumpeter, Brewer. The augmented fleet sailed on to the island of La Brava, which Drake planned to make his last port of call. Here he intended to put ashore the captured Portuguese—with the exception of Nuño da Silva, who had a useful knowledge of the Brazilian coast.

The first real whisper of the wind of trouble was heard at La Brava. The trumpeter Brewer suddenly came over to Drake's flagship and told him that Thomas Doughty had been pilfering articles from the Portuguese ships. The fact that the cargo had even been touched was enough to infuriate Drake for he had given strict orders that it should be kept under seal, and that none of it should be broken out until they had left La Brava. Drake's quick temper flamed up and, 'not without some great oaths', he took Doughty to task. There could be no doubt that Doughty was indeed in possession of some goods belonging to the Portuguese prisoners, but he maintained that these were gifts. He denied the charge of tampering with the cargo, going so far as to claim that Drake's young brother was the culprit—something that seems extremely unlikely. Doughty was ordered by Drake to report back aboard the *Pelican*, while Thomas Drake was given command of the prize ship. One curious thing about this incident is that Drake himself now stayed aboard the *Mary* with his brother. Less curious perhaps, but sensible, is that a reconciliation was effected with Doughty, who was put in charge of the gentlemen-adventurers in the *Pelican*. It is hardly surprising that many of the men aboard the *Pelican*, not knowing about the recent trouble, assumed that Doughty enjoyed their admiral's complete confidence, and even that he was in command of the whole ship. Doughty reinforced this impression by making a speech to the crew when he came on board. This was to the effect that he had heard there had been some quarrelling and dissension among them, and that they must now 'be honest men' and work in unison together.

The usual rivalries and arguments had broken out between the gentlemen-adventurers and the marine officers, something that constantly bedevilled life aboard ships at that time. Drake probably felt that Doughty would be able to handle the gentlemen better than he could, and preferred to sail in the captured *Mary*—where there would be no such troubles, since there were only seamen aboard her. He knew how to handle seamen, but his previous voyages had given him little experience in dealing with gentlemen, touchy about their rights, and unfamiliar with ships and the sea.

In any case Doughty's transfer to the *Pelican* is evidence that despite their recent quarrel Drake still felt he could trust him. Like many men quick to anger he was also quick to forgive. Doughty, certainly, was not of Drake's straightforward temperament. Whether he was Burghley's man or not, and whatever he may have intended to do before the incident at La Brava, it is certain that from now on he was bent on inciting a mutiny.

CHAPTER EIGHT

Straits of Magellan

In the days of the great 19th-century clipper ships, the Doldrums were
still something of a bane to sailors. They were disliked by captains and
officers—who knew enough in any case to stay in that airless belt for as
short a time as possible—because the delays made their voyages un-
economic. Their crews also hated the area for the oppressive fickle
weather.

Whatever his experience of ship-handling and of navigation, Drake
had never before crossed the Equator. He followed the usual practice
of the time and tried to take as direct a route as he could from the
African shoreline to the coast of South America. Inevitably he fell foul
of the Doldrums, that sour region where few winds blow. The 16-
century practice of trying to sail as direct a course as possible, instead
of going west and then coasting down the continent, meant that they
crossed the central area of calms.

Nowadays, a well-found sailing yacht, with all modern navigational
knowledge at her disposal, must inevitably expect to 'hang fire' for
some time when making her way over to South America. The Admiralty Instructions for Sailing Ships in *Ocean Passages for the World*
rightly cautions: 'In considering where to cross the equator it is
necessary to bear in mind that if a vessel crosses far to the Westward
there will be less interval of doldrum to cross, *but it may be requisite to
tack to weather the coast of South America, and these crossings vary during
the year....*'

Drake had a slow and tedious crossing, and it was over two months
before the first sight of land. The Doldrums were always the potential
breeding-ground of mutiny, and with a man like Doughty in a ship,
and a crew who had all been lured into believing that they were only
going to Alexandria, it was hardly surprising that trouble should break
out. While acknowledging the superstitious climate of opinion in
which Drake and his company lived, historians have tended to ignore
the sheer fractious boredom which creeps over men confined within
small ships for days on end. Minute personal characteristics become

unendurable, and men can find it difficult to see any good in their best friends.

Even today, on the comparatively pleasant trade-wind crossing from Europe to the West Indies, men step ashore off sailing yachts never to speak to one another again. Only too often modern sailing expeditions bound round the world from England break up in dissension on the coast of America, the West Indies or even as far back as the Canary Islands. If such things can happen in the mid-20th century, when no members of a crew are in superstitious fear of the sea, and when all the world is accurately charted, how easy it must have been four hundred years ago. If yachtsmen sailing free, and for their own pleasure, can fall out and become devoured by the canker of mutual dislike, what should one expect of reluctantly conscripted sailors, and 'gentlemen' at logger-heads with marine officers?

It was little more than a century since men had believed that the world came to an end somewhere south of the Canary Islands. The Atlantic had then been known as the Ocean of Darkness, where it was believed that '. . . there were magnetic rocks that made a compass spin like a wheel, rocks that would draw the iron fastenings from a ship's side. The pitch would boil in the seams, the caulking would be lost, and the ships would sink. If you escaped these hazards, worse was to come. As you neared the outermost limits of the earth, you would be caught in the steady flow of water that poured day and night over the edge. It was not an old wives' tale—sailors themselves would tell you that you could see the edge of the world running away downhill. It dropped down in a great shimmering curve, and if you went too far south, the hill would grow steeper and you could never sail back. Then the eternally rushing water would catch you and sweep you away, into the darkness.'

Three generations of sailors had exploded such superstitions—at any rate among the educated. Drake and his officers knew that the world was round, while his sailors must have known it in theory. But between Drake, the sea-officers, the gentlemen-adventurers, and the sailors, there was one common bond of ignorance and superstition. All of them believed, as implicitly as they believed in their Faith, that the Powers of Darkness were still physically active in the world. Belief in witches, wizards, and their familiars, was commonplace. At Salem, in New England, in 1692, hundreds of witches were arrested, tried, and many of them burned. This took place more than a century after Drake's voyage round the world. (Even in 1963, in the New Forest area of England, a 'witch' was compelled to leave her house because her neighbours genuinely believed in her powers.)

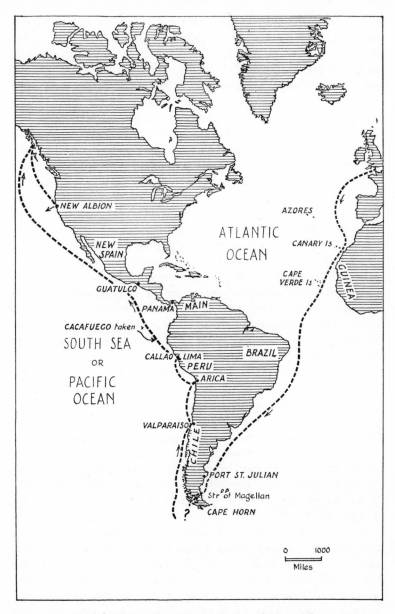

Drake's Outward Voyage to Peru and New Albion

The baffling winds—or lack of them—the long and oppressive conditions, foul water which bred sickness, and a predisposition on the part of Doughty to indulge in intrigue under any circumstances, combined to make Drake feel that something was going badly wrong with his expedition. There can be no doubt that during the passage Doughty did his best to subvert the allegiance of the ship's officers aboard the *Pelican*, as well as encouraging sedition among the crew.

The ships were in mid-ocean, idly rolling in a flat calm, when a boat was sent over by Drake from the *Mary* to his flagship to inquire, in the normal course of events, how things were going aboard her. Brewer (who seems to have been in Drake's confidence) was sent on this errand. He returned complaining that he had been treated with disrespect and made a victim of a crude practical joke, in which Doughty himself had taken part. On arrival he had been treated to a 'cobbey'—a sailor's rough way of greeting a shipmate by hauling down his breeches and every man 'beating him hard over the buttocks'. Doughty had no reason to like Brewer. It was largely through him that Doughty had been accused of having tampered with the cargo aboard the prize-ship at La Brava. Like the rest of the men in his ships, Drake was no doubt suffering from the effects of the heat and the infuriating calms. He saw in the ill treatment of his subordinate a deliberate affront to himself. He was infuriated.

At a time when rank and dignity were immensely important, it is not surprising that this should have been his reaction. Even today, a naval captain would rightly consider it an insult if the messenger he sent off to a ship under his command were treated with contumely and horse-play. Drake ordered Doughty to report at once on board the *Mary* and, when the latter arrived in a boat off his ship's side, he called out: 'Stay there, Thomas Doughty, for I must send you to another place!' He then ordered the sailors to row him over to the supply ship *Swan*, and sent instructions to her captain for Doughty to be held there as a prisoner.

Some reports suggest that Drake distrusted Doughty even before they had left Plymouth. If this was so, he certainly gave no sign of it until the incident at La Brava, and even then he quickly patched up the quarrel and restored Doughty to a position of authority. It is not impossible that Drake was coolly giving the man enough rope with which to hang himself. Drake was accustomed to rough and uncomplicated sailors, and used to dealing with their simple angers and complaints, but a man like Doughty was too complex. When the time came, Drake would be forced to act like Alexander and cut the Gordian knot.

At last, after fifty-four days at sea, the ships finally came in sight of the Brazilian coast—all of them on short commons, and all of them exacerbated by the calms, by slatting sails, and idle weather. They made land a little north of the River Plate, and immediately ran into the kind of weather which still makes this coast an awkward one for navigators. Sudden storms arose, unlooked-for fogs descended, and the ships kept losing contact with one another. First the *Christopher* disappeared, then —Drake having transferred to the *Pelican* at some point during their ocean passage—the *Mary* went missing, and at the same time the *Swan*.

They were now on the coast which the Portuguese Pilot, Nuño da Silva, no doubt described to Drake in the words of contemporary Portuguese charts as 'the Land of Demons'. The sudden off-shore winds of hurricane force which afflict this part of South America, the shifting banks and the prevalence of shoals, were enough in themselves to try the nerves of the most seasoned navigator with the best of charts. But to be told by one's pilot that the natives of the area had only preserved their freedom from the Portuguese by their magical abilities was to spread the fog of superstition over the worries that already existed. 'Ministering spirits' were said to dwell here and to have 'made a wreck of vessels', while one account of Drake's voyage has it that: 'Being discovered at sea by the inhabitants of the country, they [the natives] made upon the coast great fires for a sacrifice (as we learned) to the devils; about which they used conjurations, making heaps of sand and other ceremonies, that when any ship shall go about to stay on the coast, not only sands may be gathered together in every place, but also that storms and tempests may arise to the casting away of ships and men'. It may be that, from accounts of Drake's experiences off this coast, Shakespeare, combining them with stories about the 'remote Bermudas', fashioned his wizard-ridden 'Prospero's Isle'.

Books seemed magical to the illiterate in those days. A man like Thomas Doughty, as 'book-learned' as was his contemporary the mathematician and astrologer, John Dee, was naturally suspected of having access to the secret arts. (John Dee, it is worth remembering was even consulted by Queen Elizabeth as to a propitious day for her coronation, and his *speculum* or magic mirror can still be seen in the British Museum.) At a time when millions of people in the so-called 'rational' western world still consult their horoscopes in their daily papers, it should not be too difficult to understand the mental climate of the Elizabethans.

Doughty's brother, John, intent no doubt on securing Thomas's influence over the men, had gone so far as to boast that 'he and his brother could conjure as well as any men and that they could raise the devil and make him to meet any man in the likeness of a bear, a lion, or

a man in harness [armour].' The combination of this dangerous boast-
ing, allied with Thomas Doughty's treacherous tendencies, was to lead
to disaster. For all that Drake knew, believed, and was prepared to
admit, the latter might well:

> have bedimm'd
> The noontide sun, call'd forth the mutinous winds,
> And 'twixt the green sea and the azured vault
> Set roaring war: to the dread rattling thunder
> Have I given fire, and rifted Jove's stout oak
> With his own bolt: the strong-based promontory
> Have I made shake: and by the spurs pluck'd up
> The pine and cedar: graves, at my command,
> Have waked their sleepers, oped, and let them forth
> by my so potent art. . . .

Drake was bemused by the weather they encountered off the coast
of South America. Time and time again the ships parted company in
baffling mists, or high winds arose that spewed sand as thick as a
Channel fog across their passage. Having spent about a fortnight in the
estuary of the River Plate, the fleet coasted down towards Port St.
Julian. Here the squadron—re-united at last—arrived on the 18th June,
1578. The storeship *Swan*, which had been missing for some days, had
rejoined them at Port Desire, a little further north. They were now
only two hundred miles from the entrance to the Strait of Magellan,
and Drake would soon have to reveal not only to his officers, but to his
men, the project on which they were really bound. It is possible that
he had hinted at it when they were about to leave the Cape Verde
Islands—and this may well have led to Doughty's conduct from there
on. They were about to enter one of the most dangerous areas in the
world, and to make the passage of the Strait which few living men had
ever seen.

Ever since leaving Africa there had been trouble brewing—and
possibly even before then. The time had now come to act, for the
enterprise upon which they were bound called for the same kind of
unity that had belonged to Drake's 'band of brothers' in the old days
off the Spanish Main. The size and composition of the present fleet had
always proved something of a problem, and the different outlook of his
gentlemen-adventurers from his seamen had proved nothing but a
further burden. It was absolutely essential that any cancers should be
removed, if necessary by the surgeon's knife.

Port St. Julian was the harbour where, fifty-eight years before,
Magellan had wintered and prepared his small fleet for his unique,

Daedalus-like flight from one world into another. Drake followed his great predecessor probably because his Portuguese pilot had the anchorage clearly marked on his charts. Port St. Julian was, in any case, the last suitable place where ships could make ready and prepare for the hazardous passage that lay ahead. Brooding over the desolate anchorage there lay the knowledge that it was here that Magellan himself had been forced to deal with a mutiny, and had hanged the officers who were its ring-leaders. The anchorage was certainly haunted—in the sense that empty and inhuman landscapes, where violent actions have taken place, seem to remain heavy with what they have witnessed. Rocks, shingle, sand and sea had nothing here to commemorate except the gallows that Magellan's men had erected, and the memory of the choking cries with which the mutineers had died.

Hardly had the English landed when they found that the harsh coast was matched by the nature of its inhabitants. A party of Patagonians made an immediate attack upon them. Robert Winter, one of the gentleman-adventurers, was hit in the lung by an arrow and died from his wound two days later, while Drake's gunner was killed outright. Drake took a quick revenge, seized the musket belonging to his dead gunner 'and priming it anew, made a shot at him [the Patagonian] which first began the quarrel, and striking him in the paunch with hail shot, sent his guts abroad with great torment, as it seemed by his cry, which was so hideous and terrible a roar, as if ten bulls had joined together in roaring.'

In their previous encounters with the natives of South America, Drake and his men had managed to establi h friendly relations. But, like an augury of what was to follow and of the Dante-esque world into which they were venturing, this first incident set a seal of gloom upon the anchorage. As if to confirm any forebodings, they now found an old spruce-mast near the beach—the remains of the gibbet, they conjectured, on which Magellan had hanged his mutineers. This was soon confirmed when, digging around its base, they found the remains of skeletons. It was an age when the harsh reality of death was familiar to every man, not concealed under an antiseptic hush. It was quite natural that the cooper of the *Pelican* cut sections out of the gibbet and made tankards from them, 'for such of the company as would drink in them'.

The moment had come, and 'In this port,' as Hakluyt tells the story, 'our General began to inquire diligently of the actions of Mr. Thomas Doughty, and found them not to be such as he looked for, but tending rather to contention of mutiny, or some other disorder. . . .'

On one of the bare rocky islands which starred the anchorage, Drake called all the company together and a trial began which Sir Julian Corbett described as partaking 'rather of the nature of a Lynch Court than a court-martial'. Such words were easy enough for a historian to write in the comparative security of 19th-century England; words suggesting that life can always be conducted according to a secure framework of laws designed to operate within a solid and controlled society. Men who within comparatively recent years have engaged in partisan activities within enemy-held territory know well enough that there is not always time to bother with the formalities of the law— especially when existence itself is at stake.

Drake's charge against Doughty was that: 'You have here sought by divers means, inasmuch as you may, to discredit me to the great hindrance and overthrow of this voyage, besides other great matters where I have to charge you withal. . . .' Doughty replied that he was willing to be tried in England, but that if Drake intended to try him then and there, 'he hoped that his commission was good'. Now it is an important fact that, in his reported speech to the crew when he first joined the *Pelican* in the Cape Verde Islands, Doughty had said that the General (Drake) had a commission from the Queen which entitled him, if need be, to pronounce the death sentence. This seems to be confirmed by the report of the Portuguese pilot, Nuño da Silva (who certainly can have had no axe to grind in Drake's favour) that Drake produced his commission from the Queen during the trial and read it out. 'All present saw the papers were his and from her [Queen Elizabeth] and that it was by her authority that he was executing Doughty.'

Drake empanelled a jury of forty men, among whom were some of Doughty's principal supporters. One of these was Leonard Vicary, a lawyer who is known to have been a close associate of the prisoner. (It was Vicary who had been largely responsible for patching up the quarrel between Doughty and Drake at La Brava.) There is little of a 'Lynch Court' in all of this, and Drake's conduct of the whole trial seems to have been as close as he could make it to a trial by jury in England at that time. Winter, Vice-Admiral of the fleet, was appointed foreman of the jury.

The climax of the case came when a witness, Edward Bright, said that he had heard Doughty plotting against the whole expedition in Drake's garden at Plymouth. The prisoner does not appear to have denied this. Bright went on to say: 'It fell out upon further talk that Master Doughty said that my Lord Treasurer [Lord Burghley] had a plot of the voyage.' At this point Drake himself burst out: 'No, that he hath not!' Doughty, however, maintained that Lord Burghley had

The *Golden Hind*: water-colour reconstruction by a modern artist
(*By permission of the Trustees of the National Maritime Museum*)

e Drake coat of arms
odern Portraits Ltd., Plymouth)

Buckland Abbey
(Modern Portraits Ltd., Plymouth)

indeed known the object of the expedition. Drake asked him 'How?', to which Doughty replied, 'He had it from me.'

The amazing thing about this admission was that with it Doughty sealed his own fate. He was confessing that he had found out the secret purpose of the expedition, and had revealed it to the one man whom Queen Elizabeth had said must never know about it. Looking back in detachment four hundred years later upon the whole evidence, it seems likely that Doughty was Burghley's agent from the very beginning, and that he had been entrusted with the task of preventing Drake from embroiling England with Spain by a series of piratical raids. Drake's reaction was violent but natural under the circumstances.

'Lo! my masters,' he cried, 'what this fellow hath done! God will have all his treachery known. For Her Majesty gave me special commandment that of all men my Lord Treasurer should not know it. But see how his own mouth hath betrayed him!'

Some historians have cast doubts upon the prisoner's admission, but since one of the accounts most favourable to Doughty (and most prejudicial to Drake) records it, there seems to be no reason for treating it with suspicion. Doughty, it would seem clear enough, thought that the mention of Burghley's name would be sufficient to deter Drake from any violent action. He had made a great mistake, for Drake—with or without the Queen's commission—would most probably have acted as he did. Curiously enough, despite all previous references to Doughty's being a wizard, this was never mentioned in the trial, which was conducted on purely factual grounds.

The question Drake finally asked the jury was: 'Is this man a traitor?' The answer they returned was a unanimous 'Yes'. Drake called for a show of hands from the jury as to whether the prisoner should die. So far as we know there were no dissentients. Drake then pronounced Captain Thomas Doughty 'the child of death and 'persuaded him withal that he would by these means make him the servant of God'. The execution was to take place in two days' time.

Apparently Drake was still willing to spare Doughty's life if a way out could be found that would not endanger the expedition. The condemned man proposed that they should put him ashore somewhere in Peru, while Winter, Captain of the *Elizabeth* and foreman of the jury, suggested that he should keep him in custody until their return to England.

Peru was clearly out of the question, for Doughty must inevitably reveal the expedition's objects, either willingly, or under torture, to the Spaniards. Drake's refusal of Winter's offer is only explicable on the ground that he had determined to make an end of Doughty. He may have feared that, even as a prisoner below hatches, Doughty would still contrive to stir up trouble. But once he knew that Doughty had betrayed the secret of the expedition to Burghley, remembering the Queen's words, he no doubt felt that he had her sanction to execute him. There is always a third possibility to account for Drake's apparent determination to remove Doughty—that he felt himself personally insulted. Drake was proud and vain. He was also touchy about his humble origins. He may have felt that in Doughty he had made, for the first time in his life, a friend among 'the gentry'. To have this confidence and friendship betrayed possibly filled him with bitterness and resentment. The thought is unattractive, but so are many 'great' men. Drake would not have risen to the top in that day and age if he had been a product of the public-school code of Dr. Arnold.

Doughty's behaviour in the last two days of his life was exemplary. Chaplain Fletcher, who was disposed in Doughty's favour, had little doubt that an innocent man was being sacrificed for some obscure reason of the General's. 'But how true it was they charged him upon their oath,' he wrote, 'I know not: but he utterly denied it upon his salvation, at the hour of communicating the sacrament of the body and blood of Christ, at the hour and moment of his death, affirming that he was innocent of such things whereof he was accused, judged, and suffered death for.' There is no reason to disbelieve Fletcher's account— for why should a man lie when he takes the Last Sacrament? Yet it would hardly be the first, nor the last time, that such a thing may have happened.

The fact that Doughty and Drake took Communion together with Chaplain Fletcher officiating before the execution may seem strange. The two men then sat down, and 'dined at the same table together as cheerfully in sobriety as ever in their lives they had done aforetime, each cheering up the other and taking their leave by drinking to each other, as if some journey only had been at hand'. But, to their way of thinking, nothing more than 'some journey' was at hand. The fact that a man so soon to lose his life could take Communion, and afterwards eat a meal with the man who had condemned him, suggests also that he accepted without question the judgement passed upon him. Doughty may well have been a traitor to the project envisaged by Drake and Queen Elizabeth, but he understood what later generations of Englishmen were to call 'the code of a gentleman'. If he had lived three or four hundred years later, he would almost certainly have put a revolver to his head to spare everyone further embarrassment.

Before the execution took place, Doughty asked for a few minutes' private conversation with Drake. There is no record of what the two men talked about, and afterwards he was taken away for execution. To the very last Doughty conducted himself with great dignity. Could we but know his last words to Drake, they would furnish the answer to the whole sinister affair. At the moment of death did he maintain his innocence to his Captain and Judge? And if he did so, what is one to make of Drake's remark, and after the sword had plunged down and taken off Doughty's head:—'Lo! This is the end of traitors.'

From what we know of Drake's character, as evidenced throughout the whole of his life, it is hard to credit that he uttered those words unless he believed them. He was a hard man, and ruthless to his enemies, but it is difficult to believe that he countenanced a cynical murder. In any case, what had he to gain from such an act? It was something that must automatically set all Doughty's friends and supporters against him.

Doughty was dead, and it was now all-important that the whole atmosphere should be cleared. The issues had to be put simply before the soldiers, sailors and gentlemen, and any lingering shreds of suspicion, doubt, or mutiny, blown to the winds. With the Strait of Magellan ahead of them, and beyond that a raid into the Spanish preserves of the Pacific, it was not only essential that the ships should be in good condition, but that the men should be united and resolute. It was now July, mid-winter in that part of the world, and there could be no chance of passing the Strait until the nights began to grow shorter. Even though the main source of trouble might have been removed by the execution of Thomas Doughty, his brother still remained in the fleet. Drake decided to deal once and for all with any potential mutineers. As he had long ago learned with Hawkins, on the voyage to San Juan de Ulua, trouble on expeditions of this nature usually arose through friction between the military and the sea officers—the one despising the other as 'common fellows', while the sea officers regarded the soldiers with the contempt they reserved for all landsmen.

On the 11th August, 1578, every man in the fleet was ordered by Drake to make their confession to Chaplain Fletcher, and there to receive the sacrament. Having thus given spiritual matters priority, he proceeded to deal with material problems. When the Chaplain somewhat naturally proposed that he should preach a sermon to the assembled company Drake cut him short with the reply: 'Nay, soft, Master Fletcher, I must preach this day myself.' He then made his famous address, which has ever since been taken as the basis of all disciplinary rules for governing men at sea. At the time, his words were startling, revolutionary even, and must have astounded the sailors almost as much as the gentlemen. He reminded them all of the immense hazards of the voyage that lay ahead, and that the real difficulties were only beginning. There must be an end, he said, to the discords and quarrelling between two factions; and all must realise that they were engaged on the same task, and must share the burdens. 'By the life of God,' he thundered, 'it doth even take my wits from me to think on it! Here is such controversy between the sailors and the gentlemen, and such stomaching between the gentleman and sailors, that it doth even make me mad to hear it. But, my masters, I must have it left. For I must have the gentlemen to haul and draw with the mariner and the mariner with the gentlemen. What! Let us show ourselves all to be of a company and let us not give occasion to the enemy to rejoice at our decay and overthrow. I would know him, that would refuse to set his hand to a rope, but I know there is not any such here. . . .' His last words were heavy with irony.

If there were any who did not like the idea of the voyage, he would let them have the *Marigold* and they might make their way back to England in her. 'But let them take heed,' he added, 'that they go homeward. For if I find them in my way I will surely sink them.'

His tactics worked. Not a hand was raised, not a suggestion was made that a single man wanted to abandon the expedition. Having established his authority over the sailors, the gentlemen, and the soldiers, Drake now made it clear to all that he had total authority. He turned to the ship's officers and dismissed them all from their posts. When Captains Winter and Thomas protested, Drake asked them if there was any reason why he should not dismiss them—a question to which they could find no answer. He accepted their silence, and went on—for the last time—to refer to the execution of Doughty. 'More there are,' Drake said, 'who deserved no other fate, but as I am a gentleman, there shall no more die.' In conclusion, having told them all how the venture had come about, he revealed what influential men were behind it. He showed them the letters and documents that proved his statements, and finally produced the proof of the Queen's interest—the bill of her share in the expedition.

From that moment on he had all of them, captains, gentlemen, soldiers, and sailors, in the palm of his hand. He had enforced his will and his authority, and so—with a munificent gesture—he reinstated the ship's officers to their former positions in front of the whole company. He had deprived them of their offices and he now restored them.

All that remained to do before making their way south to the Strait was to break up the storeships, and transfer their men, stores and victuals. Drake's reduced fleet now consisted of the *Elizabeth*, the

Marigold, and his own flagship the *Pelican*. As if to show that even in small matters a new spirit was animating the enterprise, he renamed her the *Golden Hind*, after the device of Sir Christopher Hatton's crest. This, quite apart from anything else, was a politic move. Doughty had been a servant of Hatton, and by associating Hatton so openly with the voyage, Drake must have intended to allay any enmities at court, where Hatton was now a prime favourite. The most important thing now was that the *Golden Hind* should be associated with success and not with failure.

On the 20th August, the three ships reached the lean headland of the end of South America and the mouth of the Strait. As a symbol of his intentions and a reminder to them all of their duties, Drake 'caused his fleet, in homage to our sovereign Lady the Queen's Majesty, to strike their topsails upon the bunt. . . .' The airy topsails dipped to signify their devotion, and to acknowledge that the Queen had full rights and interest in any discoveries that they might make. On their starboard hand the towering cliffs ran up against a bleak sky, and ahead of them lay the grim entrance to the Strait. On the one side was Tierra del Fuego with its volcanoes and its peaks of eternal snow, and on the other the curtain of cliffs that marked the end of the continent. Tomorrow they would turn westward and attempt the passage. Ahead lay the confined waters where no man since Magellan had ever sailed and survived.

CHAPTER NINE

Into the Great South Sea

THE Magellan Strait, which separates Patagonia from the Archipelago of Tierra del Fuego, is one of the most inaccessible and lonely places in the world. Nowadays no sailing ship ever passes this way, save that of the rare and eccentric yachtsman bound on some personal quest. Except for the passage of occasional steamships, the Strait has returned to its time-haunted silence.

'From Cape Virgins to Cape Negro,' says the *Admiralty Pilot*, 'about 100 miles west-south-westward, the land is comparatively low and covered with grass, but not a tree is visible. Throughout this distance, the depth rarely exceeds 30 or 40 fathoms, and there are many banks and shoals; the tidal streams are rapid, the tide rising nearly 40 feet. . . . Westward of Cape Froward, glaciers descend nearly to the sea in places, and frequently crown the precipices.'

There is no lack of variety in the Strait, for out of the low flat lands of the first section of the east-to-west passage, the navigator soon finds himself in a fiord-like Norwegian world, where squalls descend without warning, and where—worst of all—lone pinnacle rocks spring up from the bed of the channel. Sometimes these razor-sharp rocks can be detected from the kelp that clings around their heads, but, 'when the tidal stream is strong, kelp is often quite "run under" or kept out of sight below the surface.'

The dangers of the Strait are many—violent tides, squalls, concealed rocks and banks, and the unlikelihood of any help if a ship gets into danger. The modern Patagonians are not enemies of all the human race, as they were in Drake's day, but even so the voyager is warned that, although 'Shepherds would give any assistance to shipwrecked mariners,' yet, 'in winter, communication with the *estancias* is more difficult, as the ground becomes swampy or frozen over.' It is a hard area still; even with modern charts, sounding equipment, and with engines powerful enough to give a ship control over her movements.

When Drake and his men sailed through here, the Strait was literally the end of the earth. Only masterly seamanship, careful pilotage, luck and

endurance, can have enabled them to follow Magellan, their only predecessor. It is not surprising that Drake was determined to establish the
complete loyalty of his crew before attempting to make the passage.

They were lucky with their weather. Drake's ships managed to get
through the Strait—some 300 miles of sailing—in only sixteen days. It
was often necessary for them to send their rowing boats ahead to chart
the way; they landed and reprovisioned with penguins (which they
salted down); and sometimes they had to get their boats to tow them.
Often, again, they had to brail up their sails, and lie to anchor. The great
Magellan himself (though we must make allowances for the fact that
his ships were those of an earlier period, and that he was making the
very first voyage in these waters) took 37 days to get through the
straits. Drake's successors later in the 16th century—Richard Hawkins
and Thomas Cavendish—were to take 46 and 49 days respectively.

Drake must have had a fair wind nearly all the way. He did not suffer
from the baffling head-winds that are liable to afflict sailors when they
get into the far end of the Straits. Here it is not uncommon to meet the
Pacific westerlies, funnelling through the narrow passage which
begins at Cape Froward and stretches for about 120 miles to Tamar
Island. In this area, where the channel is often less than a mile wide,
fanged by rocks and darkened by sheer cliffs, the navigator of a sailing
vessel is in a hell that is difficult for the landsman to imagine. There is
often no slack water between tides, for the moment that one tide has
ceased running, the sea turns and flows from the opposite direction.

In Drake's time, there was always the added concern that, just to the
south of them—where they saw the volcanoes smoke all night on the
island of Tierra del Fuego—there might lie a vast and unknown
continent. He had reason to believe that, when and if he did finally
make his way out into the Pacific, he might find himself on an uncharted shore.

On the 6th September, 1578, the ships struggled out into the
Pacific, the 'Peaceful Ocean' as Magellan had called it. Magellan had
been lucky in his first sight of this great expanse of unknown water—as
lucky as Drake had been in his quick passage through the Straits.
But the treacherous area of Desolation Island was quick to show that
his trials were only beginning. On Cape Pillar, at the north-western
end of the island, Drake had planned to erect a monument com-
memorating the expedition, and giving credit for it to the Queen. But
the wind began to pipe up against him and, far from being able to make
a landing on this lonely point, he found it was all he could do to make
an offing from the foam-ridged outriders of the shore.

At last his dream was realised—he had taken an English ship into the

Pacific. But it was only to find that this was a far call from the Caribbean, where the curt waves fell on coral-sand beaches. Like any good
seaman, Drake did his best to get his ships clear of the coast. He headed
in a north-westerly direction, for that was how the contemporary
Spanish charts showed the trend of the continent. Then, two days out
from the bitter mouth of the Straits, a gale struck from the north-east.
Day after day the wind screamed down from the same quarter, and
day after day the ships fled southward before it. '. . . God by a contrary
wind and intolerable tempest seemed to set himself against us.'

It is easy enough in these days of steamship travel (when men still
carefully avoid the area of Cape Horn) to make light of the sufferings
of these early navigators. But the *Admiralty Pilot* (1956) still cautions
mariners destined for this part of the world: 'Most strong winds or
gales are from west or north-west. . . . In all these regions at least half,
and in the windiest part fully two-thirds, of the winds are force 7 and
more, or gales of force 8 or more. There are occasional periods in most
years when the wind blows with hurricane strength. . . . During the
strongest williwaws, which occur most often westward of Cape
Froward and near the main coastline adjoining the stormiest region at
sea, the wind almost certainly exceeds 100 knots.'

A wind of 100 knots would cause a modern 10,000-ton steamship to
heave-to, while a small sailing vessel of Drake's period could do
nothing but run before it. But, as far as Drake knew, to run to the
south-west before such a wind meant that he would probably find
himself on the coast of *Terra Australis*. On the 15th September as the
ships drifted helplessly in these unfamiliar seas, an eclipse of the moon
seemed to add substance to the sailors' fears that even the powers of
heaven were leagued against them.

For nearly a month gale force winds continued from the same
direction. On the 30th September the *Marigold* parted company during
the dark hours, and disappeared, never to be seen again. Captain
Winter of the *Elizabeth* commented: 'That night was the most tem-
pestuous night that was ever seen in this outrageous weather.' It is
possible that the unfortunate *Marigold* tried to run back for the illusory
safety of the Straits and was wrecked on one of the innumerable rocks
and islets near the entrance. Thomas Cavendish, who followed Drake
as a circumnavigator in 1586, described a wreck in the Straits as being
that of the *John Thomas*. There was no ship with such a name, but John
Thomas was indeed the name of the *Marigold*'s captain. Cavendish
presumably established that the wreck was a British vessel. We may
take it that it was here, in this grim world, that the men of the *Marigold*
met their deaths.

Drake and Winter were now blown so far to the south that their observations established them as being in Latitude 57° South. That is to say, they were some 300 miles below the Straits, far below Cape Horn and the Wollaston Islands, those savage outcrops of the South American continent. Drake now saw for himself that Magellan had been mistaken. There was no vast continent south of the known land, only the endless acres of the sea, and the roaring march of the uninterrupted winds and waves that girdle the earth. *Terra Australis* did not exist, but the Atlantic and the Pacific ocean were united, and 'met in a most large and free scope'.

This discovery, which Drake and his companions made inadvertently, was the most important event in the circumnavigation—geographically speaking. It was a discovery which he later took care to keep secret from the Spaniards, for the knowledge that men could sail free round the southern tip of America might have proved of immense value to them. In fact, so dangerous are the winds and weather likely to be encountered in this area that the 'Roaring Forties' would be avoided by mariners for many years, until shipbuilders had produced thoroughly efficient, seaworthy craft that could stand up to the conditions.

It was on the 7th October, 1578, over a month since he and his small squadron had entered the Pacific, that Drake in the *Golden Hind* and Winter in the *Elizabeth* managed to struggle back to the western coast of Chile near the mouth of the Straits. It was a remarkable enough achievement that they managed to keep in contact at all and, after all their trials, it might have seemed only justice that the weather should now give them some respite. But they had hardly dropped anchor before the wind piped up again and, during a violent squall, the *Golden Hind* parted her cable. Drake was forced to stand out to sea for safety.

John Barrow commented that the *Elizabeth* 'remained in the port without any attempt to follow the Admiral'. But Captain Winter can hardly be blamed for behaving in a perfectly seamanlike manner. He assumed no doubt that, as soon as Drake could manage it, he would come back to the anchorage, or at any rate rendezvous with the *Elizabeth* somewhere in the mouth of the Strait. He was not to know that his admiral was once again caught by the same kind of hurricane-strength weather, and that he would once more be compelled to drive before it for nearly a month.

Winter, as his own account quite clearly shows, did attempt to stand by his admiral, but could not do so under the conditions prevailing. He later anchored in the entrance to the Strait, waited there for several days, and lighted fires to indicate his position. Finally he was driven back, further down the winding channel, by the onset of strong northerlies. Drake at some time or other had clearly spoken to Winter of some intention to go to the Moluccas—the 'Spice Islands' of the Malay archipelago. Winter, possibly convinced that Drake had already made off in that direction, tried to prevail on his crew to take the ship there. But the men, hired originally for a quiet voyage to Alexandria, had had enough, and the Master of the ship backed them up in their determination to abandon the whole venture and return home. Winter found himself alone and unsupported, and gave in to their demands.

The *Elizabeth* made her way back down the harsh Strait, and set course for England. Winter has sometimes been blamed for his conduct, but he no more deserted Drake than the latter deserted Hawkins at San Juan de Ulua. The only thing that can possibly be held against Winter is that, as captain of his ship, he allowed himself to be prevailed upon by her Master and crew, rather than bending them to his own will. But it is not given to all men to be of Drake's calibre—and that would seem the only fair criticism that can be held against Winter. He had proved himself, in everything else up to this moment, to be an honest and loyal officer, and a good seaman into the bargain.

Drake meanwhile had been driven back for the second time into the South Sea, and into that area south of Cape Horn where, four centuries later, ship after ship—the perfection of 19th-century technology and the high peak of sailing-ship design—was to be dismasted, wrecked, or lost at sea with all hands. The soundness of the *Golden Hind*, the endurance of her crew and the excellence of her captain are all borne out by the fact that so small a 16th-century vessel could live for so long in the worst seas in the world. For some weeks the battered *Hind* ran back and forth among the islands that fringe the continent, taking shelter where and when she could. During one lull in the weather Drake managed to land on a small island which was, as far as he could see, the southernmost point in that wild area. He took his instruments ashore with him, and by his calculations, 'the outermost cape of all these headlands stands near in 56 degrees. . . .' It is still disputed by historians and geographers whether Drake did in fact discover Cape Horn, but there is every likelihood that he did. The layman will almost certainly give him 'the benefit of the doubt', for the discrepancy between his measurements of latitude and the modern measurement (Lat: 55° 59′ S) is remarkably small. When at sea Drake usually took his latitude to within half a degree only—not so surprising in a small sailing vessel—but ashore he was naturally more careful and accurate. One thing is certain, that in Hondius's celebrated map of the world, which shows both Drake's voyage and that of his successor, Cavendish, there is a strait of open sea shown before one comes to the uncharted Antarctic continent. Hondius credits Drake with having charted the islands which lie to the south of Tierra del Fuego, and there is no reason to disbelieve him.

But Drake, whatever some of the investors in his voyage may have thought, had not come out as geographer, nor to make contact with the rulers and people of an unknown continent. His interest lay in that western seaboard of South America, where the Spanish ships coasted happily up and down, totally unaware that there would soon be 'a dragon' in their company. At long last the *Golden Hind* had a wind astern. For the first time since her passage through the Strait of Magellan she was able to run before a favourable wind, and she now made her northing up to the entrance where Drake hoped to rendez-vous with his two missing ships. He followed his Spanish charts and continued to sail north-west, but when no sight of land appeared, and knowing that it must surely lie somewhere on his starboard hand, he turned in that direction. By the 15th November he had reached the latitude of $45\frac{1}{2}$ degrees. Ten days later, shaping a north-easterly course he came in sight of Mocha Island some four hundred miles further north, and only about 50 miles off the coast of Chile.

His troubles were not at an end. The Indians who inhabited Mocha had had long years to become acquainted with the cruelty of white-skinned and bearded strangers in sailing vessels. Drake, who was used to the friendship which had been shown him in the past by Indians, Cimaroons and Spanish Negro slaves, allowed himself and his crew to be taken by surprise. They landed quite openly, with the peaceful intention of watering ship and getting what provisions they could, only to find themselves the victims of a sudden and unexpected attack just as they were beaching one of their boats. Drake himself was hit twice by arrows—once almost fatally in the face—while all the other men in the boat's crew were also wounded.

They were lucky that these Indians were not using poisoned arrows, for they had little enough medical comfort aboard the ship. One of the surgeons who had embarked on the voyage had died; one was with Winter in the *Elizabeth*; and all that remained was a young surgeon's apprentice, a boy 'whose good will was more than any skill he had'. Their hard physical condition, coupled with Drake's own abilities as physician and surgeon, healed them. Even so, he lost two men in his brief skirmish; his gunner, and his faithful Negro, Diego, who had been his constant servant and companion ever since the raid on Nombre de Dios six years before. Chaplain Fletcher in his comments on this

incident remarked that the natives in this place worshipped 'Settabos—
that is the divell, whom they name their great God'. One wonders
whether Shakespeare was not familiar with some of the accounts of
Drake's voyage, for where else did he find 'Setebos', Caliban's deity?

Despite this unprovoked attack, and the losses that he had sustained,
Drake would not allow his men to use the cannon against the natives
assembled on the shore. He had come to make war against Spaniards.
He and his men had unfortunately been mistaken for the enemy, but
that was no reason for acting as Spaniards would have done. In fact, in
his opinion, the Indians ought to be commended for the spirit they had
shown against men whom they had assumed to be their persecutors.

At last, after all his difficulties—sedition, attempted mutiny, the
execution of Doughty, the almost unbelievable hardships of his
passage through the Straits, and the subsequent two months in the
region of Cape Horn—Drake was on the eve of success. It is Robert
the Bruce who has gone down in legend as the epitome of determination and dogged resolution, but it is doubtful whether any man in
history has ever exhibited these qualities more than Francis Drake.
Putting Mocha Island astern of him, he sailed on up the coastline and
dropped anchor in a small bay a little north of Valparaiso. Here they
found an Indian out fishing in a canoe, and Drake at once showed his
usual friendliness, gave him presents, and received in return the useful
information that a large merchantman had recently put into Valparaiso. The Indian, not content with seeing that provisions were
brought off to the ship by his tribe, volunteered to pilot the *Golden
Hind* down to Valparaiso. As the Narrative remarks: 'In him we might
see a most lively pattern of the harmless disposition of that people; and
how grievous a thing it is that they should, by any means, be so abused
as all those are, whome the Spaniards have any command or power
over.'

On the 5th December, 1578, the Great Raid began. Drake swooped
down on Valparaiso, little more than a small fishing port in those days,
and found the reported merchantmen at anchor in the harbour. Only
eight of her crew were aboard and they, very naturally not suspecting
that this could be anything other than a fellow Spanish vessel, called
over and invited the newcomers to come and take a little wine with
them. The English were only too eager to respond, and Drake's
faithful old carpenter, Thomas Moone, pulled across with a boatload
of men. No sooner were they alongside the ship, than Moone and his
comrades leaped aboard, Moone laying about him with his fists—a
most unLatin habit—and shouting out to the astonished crew: 'Below,
dogs! Get below!' Only one man managed to escape, jumping over-

board, and swimming ashore to raise the alarm in the town. The rest of the crew were quickly shut below hatches, while the raiders examined their prize. She proved to be a happy augury of what was to come, for she had a good amount of gold on board, as well as plenty of the wines they had been asked to try.

At the news that the heretics were upon them, the inhabitants of Valparaiso took to the hills, while Drake landed with his men and captured the town. They embarked some more wine, but little else of value except some ecclesiastical silverware, which he gave to Chaplain Fletcher for use aboard ship in the Protestant service (a thought that must have appealed to him). At the same time they managed to stock up with fresh fruit, meat, and other provisions. No less important was the capture of the master of the Spanish ship, a Greek by birth, whom Drake took aboard the *Golden Hind* to pilot them up to Lima.

After lying three days at anchor in the harbour, while his men completed the transfer of the gold, wine and stores, Drake hove in the anchor and sailed out to sea. The terrified inhabitants, none of whom can ever have seen a foreign man-of-war before, came down to their rifled town and their looted merchantman. That 'Drake' who had last been heard of some years before on the Caribbean seaboard had now arrived—by some almost magical means—in the undefended Pacific. Much though they must have wished to convey the news as quickly as possible to all the other ports and anchorages up the coast, there was little they could do about it. In those days, few roads, and no regular system of post-horses connected the scattered settlements, and it was largely by means of visiting coasters and merchantmen that news passed from one place to another. Drake was now out amongst this unsuspecting quarry like a hawk.

He had still not given up all hope of finding the *Marigold* and the *Elizabeth*. Acting on the assumption that they had survived the weather off the Strait, and then followed much the same course as himself, he spent some weeks casting up and down the coast in search of them, using one of his pinnaces to help him in the search. The only place where they ran into any trouble was at the mouth of the Co-quimbo river, where the pinnace's crew was attacked by a band of armed Spaniards, and one of the seamen was shot dead. Drake moved on a few miles north from here, and found a good anchorage in Salada Bay. Before sailing any further northward, he needed to careen the *Hind*, recaulk her as necessary, and tallow and tar her against the attacks of marine worm. No doubt, too, after all that she had been through, bowsprit and masts were in need of inspection, yards had to be sent down, running-rigging overhauled, and her standing-rigging set up taut and hard. The heavy guns which had been stowed below in the hold throughout their passage were now brought up, and mounted on the gun deck. While the crew got on with the work, Drake took some men in the pinnace and sailed south, still hoping against hope to catch sight of either of his missing companions. But the *Marigold* had long been a wreck, and the *Elizabeth* was already far away on the other side of the continent, bound home for England.

One result of Drake's sudden and totally unexpected arrival off the Chilean coast was that, as word gradually got around that the heretics were in the Southern Sea, the Governor of Chile was compelled to divert what few forces he had to the protection of his towns and ports. Since the panic continued a long time after Drake had moved up north to Peru—long after he had, in fact, set sail across the Pacific for the East Indies—the Spanish troops were kept mobilised all along the coast. Inadvertently, Drake did the native Indians a very good turn, for the Governor had just been on the point of bringing them all to subjection. This unexpected diversion of his forces saved the Indians from defeat and enslavement, at least for a few more years.

With the *Hind* clean, sweet, rerigged, and ready for action, Drake moved on—always with the idea of Lima on his mind, and beyond that, like a distant dream, the city of Panama. Hoping no doubt that any merchant ships would be to seaward of them and that therefore he would be invisible against the land, Drake sailed so close inshore that 'any person travelling on land could be distinctly seen'.

One incident alone reveals the light-hearted and youthful way in which these young men 'troubled' the great empire of Spain. At the Pisagua river, in the far north of Chile, a party had gone ashore to get water, and came across a Spaniard taking a quiet siesta on the river bank. Beside him was a bundle which the men opened, only to find that it contained thirteen bars of silver, worth some four thousand ducats. These they cheerfully 'removed without waking him'. Centuries divide us from that sleeping man, but one has a vivid picture of the expression on his face when he woke up to find that his wealth had flown, as if the devil had taken it. Incidents like this, multiplied time and time again, gave Drake the laughing admiration of his own men, and the reputation among the enemy of being a magician.

Landing on another occasion to water, they came across a Spaniard driving eight llamas in front of him, and each of these strange and unfamiliar beasts was laden with a hundred pounds of silver. 'We could not endure to see a gentleman Spaniard turned carrier. . . . We offered our services and became drovers: only his directions were not so perfect that we could keep the way he intended.' Leaving the Spaniard to rage or weep at his loss, they drove the llamas down to the shore and happily embarked the silver in their boats.

At Arica, frontier-town of Peru, and the port where the wealth from the famous Potosi mines was embarked for Panama, they had little success, capturing only about one hundredweight of silver from two small vessels at anchor in the harbour. They heard, though, from a Negro watchman aboard one of these ships that they had only just missed a most valuable prize—a treasure ship which had sailed up the coast a few hours before. Drake hastened after her, but when he did come up with her, he found that she had landed her silver on seeing the strange sail, and that a strong guard had been placed over it. By now, Drake must have been growing concerned at the way in which his presence was being advertised along the coast, and have feared that the news might reach Lima before he did. He took the treasure ship captive and towed her out to sea along with two other smaller prizes. Then, setting all sail on them, he let the offshore winds drive them out and away into the emptiness of the Pacific. At least he had lost his enemies three useful vessels.

On the 15th February unable to resist so important a port as Callao, Drake stole in during the dark hours and quietly, and almost casually, dropped anchor. The alarm had clearly not reached the port. Soon afterwards, a merchantman from Panama came in and anchored comfortably next to the *Golden Hind*. One of her men called out and asked what ship it was, and received the reply that she was from Chile, 'Captain—Michael Angelo.' A man rowed over to see, as he thought, an old friend. Suddenly he saw that she was armed with large cannon—something never seen on the peaceful Pacific coast. He splashed away into the night and gave the alarm. Drake had captured little of value, and saw that he must leave quickly, but first of all he made sure that the Spaniards would be unable to pursue him. Before he left, he got his men to row round in one of the boats and cut the cables of all the ships lying at anchor in Callao—with the result that some drifted together, some on to the shore, and all were in a state of total confusion.

Standing out to sea after the Panama merchantman, which had quickly made off on discovering the *Hind*'s identity, Drake overtook her and captured her after one shot. There was little of value on board, but one most important piece of news did result from her capture. Drake learned that, only a little ahead of him bound up the coast for Panama, was an immensely rich treasure ship, *Nuestra Señora de la Concepcion*. This was her official name, and she was also described as 'The Great Glory of the South Sea', but Spanish seamen had nick-named her somewhat irreverently the *Cacafuego*, or 'Shitfire'.

Drake prepared to give chase. Although delayed for a time by the weather falling calm, it was not long before he got a favourable wind. Setting every stitch of sail, he went bowling up the coast after the quarry. On his way he encountered a number of small vessels, from whom he received further news of the treasure ship, always a little ahead of them. Then the wind increased, and the *Golden Hind*, with a bone between her teeth, began to show her best turn of speed. Their hopes began to rise, and Drake promised a golden chain to the man who should first sight the *Cacafuego*.

They crossed the line and then, on the afternoon of the 1st March, 1579, near Cape San Francisco, some fifty miles north of the equator, Drake's nephew called down from the masthead. He had sighted the *Cacafuego*'s sails on the horizon! Not wishing to come up with the enemy until after dark, and hoping to take her by surprise, Drake had water-filled wine casks trailed over the stern to reduce the *Hind*'s way. He need not have bothered. The Spanish treasure ship was neither well armed, nor in the slightest degree aware that an enemy was on her heels. On the contrary, her captain, San Juan de Anton, sighted the sail lifting over the horizon astern of him, and courteously put his ship about. He stood back towards the *Golden Hind*, hoping to exchange news and talk to a fellow-mariner on this lonely coast.

As the two vessels neared one another, the English gunners waited below with their slow-matches smouldering in case it should come to action. The unsuspecting Spaniard called over and asked them who they were. 'A ship from Chile!' came the reply. The two vessels were almost alongside when suddenly the cry went up: 'English! Strike sail!' This was followed by Drake's voice: 'Strike sail, Señor Juan de Anton, unless you wish to go to the bottom!'

Although taken totally unawares, the Spaniard replied with courage that he refused to surrender. Let them come aboard and try to take his ship! But his own guns were unmanned, and the first volley of shot and arrows from the English was sufficient for the capture of the *Cacafuego*. Her mizzen-mast, cut through by chain-shot, fell over-board, and her men fled below as forty English sailors swarmed over the side. The Spanish captain found himself alone on the deck of his ship. He had no option but to surrender to Drake, who was already confidently beginning to take off his coat of mail and his helmet. Drake put a hand on the Spanish captain's shoulder. 'Accept with patience,' he said, 'what is the usage of war.'

Juan de Anton was led below, while Drake put a prize crew aboard the *Cacafuego*. Whatever he or they may have hoped for, their prize exceeded any of their dreams. With the capture of this one ship alone,

Drake's whole voyage was made. She contained an almost incredible quantity of treasure. The losses that Hawkins, Drake and others, had suffered in previous years were made good over and over again by the fortune that lay stowed in 'The Great Glory of the South Sea'. For two or three days the ships sailed in company together, as gradually the holds of the *Cacafuego* were emptied.

Eighty pounds of bar gold, thirteen chests of pieces of eight, jewels, pearls, and plate all carefully boxed, were passed across from one ship to the other. The old *Pelican* now genuinely merited her name, the *Golden Hind*. But quite apart from all the gold, the *Cacafuego* was laden with no less than twenty-six tons of silver. Bar after bar of it went down into the lower hold and the bilges of Drake's vessel, so that she was literally ballasted with Peruvian silver. As one of the Spanish crew wrily remarked: 'You may let your ship for the future be called *Cacafuego*, and ours the *Cacaplata* [Shit-silver].'

It is impossible to calculate the exact value of the treasure captured by Drake on that March day off the coastline of Ecuador. It is doubtful even whether its total value was known in his own lifetime and, as we do not know what was the exact division of the profits when Drake reached home, we can have no idea how much of it became his. One Spanish authority has it that the total value of the treasure in the *Cacafuego* was about 800,000 *pesos*. But when it comes to calculating things like pearls and emeralds, such figures can never be accurate.

In a single brief engagement, Drake had made himself one of the richest men in England. He had also given the Queen and the other investors a greater return for their money than they can ever have dreamed of. By doing so, he had made himself important and valued in those very quarters from which all patronage came. It was a truly 'golden' moment in an astounding life. If any man has ever earned a fortune by resolution, and by refusal to accept defeat either at the hands of man, or of wind and weather, it was most certainly Francis Drake.

CHAPTER TEN

New Albion

QUITE apart from all Drake's other depredations up and down the coast, the capture of the great treasure ship meant that the whole of South America was roused against him. There could be no further thought of making an attempt on Lima, let alone of attacking Panama. He had heard by this time that John Oxenham, who had preceded him into the Pacific (by building a boat with the help of Cimaroons and landing it in the Bay of Panama), had been captured, and was in the hands of the Inquisition. If there had ever been any plan to link up and raid Panama together, the loss of Oxenham and his men had already put an end to it. With three ships, Drake might well have attempted Panama on his own, or even with two, but it was an impossible task for a single vessel. In any case, the *Hind* could carry no more, for her seams were literally opening up under the weight of silver in her bilges. It was time to disappear.

Juan de Anton, who had been most courteously treated throughout his enforced stay, was given back his ship. Drake also handed him a letter for Captain John Winter, in case the Spaniard should ever meet him. It was obvious that Drake had not given up hope that the *Elizabeth* might be somewhere in the Pacific. In its mixture of humanity, piety and simple sincerity, the letter gives an insight into Drake's character, and into that side of it which is not always apparent when tracing his meteoric course through history.

'Master Winter,' Drake wrote,

'If it pleaseth God you should chance to meet with this ship of Señor Juan de Anton, I pray you use him well; according to my word and promise given them; and if you want anything that is in this ship of Juan de Anton, I pray you pay them double the value of it, which I will satisfy again; and command your men not to do any hurt. And what composition or agreement we have made, at my return [to England] I will by God's help perform, although I am in doubt that this letter will ever come into your hands. Beseeching God, the Saviour of all the World, to have us in His keeping, to whom only I give all honour, praise and glory. What I have written is not only to you Mr. Winter, but also Mr. Thomas, Mr. Charles, Mr. Caube, and Mr. Anthony, with all our other good friends, whom I commit to the tuition of Him that with His blood redeemed us. And am in good hope that we shall be in no more trouble, but that He will defend you from all danger, and bring us to our desired haven. To Whom be all honour, glory and praise for ever and ever. Amen.

'Your sorrowful captain, whose heart is heavy for you, Francis Drake.'

Drake had not forgotten the fate of Oxenham. He had already sent a message by a released prisoner to the Viceroy, warning him not to execute Oxenham or any other Englishmen. Oxenham, nevertheless, was hanged the following year (just as Drake would have been had he been caught). It is sad to think that the success of Drake's raid may well have hastened his death.

Drake told the captain of the *Cacafuego* the various ways by which he could return to England. It was more or less the same tale that he told to other Spanish prisoners, but he never indicated a preference for any particular route. (The last people on earth to whom he would have confided his real intentions were the Spaniards.) He showed San Juan de Anton a chart of the world, and told him that he had four available routes: firstly, back through the Strait of Magellan; secondly, across the Pacific to the Moluccas and so home via the Cape of Good Hope; and thirdly, by the way of Norway. There was a fourth route, he said, which he would not name. The confusion which seems to have arisen here among historians and cartographers is that many have thought that Drake meant by the 'un-named fourth route' the famous north-West Passage which many cartographers and navigators then believed to exist somewhere north of California. What then is one to make of 'by way of Norway'? This surely must mean the North-West passage (north of the continent of America), for what else could a man mean who talked of sailing home from the Pacific 'by way of Norway'? The fourth route of which Drake spoke—and which he was determined to keep secret from his enemies— was undoubtedly that way round Cape Horn which he had discovered. It is very doubtful, having encountered not once but twice the terrible weather in that region, that he ever had it seriously in mind. But he did indeed always know that there was an escape route available into the Atlantic, which no one else knew.

Parting from the *Cacafuego* and her captain with every show of good will, Drake sailed the deep-laden *Golden Hind* northwards towards the coast of modern Nicaragua. Not far offshore, he captured a small ship bound for Panama. In her he found a most valuable prize—two pilots who were intending to take ship from Panama for Manila, and who had with them all the charts and sailing directions necessary for the trans-Pacific voyage. It is always possible to believe that Drake had intended from the very beginning to make a circumnavigation. It is equally likely, knowing what a brilliant opportunist he was, that he now quietly made up his mind to take the Pacific route home.

Not long after this, on the 4th April, 1579, he ran across a Spanish merchantman laden with silks and porcelain from China. Her captain was a gentleman called Don Francisco de Zarate, and it is from his report to the Viceroy—Drake's old enemy Don Martin Enriquez—that we gain a vivid portrait of the man and his ship in these summer days of his life.

Drake, incidentally, had never forgotten Don Martin Enriquez, the man who had done Hawkins and himself such wrong at San Juan de Ulua. One of his first questions to the Spanish captain was whether by any chance he had any relations of Don Martin Enriquez on board his ship. It is clear that this was something he had asked several times before during his passage up the Pacific coast of America. He hoped no doubt to exchange any relatives of the Viceroy for John Oxenham and his men.

'This Drake,' as Don Francisco de Zarate later reported to the Viceroy, 'is a cousin of John Hawkins, and the same man that sacked Nombre de Dios five years ago. He seems to be about thirty-five years old and has a reddish beard. Of middle height and thick-set, he is one of the greatest sailors in the world, both in his skill and his command of men. His ship is a war-vessel of about four hundred tons [a great exaggeration, but natural in the circumstances]. She is a good, fast sailing vessel, and has a crew of about one hundred skilled men, all of them well-trained and young. He treats all of his men with affection, and they treat him with respect. He has also nine or ten gentlemen with him, members of good families in England, who are members of his council. On every occasion, however unimportant, he calls them together and listens to what they have to say before giving his orders—although, in fact, he pays no real attention to any one. Drake has no single favourite, and the gentlemen I mention are all equally invited to his table, along with a Portuguese pilot he brought from England [Nuño da Silva from the Cape Verde Islands]. The latter never spoke a word the whole time I was present. The Captain is served on parcel-gilt silver plate, all of which is engraved with his arms. He has many delicacies served, as well as scents. He says that the Queen herself gave many of these things to him. . . .'

Don Francisco went on to describe how well armed the ship was, and how she was sheathed for better protection under water. (This was probably by a method that John Hawkins himself had invented, whereby elm-planks were nailed over pieces of felt above the real planking. The Spaniards used lead sheathing, which was expensive and heavy.) Drake and his officers dined together, to the music of violins—a welcome sign of civilisation in Zarate's eyes—but far more extraordinary was the fact that his men drew regular wages. As compared to the normal practise among privateers or pirates, Zarate noted that 'when they came to capture our ship, not a single one of them dared take anything without his orders'. Drake, in fact, typically, was establishing that his was a properly disciplined naval vessel.

It is clear from Don Francisco de Zarate's account, and indeed from the remarks of other Spaniards who were captured by Drake, that what really surprised them was the fact that almost everything was run so differently from a Spanish ship. Their own officers and gentlemen never had anything to do with common seamen, and indeed the gentlemen had as little as possible to do with the marine officers. The caste system in Spain, as to this day, was far stronger than in England. Drake who, as another Spaniard wrote, fell upon their empire 'like a visitation from heaven' was no roughneck, rum-swilling vagabond. He conducted himself like a gentleman, insisted on the strictest discipline among his officers and men, and treated his prisoners with the greatest courtesy. It is little wonder that Don Francisco de Zarate was impressed. He had never met, nor heard of, anyone like Drake before.

As The World Encompassed has it: 'The main ocean by right is the Lord's alone, and by nature left free for all men to deal withal, as very sufficient for all men's use, and large enough for all men's industry. And therefore that valiant enterprise, accompanied with happy success, which that rare and thrice worthy Captain, Francis Drake, achieved, in first turning up a furrow about the whole world, doth not only overmatch the ancient Argonauts, but also outreacheth, in many respects, that noble mariner Magellan, and by far surpasseth his crowned victory. But hereof let posterity judge.' It was now that, having sent Don Francisco de Zarate on his way, Drake was about to undertake in a small and overladen ship the circumnavigation of the world.

He sailed on north, entered Guatulco, a port in Guatemala, captured it, and stayed there three days to water and provision. Behind him he left the whole of Spanish America in a turmoil: warships out chasing him in the direction of Panama, every port, anchorage and coastal township on the alert, troops diverted from their main object—the suppression of the Indians—and the Viceroy no doubt wishing that he had blown the heretic to pieces years before at San Juan de Ulua. Another piece of news which the Viceroy received from Don Francisco de Zarate, and which must have proved almost as depressing as the loss of the treasure ship, was that Drake had aboard his ship 'painters, who depict the coastline in all its true colours. This was something that troubled me a great deal, for whoever follows him can easily find his way. . . .'

Added to the recent knowledge that he had captured two China pilots and taken all their charts and pilotage information from them, the Spaniards must have been very uneasy. They saw that their monopoly of the New World was coming to an end. They had been first on the shores of America, first into the Pacific, and they had very naturally tried—in the circumstances of their day and age—to keep everything secret about this area.

It was on the 15th April that the heavily laden ship arrived at Guatulco. All the town was silent, and no word had been received that strangers and enemies were upon their quiet and sun-drenched coast. The authorities were all occupied in court, trying three Negroes, who were accused of conspiring to burn down the town. In a matter of minutes the tables were turned; the Negroes freed; and the Chief Justice and other leading citizens were carried off as prisoners to the *Golden Hind*. For three days Drake lay at anchor in Guatulco, getting bread and fresh provisions out of the town, but little loot—although Thomas Moone, ever to the fore on these occasions, did manage to seize a gold chain and some jewellery from a gentleman whom he found running for the safety of the country. The small church was sacked, and 'the images' were broken. Militant Protestants like Drake were usually humane in their treatment of the enemy, but the trappings of Roman Catholicism always had a bad effect on them.

The strict character of Drake's own religious observances on board his ship is borne out by the evidence of the Factor of Guatulco, one of the prisoners. He describes how prayers were said twice a day, the Chaplain ministering to the crew and Drake taking the service for the officers. These services seem to have lasted for about an hour, after which there was music and singing, and Drake's young nephew danced for them. It all seemed very curious, and the Spaniard clearly could not make out where the service ended, and where secular pleasures began. When he and the other prisoners were put ashore before the ship left, the Portuguese pilot, Nuño da Silva, who had been with Drake ever since the Cape Verde Islands, was also released and put aboard a ship bound for Panama. Drake has been accused by some critics of inhumanity for this action, but there seems nothing whatever to justify the charge. Spain and Portugal were allies; the pilot had not willingly embarked with Drake in the first place; and he certainly made no complaints about his treatment in his own testimony. It seems only natural that Drake, whether he was about to attempt the North-West Passage or return home across the Pacific, should put Nuño da Silva ashore in the last Spanish port he visited.

On the 16th April, 1579, the *Golden Hind* weighed anchor and sailed north. The Spaniards were not to see her again. But they could never be sure that she was not still lurking off their coasts, nor could they tell whether the other two ships, which they knew had come out with her from England, were not likely to arrive at any moment—and possibly repeat Drake's success. The latest news from Guatulco added to the panic. Hundreds of miles away, on the coastlines of Peru and Chile, soldiers were still being mustered, towns previously without any defences were being equipped with a few simple guns, and primitive fortifications were being erected. The whole of the Pacific trade, which had flowed easily and unmolested for several decades, now realised the danger. Even simple coasters, carrying wine and stores, were asking for arquebusiers to protect them. On the Caribbean side of the Isthmus of Panama, guards stood watching the western gates of Nombre de Dios, and the mule-trains travelled under heavier escort than usual. It was believed by some that Drake would sink his ship somewhere on the Pacific coast and then march overland with the treasure, capturing anything else that lay in his path. His final intention, they conjectured, might well be to capture a Spanish ship on the Caribbean coast, embark all his plunder in her, and sail for home that way. Such a feat, of course, was totally impossible for a ship's crew of less than a hundred men, but it is evidence of the Spanish alarm that it was even considered. Never in history has one ship managed to alter the course of so many lives, or to disrupt to such an extent the workings of a vast empire. If the *Golden Hind* had sunk off the coastline of California, taking all her crew with her, she and her Captain would still have earned their immortality.

Leaving Guatulco, Drake steered out almost due west into the ocean, to avoid the prevailing north-westerly winds off the coastline. Then, having made a good offing from the shore, he put the *Hind* about, and came back on the other tack towards the unknown coastline north of the Spanish colonies.

From Latitude 42° North, the weather steadily deteriorated. They were now well north of Cape Mendocino on the Californian coast. The rigging grew solid with ice, meat froze soon after being taken from the oven, and all the ship's company—with one notable exception—were downhearted. But Drake kept on standing to the north until, from one account, by the first week in June, he was in Latitude 48° North. This put him on a parallel with Vancouver and it was here or hereabouts that, 'there followed most vile, thick and stinking fogs, till the gusts of wind again removed them'. According to all the information and theories of the time, Drake must have expected to find that the continent now trended away to the east. But even his determination failed when he found that, far from this being the case, the harsh and unfamiliar coastline with its icy weather, fogs and freezing wind, still hauled out on his port bow. The land seemed to run north and west for ever.

The *Hind* came to anchor in an open bay somewhere in the area of 48° North, and Drake realised that all contemporary beliefs about this part of America were wrong. If the North-West Passage did indeed exist, then it was clearly many miles further north. It was no time to embark on a possibly fruitless voyage of exploration. He had a strained ship, badly in need of a refit, and he had a fortune in her hold. The crew, for their part, must have been more than unwilling to hazard their lives and their new wealth for some problematical discovery. But Drake would certainly have disregarded their opinions, if they had not matched his own.

Abandoning the north-west route, he coasted back down to California again and came to anchor in a small bay just north of modern San Francisco. As Robert F. Heizer wrote in *Francis Drake and the California Indians*: 'For nearly a century, historians, geographers, and anthropologists have attempted to solve the problem of locating Francis Drake's anchorage in California, but the opinion of no one investigator has been universally accepted. Indeed, it seems likely that the problem will forever remain insoluble in detail, although it may well be reduced to the possibility that one of two bays, either Drake's, or Bodega, was the scene of Drake's stay in California. . . .' The bay which has taken his name and which lies just to the east of Point Reyes off San Francisco seems to fit the evidence better than any other.

Hardly had the ship come to anchor before the native Californians, the Coast Miwok Indians, began to assemble, marvelling at this strange sea-bird that had landed off their shores. Unlike the Indians of Mocha Island off Chile, they had not suffered the misfortune of coming into contact with the Spaniards. Far from being hostile to these strange, bearded men, they were disposed to treat them like gods. This was something that Drake, with his strong religious principles, was quick to prevent, but he was as eager as ever to establish friendship and agreement with these fellow-creatures—who went naked, but knew the bow and arrow, and whose chieftains wore 'crowns made of knit work, wrought upon most curiously with feathers of divers colours'.

The *Golden Hind*, which was leaking badly, had to be hauled ashore and given a complete overhaul. Her gear had to be sent down from aloft, masts and spars carefully checked, and the vast weight of treasure had to be safely stowed ashore. Drake had a small stockade built, although it was clear by now that he had nothing to fear from the Indians. Work began immediately on getting the ship ready. Understanding that the local chieftain, or 'Hioh' as he was called, was coming to pay a visit, Drake sent him presents in advance. Previously he had managed to dissuade the Indians from worshipping him and his men by holding a church service, and by indicating that the author of all their beings was above them in the heavens. Finally the chieftain arrived. Unlike his followers, he was clothed, and had on 'a coat of the skins of conies, reaching to his waist'. With him came the royal sceptre bearer, and the 'Hioh' insisted that Drake should accept this symbol of dominion over the land. He then made signs that Drake should put upon his own head the Indian headress that was the sign of kingship. So, having been worshipped as a god and been made ruler of California, Francis Drake of Devon now took possession of the land in the name of the Queen of England. He called the country New Albion. This was in memory of his own country, and also because the white cliffs surrounding the bay reminded him of the Channel, and of those chalk headlands which had led the Romans to bestow upon England the name 'Albion', the White Land,

Something of Drake's boyish spirit must be seen in all this episode. Wearing his feathered headdress and taking for his Queen a whole new, unexplored territory must have appealed to him. He had no men, means, or intention to plant a colony, but he felt that this excellent anchorage might prove useful in days to come. It could serve either as a revictualling port on the way north to that other route round the continent (if it existed), or merely as a useful place in which to hide and careen after some further lucrative 'trading' in Philip II's empire. It is clear that he intended to lay official claim to the country for, before he left, he 'set up a monument of our being there, as also of Her Majesty's right and title to the same, namely a plate, nailed upon a fair great post, whereupon was engraven Her Majesty's name, the day and year of our arrival there, with the free giving up of the province and people into Her Majesty's hands, together with Her Highness's picture and arms,

in a piece of six pence of current English money under the plate, where-
under was also written the name of our General.' Drake for a short time
thus became the first English-speaking settler in the western hemisphere. His occupation of a part of California, temporary though it was,
preceded Raleigh's Roanoke settlement by six years.

The amazing thing is that in 1937, after the lapse of 358 years, a plate
of brass was found in the region of Drake's Bay which tallies almost
exactly with the accounts we have of it from Chaplain Fletcher. The
inscription on it reads:

BEE IT KNOWNE UNTO ALL MEN BY THESE PRESENTS JUNE 17
1579 BY THE GRACE OF GOD AND IN THE NAME OF HERR
MAJESTY QUEEN ELIZABETH OF ENGLAND AND HERR SUCCESSORS
FOREVER I TAKE POSSESSION OF THIS KINGDOME WHOSE KING
AND PEOPLE FREELY RESIGNE THEIR RIGHT AND TITLE IN THE
WHOLE LAND UNTO HERR MAJESTIES KEEPING NOW NAMED BY
ME AND TO BE KNOWNE UNTO ALL MEN AS NOVA ALBION
                      FRANCIS DRAKE.

Beneath these letters, a hole has been cut in the brass plate, of the
right size and shape to take an Elizabethan silver sixpence. For some
time controversy raged about the authenticity of this brass plate, some
people maintaining that it was no more than a clever archaeological
hoax. But the conclusion reached by two American metallurgists, who
submitted it to exhaustive tests, was that the brass was identical in its
contents and methods of manufacture to Elizabethan brass, that it
showed every sign of being the correct date, and that there could be
little doubt that this was the plate set up on Drake's instructions in
that long ago summer.

The *Golden Hind* stayed in the bay for five weeks. The Indians and
the English established an affectionate relationship, which was greatly
aided by Drake's skill in treating illness among the natives, to whom he
administered 'lotions, plasters, and ointments according to the state
of their griefs'. When they realised that their visitors were about to put
to sea, the whole tribe abandoned itself to sorrow, and 'poured out
woeful complaints and moans with bitter tears and wringing of their
hands tormenting themselves'.

As the *Hind* slipped out of the bay on the 23rd July the Indians lined
the cliffs. They stood watching the ship as she headed out into the ocean,
marvelling as 'under her stormbeaten breast cried out the hollows of
the sea'. As if imploring these strange visitors to come back to them,
they lit beacon fires on all the hills. But Drake was bound west again.
He had abandoned any thought of attempting the northern passage

round the continent. The north-easterly trades sat steady over the *Golden Hind*'s poop, and the California current swilled her in the same direction. Drake was headed for the Spice Islands and the Far East. Whether he had originally intended it or not, he was committed to circumnavigate the world.

CHAPTER ELEVEN

Beyond the Spice Islands

THE *Golden Hind* took a south-westerly course into the long, rushing acres of the Pacific. For over two months they saw no land, only the flare of sunlight on the empty ocean, and all the time, astern of them, the rushing crystal of their wake. They had taken plenty of water aboard before leaving California, as well as fresh provisions, and seals and seabirds caught on the Farellone Islands off San Francisco.

People have sometimes maintained that the anchorage used by Drake off this coast could hardly have been 'Drake's Bay'. Surely, they have said, he would have used that perfect natural harbour, San Francisco? But the English had approached the area from the north, and would certainly have sighted Drake's Bay first. When the sailors were ashore on the Farellone Islands, the mouth of San Francisco itself may quite probably have been concealed by that famous fog, which rolls in almost every day and obscures the coastline.

After 68 days the *Golden Hind* was in sight of a line of islands lying about 8° north of the equator. It was not long before the ship was surrounded by canoes, but this time the natives were very unlike the Californian Indians. Drake, against his wish or his usual practice, even had to resort to violence to get rid of them. Believing that these were the same islands where Magellan had met with a similar reception, calling them the *Ladrones*, Drake, translating the word, commented that he had touched at the 'Island of Thieves'. The Ladrones group, or the Mariananas, however, lies a long way further north, and Drake's landfall was almost certainly in the remote Palau Islands. A fortnight's further sailing brought him to the Philippine Islands on the 16th October and he coasted down them for five days. Finding a good anchorage he brought the *Golden Hind* into the largest of them, Mindanao, where he watered ship.

After their long passage the soldiers and gentlemen in the company may well have been pleased to see the high green sides of the Philippines and to smell land again. But, as Drake knew as well as any other navigator, the deep sea is safer than pilotage waters. For many weeks from now on, he would be in an area that was only very roughly charted. One error might mean the loss of his ship, his men, and all that treasure so hard-earned off the coastline of America. He worked his way carefully through numbers of unknown islands until at last, on the 3rd November, 1579, having shipped some native pilots, he arrived in sight of the famous Spice Islands,

The Portuguese had long been established here and had a monopoly of that trade which sounds relatively unimportant in this modern day. But spice was essential at that time in Europe, not only for flavouring food but for preserving meat throughout the long winters. The Portuguese, like the Spaniards, had never made any attempt to treat foreign races with anything other than callous contempt. It is hardly too much to say that, if either of these Latin nations had shown more humanity in their colonies, and towards the natives in the region of their trading posts, the British would have had far more difficulty in gaining a foothold in the world.

The Malays at this time were engaged under the Sultan Baber in a desperate war with the Portuguese, who six years before had murdered Baber's father, and desecrated his body by cutting it up into small pieces and throwing them into the sea. Drake anchored in the port at Ternate and, having found out beforehand how things stood between the Sultan and the Portuguese, sent a message to him, together with presents. Most probably the Sultan had no use for any Europeans by this time, but he was quite willing, like any sensible man, to play off one nation against another. It was not long before four magnificent canoes paddled out, with eighty rowers to each, armed troops on board, and the Sultan's principal officers in ceremonial dress. The Sultan himself followed, and it soon became clear that he was quite happy to grant the Queen of England a monopoly of trade in his islands. Drake's love of ceremonial came to the fore as he had his trumpeters sound out, and the guns of the *Hind* fired a royal salute, while he himself in his finest clothes received the Sultan's deputation. Drake obviously impressed the Sultan for, some fifty years later, the Sultan's son sent a letter to King James, in which he referred admiringly to 'the great Captain, Francis Drake' who had visited the Islands in the time of his father.

It is not clear whether Drake secured any formal treaty with the Sultan but certainly before he left he had secured the latter's friendship, which meant that any other English visitors would be sure of a good welcome and the right to trade. Queen Elizabeth herself may well have regarded Drake's activities in the Moluccas as the most important event in his whole voyage. On the silver cup which she gave him after his return, it was not the establishment of her right to New Albion that she

had engraved, but a picture of Drake's reception by the Sultan at Ternate. Indeed, as Sir Julian Corbett commented: 'The alleged treaty
became a sheet anchor of our Eastern Diplomacy for nearly a century
afterwards.' Having laden six tons of cloves beneath the already bursting
hatches of the Golden Hind, Drake sailed on, found an uninhabited islet,
and there careened the ship. They called the place 'Crab Island', and here
for nearly a month Drake and his men enjoyed a golden climate and a
well deserved rest, away from the confinement of the ship and the
eternal sound and scend of the sea. 'Among the trees night by night,
through the whole land, did show themselves an infinite swarm of
fiery worms flying through the air, whose bodies being no bigger than
our common English flies, make such a show and light, as if every
twig or tree had been a burning candle. In this place breedeth also
wonderful store of bats, as big as large hens; of cray-fishes also here
wanted no plenty, and they of exceeding bigness, one whereof was
sufficient for four hungry stomachs at a dinner, being also very good
and restoring meat, whereof we had experience; and they dig themselves holes in the earth like conies.'

Drake's intention was to get north of the Celebes as soon as possible,
but he was unable to do so on account of the strong north-easterlies
that prevailed. For nearly three weeks he had to beat up and down
among one of the most treacherous areas of the world, where the
pilotage was far more dangerous even than the passage of the Magellan
Strait. On the evening of the 9th January, 1580, while the ship was
running free before a strong wind, they suddenly struck a reef. The
overburdened Golden Hind was in greater danger than she had been at
any time since leaving England.

All night Drake and his crew worked feverishly to free her, but they
were hard and fast, with no passage ahead, and the water astern too
deep for them to lay out a kedge anchor and haul the ship off. Worst of
all, the prevailing wind was steadily driving them further on to the
reef. After morning prayers (at which Chaplain Fletcher administered
the sacrament to all hands), Drake bade them all be of good heart, telling them that now they had done what they could for their souls, they
had best look after their bodies. But, despite all their efforts throughout
that day, they found it impossible to move the ship. Drake had eight
of his guns, three tons of cloves, and a quantity of stores jettisoned—but,
noticeably, no treasure—to try and lighten the Hind. It was about 4
o'clock in the afternoon, at low water, when the ship suddenly heeled
to starboard and all hands thought that it was the end. But it was just
to starboard of her that the deep water lay. At this moment, almost
miraculously it seemed, the wind veered and they were able to hoist

sail. So, with the aid of 'this happy gale', the ship slid free into deep water.

No Captain is at his best after having grounded his ship, and Drake was no exception. Although he could hardly blame himself when sailing in uncharted waters, yet the whole incident had undoubtedly brought his nerves to breaking point. While they had been on the reef, it would seem that Chaplain Fletcher had been stupid enough to say that the disaster was a judgement on Drake for his execution of Doughty. Fletcher, as we know, had been a friend of Doughty's, and he almost certainly felt that Drake had had no authority to execute him. But he could hardly have picked a worse moment to raise this old issue, and Drake was in no mood to take the accusation lightly. He had the Chaplain brought forward and padlocked by the leg to one of the hatches, then he summoned the whole ship's company and passed judgement in the following resounding terms: 'Francis Fletcher, I do here excommunicate thee out of the Church of God and from all the benefits and graces thereof, and I denounce thee to the Devil and all his angels.' One cannot resist a smile at the picture of Drake, as he was described by one witness, sitting cross-legged on a sea chest, with a pair of shoes in his hand, solemnly excommunicating an ordained minister of the Church. But the unfortunate Chaplain must surely have thought that his last moment had come. Fletcher was forbidden, on pain of death by hanging, to come on the foredeck, and had a band put round his arm on which was written: 'Francis Fletcher, the falsest knave that liveth.' The moral of this story would seem to be: if you cannot do anything constructive when a ship runs aground, at least keep quiet.

Luckily, the *Golden Hind* had suffered no damage in her grounding. The carpenters reported no water in the well, and the ship did not seem to have been strained. She must have run up on a smoothly-sloping shelf of rock for, had she struck a jagged coral-head, she would almost certainly have torn a hole in her bottom. Credit for her escape must also be given to Hawkins' system of double-sheathing. But although they had been lucky in getting clear without harm, they were far from being out of danger.

For a whole month they tacked up and down in the Flores and Banda Seas, north of Australia, trying to find their way through that intricate necklace of islands and rocks, and out into the Indian Ocean. At last, in early March 1580, they found themselves clear of hazards and with Java lying on their starboard bow. Drake put into a port on the south coast of the island, where he and his sailors received an enthusiastic welcome from the Rajah that far outdid their reception by the Sultan of Ternate. Java at that time appears to have been ruled by as many as five 'Rajahs', 'who live as having one spirit and one mind'. It was an unusual state of affairs in the Far East, or anywhere else for that matter.

They stayed in Java for over a fortnight, giving and receiving hospitality. No doubt they were all in the highest spirits, for nearly all their dangers lay astern of them, and only the long ocean passage lay ahead. Drake was even planning to careen the *Hind* again, and get her perfectly clean from weed, when he learned from the Javanese that a number of European ships had been sighted in the area. He assumed that these were most probably Portuguese traders and, with a fortune in his holds, he had no wish to risk any engagement. On the 26th March he took the *Golden Hind* to sea, setting his course direct across the Indian Ocean for the Cape of Good Hope.

The winds were favourable, the days eventless, and the ship dropped happily down towards the tip of Africa. When she felt the Agulhas Current twisting under her stern, it was time to turn and run past the famous Cape. The weather was still fair for them and they reported that the Portuguese had put out a false impression of the area, '. . . that it is the most dangerous Cape in the world, never without intolerable storms and present danger to travellers which come near the same.' They were now once more in the Atlantic Ocean. It was two years since they had nosed their way into the Magellan Strait with the *Elizabeth* and the *Marigold* in company. This time they were alone, with only 56 men left out of their original crew of about a hundred, but with the bilges ballasted with silver, the after-quarters packed with gold bars, chests of jewellery and precious stones, and three tons of cloves scenting the air between decks.

In the thousands of miles that they sailed after leaving Java, they stopped only once. This was on the 22nd July, when they put into Sierra Leone. They stayed only two days, watering ship, and getting fresh fruit as well as a quantity of the famous tree-oysters—all of which must have been more than welcome after months at sea on biscuit and salted meat. Soon the long blue planes of the Atlantic were behind them, and the *Golden Hind* felt the tumble and pluck of the uneasy sea as they came in to the Continental Shelf, headed for the Channel. They saw no ships as they ran in towards Plymouth, and it was not until they were nearing Plymouth Sound itself that they sighted some coastal fishermen. Drake's first question was: 'Is the Queen alive and well?'

The fisherman answered: 'Her Majesty is in good health, but there is pestilence in Plymouth.'

And so, 'We safely, with joyful minds and thankful hearts to God, arrived at Plymouth, the place of our first setting forth, after we had spent two years, ten months, and some odd days beside, in seeing the wonders of the Lord in the deep, in discerning so many admirable things, in going through with so many strange adventures, in escaping out of so many dangers, and overcoming so many difficulties. . . .' It was the 26th September, 1580 when Francis Drake brought the *Golden Hind* home into harbour. She was the first English ship to sail the Pacific, the Indian Ocean, and the South Atlantic, and Drake was the first captain ever to sail his own ship around the world.

CHAPTER TWELVE

Sailor's Return

THERE was no official welcome for England's greatest seaman. Drake did not come ashore in Plymouth among the excited crowds who had gathered to acclaim him. After those years at sea, when his first instinct no doubt was to leap ashore and feel the cobbles of the quayside beneath his feet, he was virtually a prisoner in his ship—a prisoner by his own choice and by discretion.

Among the first people who came aboard to welcome the great captain home was his wife, Mary. But any question of Drake's being able to exchange the affectionate pleasantries of family gossip and local news with her was inhibited by the presence of the Mayor of Plymouth. What the latter had to say to Drake cannot have made very pleasant hearing. It was true that the Queen was well, and so were the other shareholders in Drake's venture—but these shareholders were keeping very quiet about their participation in the *Golden Hind*'s voyage. For, while Drake had been away on his epic circumnavigation, the complexion of Europe had utterly changed.

The King of Portugal had died, and Philip II was just on the verge of invading the country and making it, and all its overseas possessions, part of his empire. It was clear that he would be successful and that, having united the Spanish peninsula, he would be the most important monarch in Europe. What was more, the combined overseas possessions and trading posts of the two countries would make him indisputably the most powerful ruler in the history of the world. The whole of those African, Eastern, and American countries (which a former Pope had carefully divided between the monarchies of Spain and Portugal) was now to be united under one man. No wonder Elizabeth felt that it might have been better if Drake had never returned at all.

Rumours about Drake's exploits had been current in England for over a year. Ever since John Winter had reached home in the *Elizabeth*, in June 1578, there had been much speculation about Drake's possible whereabouts. Winter, of course, had no knowledge of what had happened, but had earned himself a good reception for his account of the outward voyage, and the passage of the Magellan Strait. Only over the question of Doughty's execution was there a dark question mark. But strict orders were given that the matter was not to be discussed until—if ever—Francis Drake should return and give his own explanation.

Over a year before Drake's return to Plymouth, despatches had reached Philip II from the Governors of Peru and Mexico with their account of his hurricane-track up the west coast of America, and of the rape of the *Cacafuego*. Mendoza, the Spanish ambassador in England, had been told to find out all he could about the venture, but particularly to report the moment that 'the pirate' returned to England. Mendoza had well-founded suspicions that not only were Privy Councillors involved in the expedition, but that the Queen herself had had some hand in it.

It was in the late summer of 1579 that despatches from English merchants in Spain brought the sensational news of Drake's capture of the treasure ship, and there was immediate panic in the City of London. The main body of the merchant fleet was just on the point of sailing for Spain, and all the investors realised that Philip was likely to order their detention when they arrived in Spanish ports, or even break off trading relations altogether. It was at moments like this that Elizabeth's careful duplicity paid dividends. She and her councillors were able to assure the Spanish ambassador and the English merchants that Drake was an independent adventurer, acting on his own account. Even if Mendoza had been able to get a look at the instructions issued to Drake's squadron before Drake left, he would have found nothing that could have compromised the Queen or any of her advisers.

The coolness of Drake's official reception was not only due to the fact that the King of Spain was now the most powerful figure in Christendom. There were other more immediate causes for concern. Ireland was in its usual volcanic state, and the rebels had recently received considerable reinforcements from Spain. What added to these anxieties was the report that Philip was having an immense fleet built. It was officially explained that it was intended to set the seal on the victory of Lepanto, by crushing the Moslem sea power in an attack on Algiers. There were many who felt that this only masked its true purpose. Some believed that the fleet was designed to act against the Protestant rebels in the Netherlands, and—having subdued one nest of heretics—it would then be turned against England.

This was the pattern of Europe when Drake returned, and this was the news that the Mayor of Plymouth brought to him. The first thing he did was to get the treasure safely under guard in Plymouth Castle. Once this was done, Drake sent a despatch to the Queen informing her of his return, as well as letters to the other investors in the voyage. He heard first from his friends at court, that the Spanish ambassador was demanding the immediate restitution of the treasure, and that the Queen was gravely displeased with him. There was no word from Elizabeth herself. Drake prepared to disappear again, and the *Golden Hind* quietly shifted her berth away from the harbour wall, and out to anchor in the lee of St. Nicholas's Island.

Then, just when he was probably thinking that his incredible success was to be officially ignored, he received a summons to report at once to the Queen. He was assured that he had nothing to fear, and that her Majesty would be interested to see some of the 'curiosities' which he had managed to collect on his voyage round the world. Drake had an ability to read between the lines, and did not misunderstand. When he left Plymouth, it was with a train of pack horses laden with all the more interesting and valuable 'curiosities'. He was received by the Queen in an audience that lasted for six hours. At the conclusion, orders were given for all the treasure to be registered and sent to the Tower of London, with a view to its restitution to its rightful owners. This was the official face that was put upon things, but privately Elizabeth was wondering how she could justify keeping it all in England.

The conclusion of all the plots and counter-plots surrounding Drake's return, and the destination of the treasure, was that all of it stayed in England. The Queen got her share, as did the other investors, and the Spanish Ambassador was left to 'burn with passion against Drake'. There were still many of Burghley's opinion that the whole episode was discreditable and extremely dangerous, and Drake was not without many detractors at Court, and particularly among the rich merchants of the City. But the fact was that he was borne forward on such a tide of popular enthusiasm that no group of individuals could stem it. The Queen, who for some time had felt herself unable to recognise Drake openly, finally changed her mind. The *Golden Hind* was sailed up Channel and round the coast to Deptford, where her crew were paid off.

On the 4th April, 1581, as an open sign of her favour, the Queen went down in state to visit the *Golden Hind*. In the presence of a huge and tumultuous crowd, she made Drake kneel before her, as it were in suppliance. The King of Spain had asked her to strike off his head and she had, as she said, a gilded sword with which to do it. Then, with her usual enchanting guile, she turned to the representative of the French government who was present, and asked him on her behalf to bestow the accolade of knighthood upon Francis Drake. Thus, in a light-hearted manner, she involved France in her official recognition of 'The Master Pirate of the Unknown World'. Drake, who a few years before had been no more than the captain of a small sailing vessel, was now not only a millionaire, but a knight, entitled to his coat of arms, and openly seen to be in the Queen's great favour. Knighthood at that period it must be remembered, was, as Doctor Johnson remarked, 'an honour . . . not made cheap by prostitution, nor ever bestowed without uncommon merit.'

The Spanish ambassador wrote bitterly to his king: 'Drake has returned to court, where he passes much time with the Queen, by whom he is highly favoured and told how great is the service he has rendered her.' His name was on every man's lips, books and ballads were written about him, and pictures of his exploits, and portraits of him were to be found in homes all over the country. England was never to have so popular a hero, nor one whose face and figure became so well known, until the days of Nelson. The Queen herself was agreed that the *Golden Hind* should be preserved as a national monument. This small but ever-famous vessel did indeed lie in a dry berth at Dept-ford for many years, until—the English awakening too late to the loss of a national treasure—she had rotted to pieces. Holinshed records that some wit even suggested that the ship should 'be fixed upon the stump of Paul's steeple, in lieu of the spire, that, being discerned far and near, it might be noted and pointed at of people with these true terms: Yonder is the bark that hath sailed round the world.' The *Golden Hind* is mentioned in a comedy by Ben Jonson, where one of the characters remarks: 'We'll have our provided supper brought aboard Sir Francis Drake's ship that hath encompassed the world, where, with full cups an banquets, we will do sacrifice for a prosperous voyage. . . .'

Drake revelled in his new-found riches, his knighthood, and his immense popularity. The only thing that marred this high noon of his life was that there were gentlemen at court, and elsewhere, who would have nothing to do with him, some even refusing small gifts which he offered them—on the grounds that they were not his to give. Always there was, as there remained to the end of his days, the whispered suggestion that there had been more behind Doughty's execution than appeared. Doughty's brother, John, who had returned in the *Golden Hind*, took an action against Drake, and the case was heard before the Lord Chief Justice. It was never proceeded with. Somehow, some hand —and one feels it can only have been the Queen's—put a stop to it. If Drake had been the monster that some of the Doughty faction suggested at that time, and have carried on suggesting ever since, it is amazing that he ever let Doughty's brother return alive. There will always remain some element of mystery here, at the core of Drake's life. It is not likely to be resolved unless Drake's own account of the voyage, which he personally handed to the Queen, should ever be discovered.

During the years that followed, Drake was engaged with Walsingham in trying to promote what both saw as the inevitable war with Spain. He was busy between London and Plymouth, where he had a town house, and where presumably the shadowy figure of his wife presided and enjoyed the porcelains and silks, and all evidences of comfort that her husband had earned on the seas. In 1581 he was made Mayor of Plymouth, and with his usual love of pomp and circumstance it is not surprising to find that one of his first actions was to issue an order that members of the town council should wear red cloaks for ceremonial occasions. He also had a great compass set up on the Hoe at the point where Smeaton's Tower now stands.

It was now, as the first citizen of Plymouth and the most famous man in the West Country, that he cast around for a country house befitting his position. He found this in Buckland Abbey, a few miles inland from Plymouth. This was a 13th-century Cistercian foundation which had been converted into a private residence, and had been sold to the Grenville family in 1541. It was the Grenvilles, indeed, who had largely converted the old Abbey buildings into a residence suitable for a family of their quality. The house was carved out of the fabric of the old church itself, and the cloisters and old domestic buildings of the monks had been demolished to make room for a pleasant garden. When the work was finished Richard Grenville had had the date 1576 carved above the fireplace in the great hall. Here he also had a plaster frieze erected, showing a knight who had put aside his war horse, contemplating those emblems of mortality, the hour glass and the skull. Richard Grenville can hardly have thought, when his new home at Buckland was complete, that in little more than four years he would have sold it to Francis Drake.

The fact that Drake had been given command of an expedition somewhat similar to one which he had earlier proposed had, as we have seen, very naturally embittered Grenville. But quite apart from this, a proud man like Richard Grenville, the descendant of a distinguished family, would never have sold the Abbey to Drake—whom he regarded as a vulgar upstart, if not worse—if he had known who the purchaser was. Drake acted with his usual canniness. He knew very well that Grenville, like Frobisher and a number of his other great contemporaries, disliked him intensely. For this reason he arranged for the negotiation to be carried out through two middlemen, Christopher Harris and John Hele. Harris, like Grenville, came from an old landed family, but he also seems to have been a close friend of Drake's. He acted for him in a number of business matters, and was ultimately named as an executor in Drake's will. But even with intermediaries acting for him, Drake still had to pay the large sum of £3,400 for the house. This may well have been a welcome addition to Grenville's finances, but he must have been an extremely angry man when he found that rich vulgarian, Sir Francis Drake, with his common Cornish wife, Mary, had settled in his beautiful old home. For Drake, who would have touched his forelock to the Grenvilles as a boy, it must have been a jewel on the breast of his triumph. Perhaps he also enjoyed the curious irony of living like an English country squire in the fabric of a church that had once been dedicated to the detestable Catholic Faith.

Drake now had a suitable home, a three-floored house of noble proportions, with one of the finest tithe barns in the whole of England on the estate. Buckland Abbey was more than adequate for a childless couple. Little land, however, went with the purchase so—in these years when he could do nothing wrong in the Queen's eyes—he set about remedying the lack of it. Elizabeth herself gave him the manor of Sherford, which had been carved out of land once belonging to Plympton Priory, while Drake bought part of Yarcombe estate. This land had belonged to the Drakes of Asshe, that old county family who in the past had hardly recognised the common branch from which Francis Drake was descended. Now, after his ennoblement, his fame, his wealth, and his friendship with the Queen, they were more than willing to call him 'cousin'.

But if in these years of fame many of the well-born and the landed gentry found Drake 'ambitious for honour, and greatly affected to popularity', the people of England took him to their hearts. They loved him and, in the words of an old ballad, he was:

> *Excelling all those that excelled before;*
> *It's feared we shall have none such any more;*
> *Effecting all he sole did undertake,*
> *Valiant, just, wise, mild, honest, godly Drake.*
> *This man when I was little I did meet*
> *As he was walking up Totnes's long street.*
> *He asked me whose I was, I answered him.*
> *He asked me if his good friend were within?*
> *A fair red orange in his hand he had,*
> *He gave it me whereof I was right glad,*

Takes and kisses me and prays God bless my boy:
Which I recall with comfort to this day.
Could he on me have breathed with his breath,
His gifts, Elias-like, after his death,
Then had I been enabled for to do
Many brave things I have a heart unto.
I have as great desire as e'er had he
To joy, annoy, friends, foes—But 'twill not be.

In 1583 Mary Drake died. So little was she regarded, or remembered
in later years, that Drake's second wife even borrowed from her
predecessor the one story that is rightfully Mary's. Before Drake set
out on his voyage round the world he is supposed to have asked Mary
to wait for him for seven years, and if he had not returned by then, to
take another husband if she wished. Despairing of him, after John
Winter had returned with his tales of the terrible conditions off South
America and the way in which he had seen Drake disappear into the
storm, Mary Drake accepted one of her suitors, and all the arrangements were made for their marriage. She and her prospective husband
had entered the church and were standing before the altar, waiting for
the minister to pronounce them man and wife, when suddenly a
cannon ball fell between them. It was a sign that Drake was still alive!
Mary refused to go through with the ceremony. When Drake married
again, his second wife adapted this story to herself—proof, if it were
needed, that he was indeed a legend in his own lifetime.

Elizabeth Sydenham, who became the second Lady Drake in 1585,
was of very different background and breeding from Mary Newman.
The daughter and heiress of Sir George Sydenham of Combe Sydenham, she was young and, tradition says, beautiful. There can be no
proof of this, for the authenticity of the only portrait supposedly
depicting her has been questioned. Legend, again uncorroborated by
evidence, says that she was a Maid-of-Honour to the Queen, and that
Drake met her at Court. The noble Sydenhams may possibly have
disliked their new son-in-law, but there seems to have been no ob-
jection to the match. Drake was not only very rich, but a favourite of
the Queen. Even so, the Sydenhams made quite sure that there was a
good marriage settlement, and Drake gave Elizabeth a life interest in
Buckland Abbey, and in his manors of Sherford, Yarcombe and
Sampford Spiney (a new acquisition).

During these years after his return from the circumnavigation, and
until his next expedition to the West Indies, Drake was busy in the
local politics of Plymouth and the West Country, as well as in his own

affairs. He was also constantly up in London, where he was involved in the innumerable schemes whereby he, and the men of his persuasion, were endeavouring to fit England for the war that they saw as inevitable. Apart from one or two projected expeditions that never came to anything—largely because the Queen liked to feel that she had Drake close at hand in the event of an invasion—the most important thing that happened was the appointment, in 1583, of a Royal Commission to inquire into the state of the Navy. Hawkins had become Treasurer of the Navy in 1577, a position which he held until his death. While John Hawkins in his own day, and ever since, has been overshadowed in the public eye by the rumbustious and dashing figure of Drake, he remains one of the most distinguished men in English history. If in later years Drake led the Navy and set a pattern of enterprise for other men to follow, it was Hawkins who built the ships and secured a sound administration. It was Hawkins who was largely responsible for the construction of new ocean-going ships of 700 and 500 tons, as well as fighting galleons of the *Revenge* class, the ships which were to help save England from defeat at the hands of Philip II.

The commission was presided over by three Ministers, who in their turn appointed what we could call 'a working subcommittee'. This included most of the great sea-captains of the age, Drake, Frobisher, Raleigh, Bingham and Fulke Greville. The names are enough in themselves to show that the old policy, which regarded the Navy primarily as a local defence force designed at times to convoy soldiers, had been discarded. It was Drake's exploits, more than anything else, which had proved that the Navy was England's best offensive weapon against an empire like that of Spain.

During these years when Drake was ashore, the international climate grew colder. In 1583 war was only narrowly avoided when a French plot to invade England, with the connivance of Spain, was brought to light. The following year plans had been made, and everything was prepared for a large expedition against the Spanish colonies (which would almost certainly have led to open war), when the Queen changed her mind and refused it permission to sail. But all the time the ships were building, and Hawkins was attending to those details that were essential for an efficient fleet. The living conditions of the sailors were improved, and it was no longer thought necessary to crowd the maximum number of men into the minimum space. A sailor's pay was raised from 6 shillings and 8 pence to 10 shillings a month, and it was laid down that the manpower in the new Navy should be in the proportion of one man to every two tons. From his own wide experience, few men knew better than Hawkins that on long sea voyages, and particularly in the tropics, nothing led to disease quicker than overcrowding and insanitary conditions. He had Drake at his elbow, and could draw upon his cousin's experience both from his early days off the Spanish Main, and from his voyage round the world.

The Spanish ambassador, Mendoza, took good and careful note of the activity in England's shipyards. He observed and reported the growing influence on the throne of this new group of men. They were not politicians and elder statesmen like Burghley, but a younger and more ruthless breed. As he wrote to his master in Spain: 'They are building ships endlessly, and are thus making themselves masters of the sea. Seeing their country with such multitudes of ships helps to swell their pride, and they think that there is no prince on earth who can come against them.'

It was in 1585, that Philip of Spain, feeling confident in the power of his united empire, and secure in the knowledge that the whole of the Portuguese fleet now belonged to him, decided on a stroke against these arrogant heretics. There had been a serious crop failure in Spain that year, corn was practically unobtainable, and famine was threatening in some of the provinces. To meet his pressing needs, Philip induced the English merchants to despatch an unusually large fleet of corn-ships to Spain. There seemed nothing strange in this. Spain was England's best customer, and this was the reason why the Queen, as well as the City of London, was always unwilling to push relations with Spain into an open rupture. Philip's feeling of security was not only material. He also felt that any action against the Protestant heretics had the Divine blessing, for had not the Pope said that there was no need for the faithful to keep their word or bond when they were dealing with heretics?

He had shown the new hardening of his resolution to have done with Holland and England, in his open offer of a reward to anyone who would shoot William, the Prince of Orange—an offer which after several unsuccessful attempts, had resulted in William's assassination in 1584. It is also likely that, if he did not have a personal hand in the famous Throckmorton plot against Queen Elizabeth in 1583, it was at least done with his connivance and even blessing.

When the unsuspecting and defenceless English corn-ships entered the Spanish harbours, they were immediately seized, their cargo confiscated, and their crews thrown into gaol. Only one vessel, the *Primrose*, which was in the harbour of Bilbao, escaped this treacherous seizure. She was quietly discharging her corn when the Corregidor, or Sheriff of Biscay, came aboard with some soldiers, to affect her arrest. Less successful than his fellow-officials in other Spanish ports, he found

himself up against a wily master and a brave crew who, far from sur-
rendering, proceeded to capture the Spaniards, up anchor, and sail
home for England with the Corregidor aboard. The seizure of the
English ships was enough in itself to have infuriated Elizabeth, but in
the Corregidor's pocket was proof of her royal brother's implication
in the plot—Philip II's writ authorising the seizure of all the English
merchant ships.

For once, Drake and the war party had the whole of England
behind them—the Queen herself, and even the City merchants, usually
so reluctant to take open action against their best customer. An
embargo was placed on all Spanish goods, a fleet was gathered at
Plymouth, and Drake was given a Royal commission to release the
impounded merchant ships. It is significant that his official instructions
were to do this and no more, but the Queen must have known well
that Drake would certainly exceed his instructions. However, no
matter what Drake did once he had been let off the leash, the Queen
knew that she could always fall back on her classic answer: 'If need be,
the gentleman careth not if I disavow him.'

CHAPTER THIRTEEN

The Glorious Year

THE largest private force that had ever been mustered in England was ready to set sail by the end of July 1585. Two naval ships, the *Elizabeth Bonaventure* of 600 tons and the *Aid* of 250 tons, were contributed by the Queen. They were valued at £10,000, 'a book-keeping fiction', as Dr. J. A. Williamson remarked, which 'enabled her to draw profit at a far greater proportionate rate than the other associates'. The Queen also contributed £10,000 in money. The other ships, financed by a joint Stock Company, included the 400-ton *Galleon Leicester*, and five 200-ton armed merchantmen. Drake's flag was hoisted in the *Bonaventure*, his Flag Captain was Thomas Fenner, and Martin Frobisher was Vice-Admiral aboard the 200-ton *Primrose*. Altogether there were 29 ships in the fleet, the bulk of the smaller vessels coming from the West Country. The Queen's cousin, Francis Knollys, was Rear-Admiral in the *Galleon Leicester*; Captain Edward Winter, son of Sir William was in command of the *Aid*; and Christopher Carleill was Lieutenant General in charge of the land forces. Among the other captains was Francis Drake's brother, Thomas Drake, while old Tom Moone, the one-time ship's carpenter, who had been with Drake round the world, was in command of the *Francis*. The total force was about 2,300 men. Drake himself was in overall command, both as Admiral and General.

One of the interesting things about the expedition was that Burghley gave it his full backing, and was in complete sympathy with its aims. So long as he had believed that there was any possibility of England and Spain co-existing in some state of apparent amity, he had always been against provoking hostilities. But he was far too great a patriot, and too astute a statesman, to believe that Spain would have any respect for a country that took arrant provocation lying down. If Burghley had lived in the 1930's he would have always sought for any reasonable rapprochement with England's enemies, but he would never have been an appeaser. It was Burghley who warned Drake, when he was lying with the assembled fleet in Plymouth Sound, that there was a

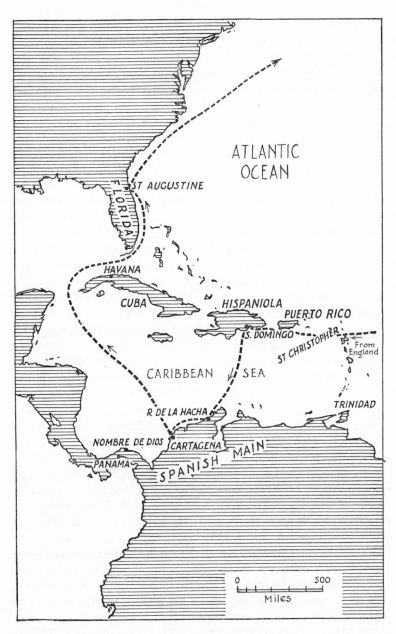

Drake in the West Indies

danger of the Queen changing her mind. He advised him to get away while the going was good.

It was just at this moment that a real complication arose—typical in its way of so much that seems mysterious about Elizabethan politics. Sir Philip Sidney suddenly arrived on board the flagship, saying that he had come to join the expedition with a troop of gentlemen-adventurers. Drake must have been appalled at the prospect. Sidney had just been made Master of the Ordinance, the highest military office in England. He was, furthermore, Elizabeth's latest favourite; Walsingham's son-in-law; at the high noon of fame and fortune; and one of the most important men in the kingdom. It was clear that at the very least he would expect to share the command, if not to become Supreme Commander of the whole expedition. Drake was more than a match for this 'golden boy'. Guessing that Sidney had slipped away without the Queen's permission, he secretly sent a messenger to the Court, to inform Elizabeth that Sidney had joined him. The result was electric, and an immediate despatch was sent down to Plymouth, ordering Sidney to return at once. This was exactly what Drake had hoped for, and the chagrined royal favourite was soon on his way back to London, wondering perhaps how Her Majesty had discovered his whereabouts so quickly. Drake had been quite prepared for the Queen's messenger to be carrying an order that Sir Philip Sidney was indeed to embark, and that he was to have command of the expedition. Just in case this had been so, Drake had had a party of seamen stationed on the road, a few miles out of Plymouth. They seized the royal messenger, and read the Queen's letter, before they let him pass. If the contents had not been what Drake wanted, there can be no doubt that he would have sailed at once, in apparent ignorance of the royal commands.

By this time he knew enough about the Queen's temperament to realise that she might still shilly-shally, and suddenly countermand his sailing orders. He was, we learn, not 'the most assured of Her Majesty's perseverance to let us go forward'. He had the last of the stores and water casks embarked in a great hurry, and indeed even left a considerable amount behind. Then on the 14th September, the wind being fair, he gave orders for the fleet to weigh and proceed. Until he was clear of the Channel, and out into the long sea-surge of the Atlantic, he could never be quite sure that a fast pinnace would not overhaul him, with orders for his immediate return.

Having left Plymouth in such haste, Drake had no intention of calling in at Falmouth to complete watering the fleet, but set course straight for Cape Finisterre. This was proof in itself that he had no intention of bothering about the merchant ships which Philip had impounded. Most

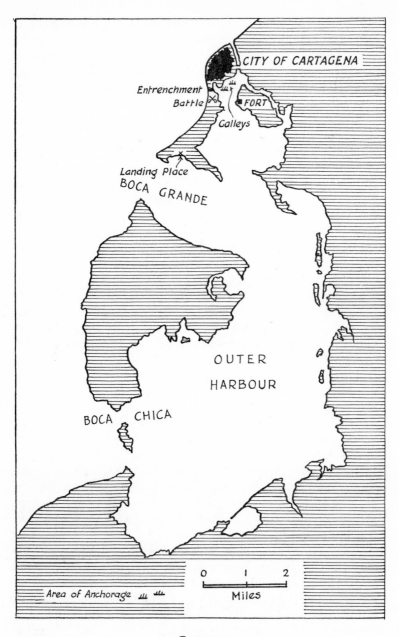

Cartagena

of them, indeed, had been set free once their grain cargoes had been
discharged, and were already on the high seas. Drake did not even bother
to make a sweep into the Biscayan ports of Spain to look for them. His
intention was always to get to the West Indies with his fine fighting
fleet, and make just the kind of havoc that he had dreamed of ever
since those early days in the little *Pascha* and the *Swan*.

He anchored just off the Bayona Islands, hard by Cape Finisterre,
and sent an armed party ashore to ask the Governor on what grounds
the British corn-ships had been seized. The latter was in no position to
offer any resistance to this large English force. He replied that the British
ships had now been freed, and that he was only too happy to see that
Drake's ships got the water and provisions they required. Bad weather
kept Drake here longer than he had expected, but his arrival off the
Spanish coast and his stay there were far-reaching in their effects. A
lesser commander, or a man of different temperament, might well have
made straight for the Canaries to water and provision. It was typical of
Drake that he should come and arrogantly drop anchor off the coast of
the most powerful ruler in Christendom, take what provisions he
wanted, and capture all the local shipping. He even managed to do a
little bit of lucrative looting, including 'stuff of the High Church, or
Cathedral of Vigo, among which was a cross of silver doubly-gilt,
having cost a great mass of money'.

Whereas Drake's previous exploits had all been on the far side of the
Atlantic, and therefore little known about in Europe (outside England
and Spain), his present action had the immediate effect of being reported
all over the continent within a few days. It seemed a deliberate and
personal challenge to the King of Spain. Where the latter's faithful
subjects saw it as an act of insolence, it put heart into the Dutch
Protestants and others, who were struggling against what at that moment seemed an invincible giant. He was already a legend in England,
but he now became one throughout Europe, and the Spanish rendering
of his name '*El Draque*', 'The Dragon', took on a real and fearful meaning.

Having carried off about 30,000 ducats' worth of plunder from Vigo,
the fleet sailed for the Canaries. *En route* they just missed the Spanish
treasure fleet homeward bound from the Indies—one thing that Drake
was always to regret. At Las Palmas, owing to bad weather, and the
fact that the town was well defended, they were unable to land, so
stood on south for the Cape Verde Islands. The towns and villages here
were impoverished and Drake can have had little expectation of profit,
but once again his long memory came into play. In 1582 William
Hawkins had been treacherously attacked at Santiago in the Cape

Verdes. Landing Carleill and a thousand men, he sacked and burned
the town. 'We consumed with fire all the houses, as well in the country
as in the town of Santiago, the hospital excepted, which we left
unconsumed.' Nearly all the inhabitants had taken to the hills and there
was no resistance, but later on some of them came across a young
English seaman straggling behind the main body, killed him and
mutilated his corpse. In revenge for this the other principal town,
Porto Praya, was sacked. Except as a further irritant to Philip II, there
was little point in this diversion from the main object of their voyage—
the West Indies. It would have been better for the fleet if they had never
gone to the Cape Verdes, for the islands were fever-ridden. The
English had not been long at sea before fever spread among the troops,
and close on 300 men were dead before the trade winds had lofted their
ships across the Atlantic.

After watering at Dominica and trading with the Carib Indians,
Drake made for the unoccupied island of St. Christopher in order to
clean and disinfect the ships, and give the sick a chance to recover. The
Christmas of 1585 was spent here and then, after a brief consultation
with the other commanders (which amounted to telling them what he
intended to do), Drake took the fleet straight for the heart of the
Spanish West Indian Empire. This was the ancient city of San Domingo
in Hispaniola, which had been founded in 1496. It was the administrative capital of the empire, and was reputed to be finer than any city
in Spain itself, with the exception of Barcelona. Drake realised that
the effect of a successful attack on this 'jewel in the Spanish crown'
would be immense. He also hoped that it would yield more than its
fair share of return for the capital investment in his expedition.

It was well known to be strongly fortified, and none of the privateers and pirates who preyed on the West Indies had ever attempted it.
Drake was not at all deterred. He had long ago learned that in this
enervating climate men soon grew relaxed and careless. The very fact
that San Domingo had never been attempted made it all the more likely
that the Governor and the military would have grown over-confident
and complacent about the state of their defences. On passage towards
the island Drake was lucky enough to capture a frigate with a local
pilot on board. The man told him that, although the entrance to the
harbour of San Domingo was difficult, it could indeed be effected. On
the other hand, he said, there was an excellent landing place further
down the coast. This was about ten miles away from the city, and it
was unlikely to be well guarded.

On 31st December the bulk of the fleet was riding to anchor in front
of this ancient and beautiful city, which had recently been described

L

by the Governor of Raleigh's new colony in Virginia as 'of fabulous wealth'. There was every indication that the English intended to make a straightforward frontal assault. In the meantime Drake had inspected the landing place down the coast, and had arranged with some friendly natives for the elimination of a Spanish picket in the area.

He now rejoined his fleet. His plans were laid and, with his usual quick eye for seeing a weakness, he had given Carleill and the soldiers their instructions. As soon as darkness fell, all the troops were embarked in light craft and frigates and made their way to the landing place. Taking charge of the foremost boat, Drake led the way through the surf and stayed there until all the men had disembarked. He learned at the same time from his local helpers that the enemy picket which had been guarding the route to the city had been wiped out.

Regaining his fleet on New Year's Day 1586, Drake brought all his ships into position close inshore off San Domingo and opened up a bombardment of the castle that guarded the narrow entrance to the harbour. The Spaniards reacted as he had expected, and concentrated all their attention on the fleet and on the small boats and pinnaces which were moving about among the ships, apparently embarking soldiers and sailors for a landing in front of the city. The garrison took up their station to repel this threatened landing, while the gunners concentrated their somewhat inefficient fire on such of the ships as came within range. Cavalry were drawn up to cover their landward flank as they stood to arms along the shore. They were hardly in position when Carleill's force, which had marched 10 miles overland, suddenly appeared in their rear. With drums beating, trumpets sounding and standards flying, they advanced in two columns on the Spanish troops. It was clear that they intended to cut off the garrison from the very town that they were defending. Taken completely by surprise, the Spaniards attempted to make back for the safety of their defences. It was too late, for Carleill's men were already upon them.

Any attempt at an organised withdrawal was quickly turned into a rout, and the English surged into the town with the fleeing defenders. Although they suffered some casualties from artillery fire, they pressed home the pursuit so fiercely that they stormed through the two seaward gates of the city in a confused struggle with the defenders. It was all over quickly. The sailors in the ships saw the Spanish soldiers taking to the boats, and making across the harbour for the safety of the country on the far side. The flag of St. George was soon flying above a tower on the main wall. San Domingo, that great and wealthy city, had been taken in a classic 'combined operation' which was the fruit of one man's genius for war.

The castle which commanded the entrance to the harbour was still in Spanish hands, but it fell easily to a night attack. On the following morning Drake led in the fleet, piloting them through at his leisure in the early sunshine, and seeing before him the rewards of victory—a large merchantman (reputedly the finest in the Indies), a number of coastal vessels, and several galleys. One of his first actions was to liberate the galley-slaves, some of whom were English and French. At the same time, he did not forget the Negro slaves whom he found in the city. Remembering his old friendship with Cimaroons, Indians, Negroes and all the native populations always hostile to their Spanish masters, he not only freed the slaves but gave them arms so that they, in their own right, could carry on the war against the Spanish enemy.

Drake was only disappointed in one thing. The town, though famous for its wealth, yielded little portable treasure in the shape of gold and silver ingots, jewellery, or uncut gemstones. The fact was that San Domingo, although the administrative centre for the Indies, had long since yielded pride of place to the other principal cities on the Isthmus of Panama in terms of wealth. But the city was still worth a large ransom, and Drake opened negotiations with the Governor who, along with all the other citizens, was hiding in the countryside.

During the course of these prolonged negotiations, a Spanish officer approached the city one morning with a flag of truce on the end of a lance. Drake sent out his personal servant, a young Negro boy, to inquire what was his mission. The Spaniard, seeing a 'despised' Negro coming out to meet him, took it as some kind of insult, and ran him through with his lance. The mortally wounded boy had just enough strength to crawl back and tell Drake what had happened, before dying at his feet.

Throughout his life Drake always showed a compassionate affection for Negroes, had them as friends and servants and, whenever he could, would set them free. (It is quite possible that he felt some guilt for having at one time engaged in the slave trade, and hoped to restore the balance a little by his subsequent conduct.) At any rate, this treatment of his Negro servant put him into one of those terrible rages which even his friends had learned to fear. He gave immediate orders for two friars, who were among his prisoners, to be taken to the place where the boy had been wounded. He had them hanged on the spot. It was the only time in his life that he ever killed a prisoner.

A message was immediately sent to the Spaniards that, unless they brought in the murderer and executed him in view of the English forces, Drake would hang two more prisoners every day. The threat was enough. Next day the Spanish officer was delivered up by his fellow-countrymen, who were compelled to hang him on the same gallows. Drake had inflicted on his enemies the knowledge that he, an Englishman and a Protestant, considered one Negro boy was entitled to the same treatment and respect as any other man on earth. Now that this savage piece of justice had been enacted, he reopened negotiations with the Governor of San Domingo.

Backwards and forwards went the messengers, the Governor protesting all along that he was totally unable to raise the sum that was demanded for the ransom of the once-proud city. Drake grew weary of the procrastination, and initiated a policy that had paid dividends in the past. '. . . For many successive days, 200 sailors from daybreak till nine o'clock, when the next began, did nothing but labour to fire these houses; yet we did not consume so much as one third part of the town.' In the end, realising that the wealth of San Domingo had been over-estimated, Drake accepted a ransom of 25,000 ducats. It was little enough in itself, but the capture of San Domingo with such insolent ease was worth an incalculable fortune. Its effect was to diminish morale throughout Philip's empire, and to raise the spirits of all those who suffered under Spanish oppression both in the New World and in Europe.

The English, with their dislike of pompous pretension and their love of a joke, had some amusement at the expense of the Spaniards. In the hall of the Governor's palace there was an immense coat-of-arms—the King of Spain's—painted on the wall beneath which the final transactions took place. Depicted in the coat-of-arms there was a terrestial globe, and on it was written the motto, '*Non sufficit Orbis*' ('The world is not enough for me'). The English, feigning ignorance of Latin, 'would not refrain from pointing it out to the Spaniards, nor from sarcastically inquiring what was meant by such a device? At which they would shake their heads and turn aside their faces, in some smiling sort, without answering anything, as if ashamed thereof.'

On the 1st February, having taken everything they needed from the city's stores, seized whatever treasure they could lay their hands on, and lived in considerable comfort for a month, the fleet made sail. The devastated city was reoccupied by the Spaniards as the ships sailed south-westerly across the Caribbean Sea. Apart from a passing blow at Rio de la Hacha—a name that Drake never forgot—he made straight for Cartagena. This was another place that Drake remembered well, though with more pleasure than Rio de la Hacha. It was past here that he had swaggered on that early adventure, in his small Spanish ship, full of her captured gold, with all his flags flying, triumphantly homeward bound. Like a magpie, he had looked the place over in those days and had seen with his bright eye, and stored away for reference in his brilliant memory that Cartagena, though apparently impossible to attack, had its weak point.

One side of the town faced the open sea and presented no possibilities for attack. The quayside area of the city faced on to a small inner harbour, which was almost land-locked and had a chain barring its narrow entrance. Beyond the spit of land which formed this basin lay the great outer harbour, sealed off from the sea by a narrow wooded promontory except at one point, the Boca Grande. There was nothing to stop ships from entering here, but once inside the main harbour it was practically impossible for them to get at the city itself, protected as Cartagena was by its spur of land and by its chain across the inner harbour-mouth. All this Drake knew, but he had seen the success of his tactics at San Domingo and he decided to apply almost exactly the same approach to this problem—with whatever minor variants the situation might demand.

It was the 9th February when Drake led his ships into the large outer harbour and immediately tacked up towards the entrance to the inner basin, giving every impression that he intended to attack the fort that protected it. Frobisher was sent to effect a diversion near the fort, while Drake and the main body of the fleet sailed up and down, as if looking for a place to land troops. The Governor and the inhabitants may well have felt even more secure than their counterparts at San Domingo, for the natural advantages of their city had been further strengthened by the best that the fortress-engineers of the day could achieve.

As soon as night fell, Drake sent off his troops in ships' boats and light craft to the mouth of the outer harbour, at the far end of the wooded peninsula. Their instructions were to make their way diagonally through the woods. Carleill led his men in person and brought them down to the seaward side of the peninsula and out on to the beach. Wading knee-deep in the sea, the men cautiously made their way up to the point where the fortifications trailed off in the water. The point was quite strongly defended but, by the tactic of having kept right along the shore itself, the English had avoided the fire of two galleys which were moored in the inner basin. and would have enfiladed them if they had attempted a head-on attack down the peninsula.

The Spaniards were not taken totally unawares, and a brief but fierce struggle took place. As at San Domingo, however, the sudden-ness of the onslaught demoralised the defenders. There was little musket fire, and it was with cold steel that the English broke the defences and swarmed into the city. As Captain Walter Biggs described it: 'Our pikes were somewhat longer than theirs and our bodies better armed, for very few of them were armed: with which advantage our swords and pikes grew too hard for them and they were driven to give place. . . .' As usual, the English made straight for the Plaza, the town's central square and its heart, where they reformed. But resistance was already at an end. The inhabitants were streaming out of the city and making for the hills, with their soldiers not very far behind them.

Next day Drake moved up the fleet and prepared to bombard the fort which guarded the mouth to the inner harbour. He found it unnecessary for, at the sight of the ships closing in on them, the gunners abandoned their position and joined the rest of Cartagena in the safety of the country. Carleill and his troops had taken the capital of the Spanish Main by a brilliant night assault, but the presiding genius behind the whole operation was clearly Drake. The capture of Cartagena is marked by that special dash and flair which were his signature.

The usual negotiations about a ransom now began, Drake demanding —as was his habit—several times the amount that he expected to get. As at San Domingo, the Spaniards temporised, so the city was sacked and looted by the troops, while all the shipping in the harbour was destroyed. They also seized all the guns from the city defences, as well as from the armed galleys in the harbour. As an operation of war it was a total success and a devastating blow to Philip's empire. In terms of plunder it was not so successful, for the inhabitants had removed most of their valuables the moment that they saw the English fleet enter the outer harbour.

During the six weeks that they were occupying the city, sickness broke out again amongst the troops. This, most probably, was not a recurrence of the fever from the Cape Verde Islands, but malaria from the mosquitoes which infested the swampy ground behind Cartagena. Sickness of one kind or another was the inevitable companion of armies and fleets in those days, when men were herded together under insanitary conditions and hygiene was hardly understood. But tropical diseases inevitably decimated armies in the 16th century—and continued to do so for centuries to come. If the conduct and morale of Spanish soldiers and seamen in the western empire seems invariably poor in comparison with that of the English, it is only fair to remark that the Spaniards were inhabiting unhealthy areas in a torpid climate. Most of them were almost certainly malaria-ridden, as well as weakened by other tropical diseases. In Europe their armies were second to none, while as later events have shown, in their own country and climate, no man can fight with greater endurance or courage than a Spaniard.

The fever and the inevitable losses of war (old Tom Moone, for one, had been killed in an ambush) faced Drake with a harsh problem. One of his main intentions had always been to realise his old dream—the capture of Panama. The question was whether he still had enough men with which to carry out this expedition, or, alternatively, whether he should hold Cartagena. He called a council of his military officers and put the problem to them. The answer he got was that, although they only had 700 fit men left, they were willing to attempt Panama over-land with the help of the Cimaroons. They were equally willing, if Drake thought it more expedient, to hold Cartagena against the Spaniards until reinforcements could reach them from England— provided always that he could guarantee to protect them from the Spanish Navy.

Drake admired their spirit, but it would seem that he had already made up his mind. He asked them therefore—since he did not feel the force was adequate for either of these projects—whether they should accept the ransom that had been offered and make their way home, or whether they should hold out for more. They replied that it would be best to accept the ransom, for the town had already been sacked and— since it had yielded less booty than had been expected—the officers would renounce their own share in the ransom, 'and do freely give and bestow the same wholly upon the poor men who have remained with us in the voyage, meaning as well the sailor as the soldier'.

It was a noble answer. Gone were the days when military officers and gentlemen would have no truck with sea officers, let alone with common soldiers and sailors. No more was there any need for him to say that he must 'have the gentlemen to haul and draw with the mariner and the mariner with the gentlemen'. His point had been taken. He had given England the strength with which to save herself from Philip II—and he had also set the pattern for all democratic armies and navies in the future.

Most historians have accepted Drake's decision not to attempt Panama with his greatly reduced force as no more than sensible, but he has been harshly criticised by some for not holding Cartagena. Had he held the city, it has been said, he would have cut the lifeline of the Spanish Empire at one stroke. No gold could have flowed from South America to Spain while an English fleet was based on Cartagena and, without the regular arrival of the treasure fleets, the Spanish economy would have collapsed. But Drake was right, and his critics have been wrong. To have sent ships back to England would have weakened his fleet, and in due course Philip II would certainly have sent an armada against the English outpost. It was more than likely that Elizabeth would have refused to reduce her home fleet or her military forces, particularly at a moment when an invasion was imminent. Without reinforcements, the English would soon have been forced to withdraw, decimated by disease, or even to yield to the Spanish forces outside the town. On the other hand, if Elizabeth had been prepared to back up her rough Devonian 'knight', Philip II would surely have chosen this as the moment to strike at England with his great armada. With Drake and Frobisher and Carleill far away in Cartagena, what an opportunity it would have been to destroy the home nest of these heretic hornets!

So Drake accepted the Governor's ransom offer of 110,000 ducats, about £40,000 in modern money. The fleet finally left Cartagena on the 31st March, all the ships undermanned, but weighted down with 240 captured guns, as well as such other booty as the Cape Verdes, San Domingo and Cartagena had yielded.

They had a hard time getting clear of the Caribbean. There were head-winds all the way, sickness aboard, and particularly bad weather off Cuba. Late in April they were still off Cape San Antonio, the westernmost point of Cuba, where they were forced to put in to water ship. Here one gets an endearing picture of Drake, something that immediately makes comprehensible the love and devotion he inspired in his men. 'I do wrong,' wrote Walter Biggs 'if I should forget the good example of the General, who, to encourage others, and to hasten the getting of water aboard, took no less pains than the meanest. Throughout the expedition, indeed, he had everywhere shown so vigilant a care and foresight in the good ordering of his fleet, accompanied with such wonderful travail of body, that doubtless, had he been the meanest person, as he was the chiefest, he had deserved the first place of honour.'

Reaching the humid surging waters of the Gulf Stream, the fleet coasted up Florida, frightening the early Spanish settlers along that coast and burning down the town of St. Augustine—just for good measure. Finally they reached Raleigh's newly-planted colony in Virginia, where 103 settlers were trying to carve a small patch of civilisation out of the wilderness. Drake offered a storeship, a pinnace, and a month's rations to help these first colonists. His offer was accepted, but unfortunately the storeship foundered during a sudden storm, and Ralph Lane, first Governor of the colony, accepted Drake's alternative offer of transportation home. Thus ended the year-old settlement of the first English-speaking Americans. But the fact that Drake was the man who took them home was in itself almost a promise that, before very long, they and others like them would be back.

It is interesting to note that these returned colonists were the first to introduce the nicotine habit into the civilised world. 'These men who were thus brought back,' wrote Camden 'were the first that I know of that brought into England that Indian plant which they call tabacca and nicotia, or tobacco, which they used against crudities, being taught it by the Indians. Certainly from that time forward, it began to grow into great request, and to be sold at a high rate, which, in short time, made men everywhere, some for wantonness, some for health sake, with insatiable desire and greediness, to suck in the stinking smoke thereof through an earthen pipe, which presently they blew out again at their nostrils: insomuch that tobacco-shops are now as ordinary in most towns, as tap-houses and taverns.'

The fleet reached Plymouth at the end of July 1586. This time there was no question of Drake's having to stay aboard ship while waiting to hear how his exploits would be received. Certainly, the venture had not been a financial success in anything like the same terms as his voyage round the world. But in military, economic, and political terms, it had produced an immense effect. With violence and effrontery he had made the greatest king on earth look a fool. He had cost the Spanish Empire an almost inestimable amount of money. Most important of all was the impression made on Europe, where Antwerp had recently capitulated to the Spanish forces, and where the flood tide of the Counter-Reformation was carrying all before it. Drake's return, and the news of his exploits, had an immense moral effect. Although 'the tide' stayed high for many months to come, it was slack-water, and the turn was almost in sight.

Spanish credit, not only moral but material, was almost ruined by his expedition to the West Indies. The Bank of Seville broke, the Bank of Venice (to which Philip II was principal debtor) trembled on the verge of bankruptcy, and the Fugger Bank at Augsburg received such reports from their correspondents that they looked averse on Spanish loans. Drake remarked in a letter to Lord Burghley: 'There is a very great gap opened, very little to the liking of the King of Spain.' Burghley himself, who had never really approved of Drake's methods, and who had an aristocratic distaste for the braggadocio in Drake's character, was forced to admit that: 'Sir Francis Drake is a fearful man to the King of Spain.'

CHAPTER FOURTEEN

The Enemy

PHILIP II, King of Spain, the son of the Emperor Charles V and Isabella of Portugal, had been born at Valladolid on the 21st May, 1527. Some fourteen years older than his great adversary, he could hardly have been more remote by birth, temperament, position and power, from the Devon preacher's son. Drake's place in history is marked by a fiery star. He burned his way upward like a rocket, impelled by the fuel of ambition and boisterous energy. Philip, on the other hand, had been destined for greatness from his birth. When he was a child, his father Charles V had impressed upon him that he was born to rule, and that he must learn to distrust the counsel of all others. The one thing that the two enemies shared in common was a passionate conviction that God was on his side.

In the whole of history no man before Philip II had ruled so large an area of the world. His titles still echo down the ages like a roll of distant thunder. From Sicily to the Netherlands, from Cape Sagres in Portugal to remote townships in Peru, and from trading outposts in Africa to the Celebes, his shadow lay over the earth. If ever a monarch might have felt justified in calling himself by that grandiloquent Eastern title, 'The Peacock of the World', it was Philip II. Yet such vainglory was far from his true nature. To understand something of Philip's character one must go to the paintings of El Greco, who united the supernatural world with the material by a sinuous line, and by a choice of subject-matter and colour that was somehow both ascetic and sensual.

Philip II, curiously enough, never understood or liked the work of the greatest painter in his empire. Although he commissioned El Greco to provide an altarpiece for the Escorial, the picture was never placed in its designed site. St. Teresa, another contemporary, would have comprehended El Greco's work better. 'I see.' she wrote, 'a white and a red of a quality that one finds nowhere in nature, for they shine more brightly than the colours that we perceive. I see pictures such as no painter has painted, whose models one finds nowhere in nature—

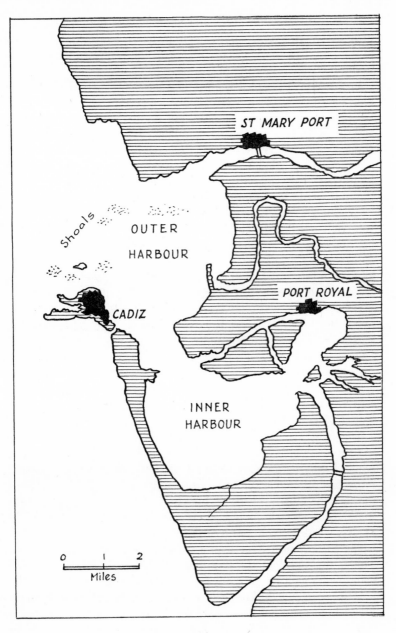

Cadiz

and yet they are nature itself, and life itself, and the greatest beauty imaginable.' St. Teresa herself, and in particular her treatise *The Castle of the Soul*, had much in common with the nature and outlook of Philip II.

In the almost personal conflict that developed between the great king and the west-country seaman one can perhaps see in a microcosm the conflict between the sensuous, but mystical, Latin temperament, and the pragmatic, but equally God-blinded, North. There was great courage displayed on both sides in the battle between Reformation and Counter-Reformation, and if there was more rude violence displayed by the one, there was far more refined cruelty displayed by the other. Philip II would have found little strange in the words of Berthold of Regensburg, a Franciscan preacher: 'Had I a sister in a country wherein were only one heretic, yet that one heretic would keep me in fear for her . . . I myself, by God's grace, am as fast rooted in the Christian faith as any Christian man should rightly be; yet, rather than dwell knowingly one brief fortnight in the same house with an heretic, I would dwell a whole year with five hundred devils!'

Francis Drake was convinced of the rightness of the Protestant cause, but he could never have subscribed to such an extravagant statement. In our own day, and reflecting the preoccupations of our own time, it is the 'cash nexus' which usually concerns historians in their treatment of the Anglo-Spanish wars. This certainly existed, as every action in Drake's life clearly reveals, but it would be a great mistake to forget the religious or, as it would be called today, 'ideological' gulf that divided the two nations.

The men have long since returned to the earth, but two buildings still survive which reveal the difference in their temperament and, it would hardly be too extravagant to say, the difference between two incompatible ways of life. On a fine summer's day one can wander through the quiet grounds of Buckland Abbey, or one can feel the sunshine soft on one's shoulders as it pours through the windows of the library, where Drake's crest is carved above the stone fireplace—and be happy to be a man. One is in a friendly, domesticated atmosphere. This is the world of the Renaissance, where it is man who tames nature—although he does not forget to give thanks to God for his benefits, or to bow the knee before His incomprehensible design. In the Escorial, on the other hand, built for the greatest monarch on earth, one is in a temple dedicated to an obscure God of Sacrifice. If the Carthaginians (and there is certainly some Carthaginian blood in Spain) had ever become Christians, this, one feels, is the kind of temple that they would have raised to the new Moloch.

The Escorial is one of the greatest buildings in the world; it is also one of the most austere. It is a church, a monastery, a mausoleum and a palace—all in one building, and in that order. Tradition has it that the building owes its origin to a vow made by Philip after the battle of St. Quentin, on the 10th August, 1557, when his army had been victorious over the French. Since the day was sacred to St. Laurence, the King vowed that he would build a monastery dedicated to the Saint. Hence its name San Lorenzo de Escorial—Escorial deriving from the small poverty-stricken village on the site that Philip finally chose.

It lies on the south-western slopes of Guadarramas, 3,500 feet above the sea, and drinks the wind like an eagle. The land around is wild and barren, baked in summer and frozen in winter. Local granite was used for the building, so that it seems to be a natural part of the harsh mountains. Henry the Navigator, that great ascetic ruler of Portugal, had chosen for his home over a century before a palace almost as austere: the towering headland of Sagres. But in Sagres there is always the sight and sound of the sea, to carry the heart and the eyes westward into the Atlantic. Looking out from the Escorial, on the other hand, it is the sky alone that feeds the mind. That motto, which Drake and his friends had laughed about at San Domingo, *Non sufficit Orbis*, might be translated, 'The World is not Enough'. It may not have been so much a vainglorious boast as a reflection of the aspirations of a mystic.

Philip was no saint, indeed he was accused in his own time of extreme licentiousness. He was, in fact, probably a good deal less immoral than most rulers (if by morality one refers to sexual *mores* alone), and he was rigidly abstemious. Totally dedicated to work, he had a sensual nature that was usually held in check by his will. His high conception of his duties as King, and as champion of the Catholic Church, made him a formidable antagonist. The building of the Escorial, which had begun in 1563, was completed twenty years later. From the moment that his army of workmen had started on the site, Philip came there increasingly often, preferring to sleep in a rough cell than in any of his magnificent palaces throughout Spain. Once the building was completed, he left it as rarely as possible, dying at last at the Escorial, in his self-chosen loneliness and austerity, on the 13th September, 1598.

At the heart of the complex of the Escorial, in a small group of rooms that were far less kingly than Elizabeth's apartments in any of her palaces, the king sat day after day, wrestling with the problems of his gigantic empire. Because he had been taught, and had learned later from his own experience, to trust few men, he undertook a volume of correspondence that would appal even the most overworked modern statesman. Where Henry the Navigator had worn a hair-shirt next to his skin, and where the saints and mystics of Spain applied the scourge to their bodies in order to drive out the devils of lust, carnality and pride, Philip II mortified his flesh by reading document after document. It was an inefficient system, for the secret of authority is to know how to delegate it, but this was something that Philip never learned. His was a personal, God-given rule, and he knew that the Almighty expected of Princes and Rulers a far higher degree of discipline than He did of common mortals.

Philip loved his children, he loved hunting and the countryside, and he had a civilised taste in pictures, architecture and decoration. In his youth he had been an amorous man—yet in later years he put almost all these things behind him. He could never have echoed the remark of Pope Leo X: 'God has given us the Papacy, let us enjoy it!' Philip, whatever his ancestry, was a Spaniard to the bone, and he was imbued with 'the tragic sense of life'. In a country that is largely austere, even though he could have lived in some of its most gentle and pleasant places, he chose of his own free will to become immured in a secular monasticism. One may still see on innumerable documents the record of his curious thin hand, commenting on this, that, and everything— even picking up grammatical faults in the dull reports of Governors and officials written thousands of miles away. It is difficult not to admire this intense industry. It is easy to despise it, but, in the final analysis, one feels a great sympathy for this lonely man. He was burdened with too many things, attempting too much, and assailed by innumerable gadflies.

Not the least of these irritants, in Philip's eyes, was that arrogant and relatively unimportant Englishman, Francis Drake. It would have been difficult for Philip to credit him with the 'Sir', for Drake was common-born and, if this was how the English dispensed their titles, it was yet another reason why they should be taught a true sense of values. For years now, Philip's advisers had been urging upon him 'the enterprise of England'. The most ardent among them were certain English Catholics, who longed to see the True Faith established once more in their country. For years, too, the King—rather like his cousin Elizabeth— had tended to prevaricate. It was not that he had no wish to see these heretics returned to the fold, and his uncomfortable northern flank covered. It was because he did, to a certain extent, realise just how difficult such a seaborne invasion was certain to be.

Philip had little knowledge of the sea himself. His was not the healthy respect of a sea-captain, who knows its dangers, but the natural dislike of a Latin for those barren acres of 'the fish-infested sea'. But now that Portugal was his, as well as a whole race of seamen trained on the

Atlantic coast (not forgetting the valuable acquisition to his naval power of their good and well-found ships), he found himself more and more inclined to consider the venture. He asked his Admiral, the Marquis of Santa Cruz, how many ships he thought would be necessary for an invasion of the island kingdom, and received the reply that about five hundred ships would be enough. Half of them would need to be 'great ships' (galleons or large armed merchantmen), and the rest could be composed of storeships and auxiliaries. From the Netherlands, the Duke of Parma, who knew far less about the sea than Santa Cruz, wrote that he could occupy England with 30,000 infantry and 4,000 cavalry. Parma also maintained that he could take the troops across the Channel—given favourable weather—without any help from the Spanish Navy. He added, though, that everything would depend on the element of surprise. Philip was not deceived, for he was no man's fool. He knew well enough that no such army or fleet of invasion barges could be assembled without word of it getting back to England.

Alone in his Spartan quarters, in his palace and temple dedicated to God on earth and above the earth, Philip wisely decided on a compromise. He never made the same mistake as Napoleon and Hitler in later centuries. He could not be bamboozled into thinking that a fleet of invasion barges could cross the Channel so long as the English fleet was in existence. Parma should have his men—and he should be reinforced overland from Italy—while the English fleet should be taken care of by a vast armada that Santa Cruz should get ready at Lisbon. Not only should this great Hispanic fleet be fitted out to destroy the English at sea, but it should also be designed to carry additional thousands of troops to link up with Parma's men. The invasion point was to be somewhere near the Thames, so that the troops could march straight on London and strike at the heart of England. The barges coming over from the Netherlands would proceed under cover of the armada, which would also bring over the 'follow-up' forces once the beach-head had been established. It was a good plan, and Philip, sitting alone in his strange secluded world in the Escorial, had divined far better than either his naval or military commander the problems which faced them. There was only one aspect that he appears to have overlooked and, being a landsman, it is not surprising that he should have done so. This was the total unpredictability of the sea.

'God's death, my lords!' remarked Queen Elizabeth on an occasion when the Polish ambassador had been rude to her, and she had answered him forcefully in Latin, 'I have been forced this day to scour up my old Latin that hath long lain rusting!' Like Drake she was addicted to plain speaking, and she could not abide the mealy-mouthed. She was indeed, as she was happy to boast, 'mere English', and would endure a great deal with patience. But once her back was against the wall, she would fight to the death. She hated war and all its stupid wastage of life, wealth and happiness, but if forced into it she could be like the proverbial bulldog. The Babington plot had broken soon after Drake's return, with all its implications that, if Elizabeth had been successfully assassinated, Philip II would have launched an invasion.

Having used Drake for some obscure project in Holland (which seems to have come to nothing) Elizabeth finally reached the conclusion that 'her little pirate', her rough but able Devonian, should be let loose once more upon the ships and trade of Spain. It was hardly any secret by now that the Enterprise of England was under way. Even to the dullest observer it was clear that the project was gathering an irresistible momentum.

Late in December 1586 Drake had his initial instructions. These were 'to impeach the provisions of Spain'—raid her supply lines and capture her shipping at sea. But by the time that his fleet had mustered, he had an even clearer direction—and far more attractive to his temperament. This was that he would make for the Spanish mainland, and 'distress the ships within the havens themselves'. He had never received this kind of *carte blanche* before and it is evidence not only of Elizabeth's growing realisation that war with Spain could not be avoided, but also of the complete trust she now had in Drake.

The *Elizabeth Bonaventure* was his flagship as before, and with him went three other galleons. There was the *Golden Lion* of 550 tons with the Vice-Admiral, William Borough, aboard; the *Dreadnought* of 400 tons commanded by Drake's old friend Thomas Fenner; and the *Rainbow* of 500 tons under Henry Bellingham. The *Rainbow* was a brand new vessel and had only been launched a few months previously. The rest of the fleet was made up by two pinnaces, a small galleon belonging to the Lord Admiral, some west-country privateers, four large merchantmen from the Turkey Company (which were almost as formidable as warships), and a number of private vessels. Altogether, there were 23 ships and about 2,000 men embarked. This was the strongest fleet that the Queen had yet sent to sea, and Drake was in all respects the Queen's admiral on the seas. The only potential source of discord lay in the appointment of William Borough as Vice-Admiral. He was an old naval veteran, Clerk of the Ships, and an excellent theorist in naval matters, but one of the old school. It is possible that he was given this appointment to act as a check on the admiral, but unfortunately—once Drake was at sea—he would accept no rules but his own.

The fleet weighed anchor and sailed on the 2nd April, 1587. As usual, Drake was in a great hurry to be gone, in case the Queen should change her mind. Even as it was, he only just got away in time. A messenger was already spurring down to Plymouth with orders that would have restricted his freedom of movement, and would in fact have forbidden him to enter any Spanish harbours. Drake had already sailed, but a fast pinnace was immediately sent after him carrying the despatch. Perhaps because its captain was a bastard son of Hawkins, the pinnace, somehow or other, never caught up with the admiral. An inquiry was held afterwards into their inability to 'find Drake', but the captain and his officers cleared themselves on oath. They had found time, however, to take a fat prize worth about £5,000, so this may have been regarded as some mitigation of their inefficiency.

After weathering a gale off Finisterre, Drake came across a homeward-bound Flemish merchantman, and learned from her that there was a great gathering of Spanish shipping in Cadiz. Drake had never been in the harbour, and knew little about it except that the entrance was reported to be difficult. A small thing like that was unlikely to deter him, and he made straight for the famous Spanish port. When his Vice-Admiral William Borough later sent to inquire for his orders, he received from Drake only the laconic: 'Follow your flagship!'

This was not at all to Borough's liking, who believed that everything should be done according to the book. Drake did indeed have a conference with the other commanders, but as a contemporary remarked, 'Though a willing hearer of other men's opinions, he was commonly a follower of his own.' Borough was later to complain that Drake never consulted his fellow admiral or his captains at any point, but merely had them aboard and entertained them. In conclusion, he either told them what he intended to do, or told them nothing at all.

By the 19th April, Drake was off Cadiz with the major part of his fleet. Despite the fact that the only safe approach for warships was through a narrow channel under the guns of the city, Drake took advantage of a favourable onshore breeze, made all sail, and steered straight into the harbour. His Vice-Admiral was aghast. According to the text-books, to take a fleet of sailing ships into a defended harbour, known to have oared galleys inside it, was neither more nor less than suicide. It is not difficult to feel some sympathy for Borough. But what Drake lacked in theory he made up for by experience, and he knew that Spanish defences were rarely as formidable as they were reputed to be. He knew also that surprise was the essence of success in war, and that the Spaniards commonly seemed to be demoralised by a headlong attack if it was pressed home with vigour and élan.

M

The sight that met his eyes as his flagship swung round the northern promontory would have proved an irresistible lure even to a man far more cautious than Drake. The outer harbour was dense with shipping, some sixty large ships at least, most of them making ready for the Enterprise of England. Loading and unloading, some waiting for their guns from Italy, others without their masts stepped, or with their yards sent down, they lay before him like a flock of fat sheep. The fact that must have horrified William Borough was that he could already see the galleys in the harbour, ready-manned for the protection of the merchantmen. What Drake was doing, according to the theory of the time, was as foolhardy as if the captain of a battleship in the last war should have sailed into an enemy harbour where there were a number of motor torpedo-boats. The oared galley had a formidable reputation, especially under conditions where it could be rapidly manœuvred against a vessel that was dependent entirely on the wind. But Drake was ever a despiser of established reputations, and he was to prove once again that his judgement was far sounder than that of the theorists.

Two galleys immediately made for the flagship with the intention of bringing their main armament, their bow chasers, to bear on her. Drake responded with a broadside, and his heavier weight of metal, and the longer range of the English guns, took effect. Hit time and again, the galleys turned and fled. Out of the ten that had initially advanced boldly to the attack—confident that the English had made every mistake possible—two fled into the inner harbour, one had to be beached to save her from sinking, while the rest retired behind a reef where they were covered by the guns of the Castle. As far as Drake was concerned they were just as well out of the way behind the reef as if he had sunk them. All the defenceless shipping of Cadiz now lay in his hands. The English were like wolves among the sheep. The Spanish ships were looted, burned, and sunk, and by nightfall Philip II's ships in Cadiz—with the exception of the shipping in the inner harbour— had all been destroyed or disabled.

Drake ordered the bulk of the fleet to anchor out of range of the shore batteries, while he and the three other royal galleons covered their flank against any further attempts by the galleys. William Borough was in a fever to be gone. Against all the rules of war they had already achieved their main objective, and he felt sure that if the wind dropped, they would be trapped in Cadiz—at the mercy of the galleys' and the town's guns. He expected no doubt, that, with day-break, Drake would order the fleet to weigh and proceed to sea. Far from it: with the first light, the Vice-Admiral was astounded to see his senior officer standing in towards the inner harbour, where two galleys

covered the anchored merchant shipping. Drake had sighted, among
the thicket of masts and spars, a huge merchant vessel belonging to no
less a person than Santa Cruz, commander of the Enterprise of England.
As far as Drake was concerned, the expedition had been a great success
from a naval point of view, but he was still determined to satisfy all the
investors in the expedition—including himself. What was needed was
a really rich piece of plunder.

Drake had no intention of taking his flagship into the narrow waters
of the inner harbour, but he rapidly organised a fleet of small boats. He
dashed in at the head of them and captured the 1,500-ton giant belonging to Santa Cruz. The inner harbour was now given over to the same
scene as the outer had been the evening before. Boatloads of English
seamen were looting, sacking, and firing the devastated ships, before
passing on to the next in line. Borough, in the meantime, had had
himself rowed across to the flagship, only to find to his horror that his
admiral was gone, and was somewhere in the inner harbour. It is not
hard to sympathise with his predicament, for he had had no orders,
except perhaps the unspoken one: 'Use your initiative.'

Returning to his own vessel, the *Golden Lion*, which by now had
come under heavy fire from the shore, he began to warp her out towards the harbour mouth. In the meantime the thing he had feared
all along took place—the wind dropped. For twelve hours Drake's
ship lay becalmed in the centre of Cadiz harbour—a situation in which,
theoretically, she should have become an easy prey to the galleys. But
as before, the range, accuracy, and weight of the English fire kept the
enemy at bay. The galleys tried time and again, with great gallantry, to
attack the *Elizabeth Bonaventure*—only to be repulsed.

Drake was 36 hours all told in Cadiz. Quite apart from the valuable
loot, his fleet had been entirely re-stored and re-victualled. Thousands
of tons of enemy shipping had been destroyed, six merchantmen laden
with provisions were prizes, and a large bulk of stores designed for the
Enterprise of England had been ruined. Shortly after midnight on the
morning of the 21st April the breeze began to draw softly on to the
land. At 2 a.m. Drake stood out to sea and rejoined his other ships.

This famous episode, which he laughingly referred to as 'singeing
the King of Spain's beard', had long-lasting repercussions throughout
Europe. It was not so much the amount of shipping destroyed. This
was considerable, but not vitally damaging to Philip's merchant fleet.
It was the very fact that Drake had been able to do it at all which
inflicted such an immense blow upon Spanish prestige. Philip found it
more and more difficult to raise money, and the great merchant bankers
now put up his rates of interest. Apart from that, the morale of Spanish

military and naval officers was shaken. They had seen the much-
vaunted galley recoil before sailing ships, and under conditions
supposedly ideal for an oared vessel. But above all it was the audacity of
the English, combined with Drake's swaggering self-confidence, that
sent a tremor of unease throughout the Spanish Empire.

All the rest of that day he lay at anchor in full view of the city 'upon
a bravado', as the report tells us, daring the galleys to come out and
fight. His challenge was refused, as were his attempts to secure the
release of English and French galley slaves. The following day the fleet
made sail and stood to the west, thus convincing the Spaniards that
Drake was off once again to ravage the West Indies. He was in fact,
bound for Cape St. Vincent. Its importance had long been realised for,
jutting out into the Atlantic Ocean, it commanded all the coastal trade
between the West Indies, Portugal, Spain, and the Mediterranean.
Drake had determined on capturing it, and it was this which finally
provoked the explosion between him and his Vice-Admiral.

Borough had been sufficiently shaken by the conduct of his admiral
at Cadiz, but he was dumbfounded when he learned that—without any
real consultation with his other commanders—Drake intended to bring
his fleet to the anchorage under the Cape and storm the fortified
heights. This was even further against the accepted rules and regulations
governing the conduct of war at sea, and the idea that a relative handful
of men should be able to take a fortified position on an almost impregnable headland seemed ludicrous in the extreme.

On the 30th April 1587, William Borough sent a long protest to his
admiral, accusing him among other things of never calling a proper
council before making a decision; of acting beyond the instructions
which Her Majesty had given him; and of treating his Vice-Admiral
with scant respect. Had Borough known Drake better, he would never
have dreamed of doing such a thing. Drake flew into a fury, had his
Vice-Admiral removed from his command, and placed him under
arrest. For the remainder of the expedition, the distinguished but
conservative old sailor was confined to quarters and, as he later put it,
'ever in doubt of my life, and expecting daily when the Admiral
would have executed upon me his bloodthirsty desire, as he did upon
Doughty'.

Drake's first attempt to capture the small but useful seaport of Lagos
was foiled by what he clearly considered was a lack of enterprise on the
part of his military leaders. He immediately sailed for Cape Sagres,
landed 800 men and took command of them himself. In theory, the
fort on its almost inaccessible promontory should have been impregnable. The result of Drake's action was proof once again that men in

secure fortifications tend to lose morale and get, as it would later be called, 'Maginot-minded'.

Drake led the attack in person, advancing at the head of the land forces up the steep slope towards the fort. They reached the main gate and, under cover of his musketeers' fire, Drake and a small body of men began to pile up faggots, pitch, and timber, against the main gate. William Borough might well have contended that this was no task for an admiral—and technically he would have been right—but Drake's presence at the most dangerous place inspired his men to vie with him in audacity. Before the fire had taken a real hold, the garrison of the fortress asked for terms. Their commander had died from wounds, and they were unnerved by this extraordinary enemy who advanced to attack what should by all right have been an impregnable position. It was evidence yet again that nothing shakes an enemy's confidence so much as the theoretically impossible. Nothing, in fact, succeeds like excess.

Drake was now master of Sagres Castle. The headland where the lonely spirit of Henry the Navigator had once brooded, yielded to the impetuous genius of an English seaman, a man who—except in his capacity for hard work—could not have been more remote from the ascetic, Catholic pioneer of ocean navigation. With the capture of the fort the other surrounding positions quickly capitulated. The fortress on St. Vincent was demolished, another nearby castle was razed to the ground, and the heavy guns on Sagres itself were thrown over the headland into the sea, where they were collected by boats from the fleet.

The English now held the point that dominated the Spanish trade routes, and Drake's inshore squadron was busy sweeping up everything that came into its path. Although not so glamorous as the raid upon Cadiz, these activities were to prove even more detrimental to Philip's war effort. It was the inshore coastal trade that carried those essentials which hardly get mentioned in comparison with gold and silver and pearls in history. But the Portuguese caravels, for instance, held barrel hoops and staves destined for Lisbon, and these were vital to the armada. At that time, everything from salted meats, dried tunny fish, to all-important water, was carried aboard ship in barrels. In the course of a week the English had captured at least fifty coastal vessels, containing not only these essentials, but also timber for oars and spars and ship-repairs. They destroyed nearly all the nets and boats of the famous Algarve tunny fisheries, upon which a large part of the economy of Portugal rested. Salted down tunny was very important during the winter months, just as in most Mediterranean countries the salt cod-fish from Newfoundland banks, *Bacalhao*, remains a staple diet of the poor to this day.

Soon after the capture of Sagres, Drake moved on to Lisbon, coming to anchor in Cascais Bay at the mouth of the Tagus River. It did not take him long to realise that Lisbon, with its well defended harbour-mouth and its river, was a very different project from Cadiz. Historians and commentators, who have taken the side of William Borough in his dispute with Drake, have often neglected the fact that, whenever Drake was faced with something he felt was beyond the forces at his disposal, he never attempted it. Foolhardy and impetuous he may have appeared to the conservatives of his day and age, but his actions were nearly always tempered by a rational assessment of the odds against him.

It was in Lisbon that the Marquis of Santa Cruz had his headquarters, and Drake—in the fashion of the day—'spurred up and down' outside the harbour challenging his enemy to come out and fight. Santa Cruz was wise. He refused the invitation and, although some galleys did make a faint-hearted attempt against the English ships, they were easily repulsed by their gunfire. Drake and his ships dallied a whole day 'in contempt of the town of Cascais', while his light craft and pinnaces comfortably swept up the local trade as it bore down towards the Tagus.

During the evening a gale began to blow up from the north, and Drake, determined not to be caught on a lee shore off that treacherous iron-bound coast, stood out to sea. He made his way back to Sagres and to his 'Engish anchorage', in the heart of King Philip's empire. It was from here that he wrote to Walsingham: 'As long as it shall please God, to give us provisions to eat and drink, and that our ships and wind and weather will permit us, you shall surely hear of us near the Cape St. Vincent. . . .'

One messenger after another came drumming up the bare hillside to the Escorial. Philip II, receiving their disturbing news, sent belated despatches to all the most important men in the kingdom. Santa Cruz was ordered to get to sea as soon as possible, the Duke of Medina Sidonia was alerted, while troops were marched and counter-marched across the Spanish peninsula in anticipation of the 'Dragon's' next move. Suddenly, on the 22nd May, 1587, the anchorage off Sagres was found empty. Cape St. Vincent was unoccupied, and the English had vanished as suddenly as they had come.

Drake had seen only too clearly that trade had practically dried up because of his presence on the coast. He had neither the men, ships, nor munitions to maintain a permanent 'Tobruk' on enemy territory, so he decided to withdraw. The Spanish messengers who spurred overland with this news to Santa Cruz, to Medina Sidonia, and to the King in his seclusion on the ridge of the Guadarramas, had no information beyond the fact that Drake and his ships were gone. The pirate had been observed sailing westward into the sunset, and once again the rumour spread that he had gone to the West Indies and the Main.

The fact of the matter was that, having decided there was nothing more that he could do upon the coast of Portugal, Drake had heard of a Spanish treasure ship Lisbon-bound from the Azores. As ever, he was determined to make a profit for his investors, as well as prosecuting his country's cause. But hardly had the English got clear of the coast, than they ran into a typical Atlantic gale. It blew for a full three days, scattered the fleet, and the *Elizabeth Bonaventure* nearly foundered. By the time that the gale had blown itself out, there were only ten vessels in company with the flag-ship.

It was at this point that the *Golden Lion* detached herself from the main body, claiming that a sail had been sighted on the horizon. Shortly after this, Captain Marchant came aboard Drake's flagship in a pinnace, saying that his crew had mutinied, complaining of the shortage of water and victuals. The *Lion* was homeward bound, with Vice-Admiral Borough still a prisoner aboard her. While the men still worked to repair the storm-damage aboard his vessel, Drake found time to summon a council and sentence Borough and all the other officers aboard the *Lion* to death. Whatever one's feelings about his reactions to Borough's initial letter, it is easy to understand that he felt himself betrayed by this open desertion. The one thing that must be remembered is that Borough can have had no part in it.

Drake was 16 days out from St. Vincent when he raised the Azores, and saw the lonely peaks of the volcanic islands rising out of the Atlantic. He and his ships in company were closing the nearest island at evening, when suddenly they sighted a large vessel, clear-cut against the sunset and the land. She was the *San Felipe*, the ship which Drake had heard about, and on whose account he had set off into the Atlantic. Portuguese-built, she was the private property of Philip II, armed like a warship, and the largest merchant vessel in the world. Totally ignorant of the fact that English men-of-war were in the area, she innocently made sail towards them, as Drake at the van of his depleted squadron came rolling towards her under a fair breeze. When both ships were well within sight of one another, the English 'hanged out flags, streamers, and pendants, that she might be out of doubt what they were. Which done, we hailed her with cannon shot. . . .' The luckless great merchantman had no chance but to yield, as Drake's other vessels now closed her and began to open fire.

The *San Felipe* proved to be the greatest single prize ever taken in Drake's lifetime. Beside her, the *Cacafuego* (which had made his fortune) was comparatively unimportant. She was laden not with the bullion of America, but had come all the way from the Far East. She carried spices and silks, the then unbelievable porcelain products of China, pearls, velvets, oriental furniture, and rough as well as cut gemstones. She was valued at the time as being worth nearly £120,000 —which Sir Julian Corbett estimated as being worth about a million in the currency of the 19th century. (In the depreciated 'paper' of our era it might be reckoned as worth some 5 million.) It is impossible to say whether Drake had had accurate information of the whereabouts of the *San Felipe*, or whether he was merely acting on an intuition that he might well come across her or other treasure ships in the area of the Azores. One thing is certain that, after this dramatic incident, the legend spread among the Spaniards that Drake had a magic mirror in the cabin of his ship which enabled him at any given moment to see what other vessels were sailing the ocean, and exactly where they were.

The capture of this great ship, a type of vessel which had never previously been taken by the English, was the crowning jewel in Drake's campaign of the year 1587. He had shown how initiative and dash could be used to make a well-found sailing fleet more dangerous than any other instrument of war. From this moment on, although many of their rulers only dimly grasped it, the English had in their hands the weapon that was to make them masters of the world. As the Venetian Ambassador put it in a despatch, 'He has done so much damage on the coasts of Spain alone that, though the King were to obtain a most signal victory against him, he would not recover one half the loss he has suffered.' The monk of the Escorial was at last forced to recognise his most dangerous enemy in the Lutheran preacher's son.

CHAPTER FIFTEEN

The Giant Stirs

'THERE must be a beginning of any good matter,' Drake had concluded his despatch from Sagres to his friend Walsingham, 'but the continuing to the end, until it be thoroughly finished yields the true glory . . . God make us all thankful again and again, that we have, although it be little, made a beginning on the coast of Spain.' But the determination and resolution that breathes out of this famous passage was not shared by England's Queen. When Drake returned, he found Elizabeth unapproachable in her intense depression over the execution of Mary Stuart which, whether feigned or not, resulted in a renewed hesitance and inactivity in English policy. It is quite possible that Elizabeth did really regret having loosed her dangerous admiral on the coast of Spain. (It must always be remembered that the despatch which never reached him had restricted his sphere of operations to the high seas alone.)

Even at this late hour, perhaps, the Queen hoped that the head-on collision between herself and her royal brother might be avoided. Drake had only increased the tension, and not content with having inflicted the gravest loss of face on Philip by his action on Cadiz, he had even landed on the shores of the peninsula. He had captured the fortress of Sagres and, in fact, engaged in a military escapade on what was technically friendly soil.

Drake may have feared that something like this would happen as soon as he was away. As on most of his voyages and expeditions, his determination to make them pay and return a good profit is not solely evidence of his own acquisitive instinct. On his return from that highly successful expedition in which he had captured San Domingo and Cartagena—causing Philip II far greater long-term distress than the recent raid on Cadiz—Drake had met with a somewhat cool reception. The Queen and the other investors got no more than 15s. for their every pound. Elizabeth was always short of money, lived very much hand-to-mouth, and voyages of this nature were something that she could not afford, however much they might damage her enemy. In the campaign of 1587, therefore, Drake had good reason to feel that he would have earned himself a favourable reception by his capture of the great carrack *San Felipe*. It was true that the Queen had no hesitation in accepting her share of the plunder. But, even while the captured oriental silks were being made into dresses for her, with pearls and cut gemstones from the *San Felipe* sewn on to the material or set scintillating in her red hair, she was writing to Parma and completely disassociating herself from Drake's recent activities.

It is understandable that Drake, whose temper was never of the best, felt highly indignant at the state of affairs that he found in England. His frustration to some extent may account for his determined persecution of his Vice-Admiral. For, whatever one may feel about the Doughty episode in Drake's life, it would seem that the only man, apart from Philip II, whom he pursued with an almost malicious hatred was William Borough. Drake had condemned his Vice-Admiral to death in his absence, but naval regulations clearly stated that a Commander's authority did not extend to such power over his principal officers. As Sir Julian Corbett pointed out, under orders laid down by King Henry VIII, 'all Captains must be obedient under their Admiral; if any be stubborn the Admiral shall set him ashore and put another in his place and write to the King and his council of his faults, truly and without malice.'

There was no precedent for Drake's action. Burghley was almost certainly alarmed by Drake's conduct on the coast of Spain. Certainly he cannot have been happy about the admiral's determination to have so distinguished and senior an officer as Borough arraigned for cowardice, mutiny and desertion. Drake's contention that Borough had prevailed upon the officers and crew of the *Lion* to mutiny and desert could hardly be substantiated by the known facts. Borough had been a prisoner aboard the *Lion* and in no position to exert any authority. It was, however, probable that it was the fact that their Vice-Admiral lay in such an ignominious position which gave the officers and men aboard the *Lion* their determination to leave Drake's flag.

In Drake's eyes, Borough's real offence lay in his protest against the attack on Cape St. Vincent. It was not until after this that Drake began to remember Borough's tardiness at Cadiz, or even to suggest that his Vice-Admiral had had his ship warped out to the harbour mouth out of cowardice—which was certainly not true. In the end, Borough was brought before a Court of Inquiry, and was acquitted on all counts. Burghley's influence is noticeable throughout the whole of this episode. The great talent of the Cecils over the centuries has been to know how to endure, and to play a waiting game. Burghley was certainly not willing, at this moment of Drake's great fame and fortune, to attempt a direct confrontation with him. He was intelligent enough to be able to value and respect Drake's services, even while disliking the man in person. But one thing he was determined on was to see that an honest and able gentleman of Borough's character was not sacrificed to some peculiar hatred of his admiral. Not only did William Borough keep his important office of Clerk of the Ships, but a few years later he was made Controller of the Navy. It is noticeable, however, that he was never again employed on active service.

Drake's persecution of Borough is one of the least attractive episodes in his life. As the previous cases of Thomas Doughty and Chaplain Fletcher have shown, he was a man who would not tolerate any interference from anybody, once he was at sea and in command. William Borough, brought up these previous incidents of Drake's high-handedness in his defence, nor did he forget to revive the old tale that Drake had 'forsaken' John Hawkins at San Juan de Ulua. The only thing that makes Drake's behaviour comprehensible is the knowledge that he suffered all his life from his humble birth. The Raleighs, Grenvilles and Frobishers always disliked him, not so much for what he had done, or the way in which he had made his fortune—but for the fact that a man of his stamp should have made a fortune at all. Always popular with his subordinates, and sympathetic to the under-dog, Drake had a 'chip on the shoulder' towards his superiors. Who knows what cool, insolent English patronage he had had to suffer during his early years, from men who considered themselves his betters? Like so many self-made men, Drake was inclined to boast. Like so many self-made men, despite his riches and his acquired position in the Establishment, he was never allowed to forget that he did not really 'belong'.

It was the last week of June when Drake reached Plymouth, and the best course of action for England would have been to revictual his fleet, and send him off again. He was kept inactive, and Santa Cruz, who had at last put to sea, was enabled to bring the whole West Indies fleet safely back to Spain. There were over 100 vessels, carrying some 14 million ducats' worth of goods and treasure, and they helped to restore Philip's immediate finances, as well as his credit in Europe. The intelligent policy for the English would have been to strike and strike again, while the enemy were still reeling from the blows that Drake had inflicted on the coast-line of Spain. Nothing was done, and the autumn of 1587 wore on.

From all over Europe reports came in that, far from being deterred, the King was pressing ahead with his preparations for the Great Enterprise. Ships were being launched on the Scheldt, Parma was having a fleet of barges built, and in Lisbon the main preparations for the invasion were going ahead without delay. Despite everything that had happened, Philip still seems to have been convinced that he could launch the invasion in the autumn of that year. Having sent Santa Cruz in pursuit of Drake (as he believed), Philip had gone ahead with his grand design. Slowly the forces built up, with the king agitating from his remote fastness for immediate action, while Santa Cruz and his officers maintained that it was now far too late in the season to launch the armada against England. By November the fleet was still not ready, and the Spanish Admiral implored the king to put off the Enterprise of England until the spring.

As the year drew to a close Europe was beset by rumour, while the superstitious maintained that 1588 might well prove to be the end of the world. Armageddon seemed in sight. It was not only the conflict between England and Spain, now seen as inevitable, that provoked the wave of ominous prophecies. It was true that, particularly in Spain, there were plenty of voices raised to point out that heretic England was at last about to get her deserts. The poet Gongora wrote of the heretic country and her Queen:

> How art thou doom'd to everlasting shame
> For her accursed sake,
> Who, for the distaff, dares to take
> The sword and sceptre in her bastard hand!
> She-wolf libidinous, and fierce for blood!
> Thou strumpet offspring of th'adult'rous bed,
> Soon may avenging heaven hurl down
> Its lightning-vengeance on thy impious head!

The immensity of the preparations throughout Spain and Portugal induced a feeling of self-confidence in the common people, whatever doubts and hesitations the King and his councillors may have had. This mood of exuberant optimism was reflected in a little jingle:

> My brother Don John
> To England is gone,
> To kill the Drake
> And the Queen to take,
> And the heretics all to destroy. . . .

But the sense of doom and catastrophe which seemed to gather over Europe as the year 1588 approached, was not only due to the impending conflict. The fact was that a number of astrologers had calculated that the year was predestined to be fateful for all mankind. As long ago as the mid-15th century, the great mathematician and astronomer, Regiomontanus, had observed that there would be an eclipse of the sun in February 1588, and two eclipses of the moon in the same year. He had further remarked that the conjunction of Jupiter, Mars and Saturn in the Moon's House, made it certain that the year would be marked by some disastrous and terrible events. '. . . If in this year complete catastrophe does not befall the world, and if the land and the ocean does not dissolve in ruin, yet the world will still endure a great upheaval. Empires will crumble, and on all sides there will be great lamentation.'

When Santa Cruz returned to Spain in October, he was immediately ordered to try and get the Armada to sea. But by now it was far ton late in the year, many of the ships were still without guns, many were re-fitting, and some had not even finished building. Through the winter of 1587, and into the spring of 1588, Santa Cruz toiled at his Herculean task of preparing the Armada. In the late autumn Drake was still down at Plymouth, this time preparing for an expedition in connection with an attempt to restore the Portuguese pretender, Don Antonio, to his throne. During these years, when he was an almost penniless hanger-on at the English court, this unfortunate Portuguese prince was involved in numerous plots and counter-plots. None of them ever came to fruition, and the current project languished like all the others. It is clear, however, that Drake was once more back in the royal favour. This was confirmed by his commission on the 23rd December, giving him command of an independent fleet of thirty ships, seven of which were to be Royal Naval vessels. A few days before this, Lord Howard of Effingham had been appointed Lord Admiral of England, or Commander-in-Chief of all the naval forces. The pattern of command for the crisis year of 1588 had taken shape.

In January, Drake was getting his squadron ready, and making preparations for what was commonly believed was to be another expedition to the West Indies. One thing that Drake did not suffer from—and it was the usual bugbear of Naval commanders in those days—was a shortage of men. Indeed so great was his fame and reputation among sailors, that men flocked to be in a squadron under his command. It was reported in Spain that he could have manned at least 200 ships with volunteers.

Irritated though Drake had been by his enforced inactivity during the autumn, his problems were small compared with those of the Marquis of Santa Cruz. 20,000 men sat idle in the ports of Spain and Portugal over that winter, which meant a heavy drain on the Spanish exchequer and an immense victualling problem. Even worse was the continued shortage of ships. At this late date he still had no more than thirteen galleons, whereas he had always calculated he would need about fifty, not to mention a large fleet of merchantmen, galleys, and small frigates. But apart from the galleons (one of which was scarcely fit for sea), he had only sixty or seventy other ships, many of them totally unfitted for their task, and almost all of them under-gunned.

Santa Cruz had been one of the prime movers of the war party against England, but he was now an ageing man of sixty-two. In these last months he must have realised that in the Enterprise of England he had undertaken a task which was beyond his powers—or, more accurately, beyond the powers of the shipyards and administrative capabilities of the Spanish Empire. Given time, no doubt, a truly formidable armada could have been raised by Spain, one which would have been quite capable of delivering a crushing blow against the English on the high seas. But time was one thing that Philip would not allow his admiral and, in any case, it was already running out for the Marquis. On the 9th February, exhausted by a lifetime in the King's service and totally worn out by the burden of the past year, Alvaro de Bazan, 1st Marquis of Santa Cruz, died in his bed in Lisbon. He had fought gallantly at Lepanto, had been one of the captors of Tunis and Velez de Gomera, and had been largely responsible for the design of the great galleons of the Indies Fleet. His efforts to subdue the Lutheran heretics of the North were not destined to be attended by such success as he had had against the Moslems of the Mediterranean.

Philip had for some time been growing increasingly irritated by his admiral, whom he unfairly held to be responsible for the fact that the Armada was not yet ready for sea. Even before Santz Cruz died, he had a successor in mind, and immediately on hearing of his Admiral's death a messenger was sent spurring off to the Duke of Medina Sidonia, appointing him Captain-General of the Ocean Sea. Philip's choice must largely have been based upon the Duke's impeccable ancestry, for he had done practically nothing to distinguish himself in war.

Born in 1550, the Duke was a sensitive and kindly man, the inheritor of one of the greatest fortunes in Spain, a devoted Catholic and, as Garrett Mattingley wrote of him, 'a grandee of such dazzling eminence that no officer in the fleet could feel insulted by his promotion, or find it beneath his dignity to obey him'. Such is not the stuff out of which great commanding officers are made.

England was fortunate (as she has been in many succeeding centuries), that, despite the English love of caste, the ranks of the nobility have always been kept open to merit and money. Drake had been raised in a harder school than the Duke, and so had many of Drake's great contemporaries—even those who were nobly-born. Medina Sidonia, it must be remarked, had no illusions about his aptitude for the task that had been given him. He wrote almost immediately to the King's secretary, protesting at his unsuitability, and stating that he had no experience of war or of the sea, and that 'I cannot feel I ought to command so important an expedition . . .' It is difficult to have anything but sympathy for Medina Sidonia. His sense of duty and his personal loyalty to the king, were to bring him no happiness. Unwillingly, and with a feeling of complete inadequacy, he took over the confused muddle that had been left behind by the death of Santa Cruz.

CHAPTER SIXTEEN

The Great Armada sails

THE spring came, and Drake was in a fever to be gone. More than ever before, he was convinced that the English policy should be to strike the enemy on his own coastline. Cadiz had taught him, if he had not known it before, that a harbour crowded with shipping was vulnerable to a sudden attack from the sea. Reports had reached him that Philip had something like 400 ships (a gross exaggeration) in Lisbon. His hope was, as he told the Italian Ubaldini, to maintain such an intensive blockade off the coasts of Spain and Portugal that nothing would be able to move. As he wrote to the Queen: 'Your Majesty shall stand assured, if the fleet comes out of Lisbon, as long as we have victual to live upon that coast, with God's assistance, they shall be fought with ... The advantage of time and place in all martial actions is half a victory; which being lost is irrecoverable.'

Drake asked for eight royal galleons and a total force of 50 ships for the expedition. The Queen gave him more than he asked for, and promised to despatch 14 large galleons and the greater part of the armed Levant merchantships to Plymouth, as well as several ships contributed by private individuals. By doing so, however, she was putting the bulk of the fleet into the Plymouth area, and this meant that the command automatically became the Lord Admiral's. Lord Howard of Effingham, accordingly, prepared for the West Country.

It was a hard spring that year, with constant bad weather, and Howard was held up by head-winds until the end of May. He was also delayed by the fact that the victuals for his fleet were late in reaching him from London. When he did get to sea to make his way to Plymouth, he ran into a south-westerly gale, and it was not until the 23rd May that the Lord Admiral arrived off the great west-country seaport. In company with him were 18 Royal Naval ships, and an attendant fleet of armed merchantmen and private vessels. Drake went out to meet him in the *Revenge*, and dipped his flag before the Lord High Admiral of the English Navy. Shortly afterwards a boat came over from the flagship to the *Revenge*, bearing the Queen's commission to

Sir Francis Drake, and making him Vice-Admiral of the whole fleet. Whatever he had done before, and however much the Queen may have been implicated in his actions, she had always left herself a loop-hole by which she could, if she so wished, 'disavow him'. But from the moment that he hoisted his Vice-Admiral's flag in full view of the fleet and under the eyes of the Lord Admiral, the Queen had openly endorsed Drake's position in the Navy and, therefore, any of his future actions. Whatever he may have felt about being deprived of an independent command, Drake accepted Lord Howard's presence with good grace. The two men were to work well with each other in the months to come.

Both men were preparing to make for the Spanish coast as soon as possible when orders reached them from London, to take up a position 'covering the approaches to England, Ireland and Scotland'. Howard angrily retorted that no such place existed. The government, however, was concerned—and rightly so—that, if the English fleet sailed, it might miss the Armada somewhere in the Bay of Biscay. If this had happened, Medina Sidonia would have been able to swoop through the Channel-mouth and land his troops on an almost undefended coast. Quite unknown to the English, the Armada had already sailed.

It was on the 25th April that the Duke of Medina Sidonia had gone to the Cathedral of Lisbon, and had taken from its altar the sanctified standard which he was to bear aboard his flagship in the crusade against the heretics. The Archbishop of Lisbon had pronounced a benediction on the Enterprise of England. Every man who took part in it was given Papal absolution and indulgence, since he was going as a soldier of Christ against the legions of the Devil. Whatever economic and military considerations may have influenced Philip and his councillors, the fact remains that the expedition was seen as a crusade. As Garrett Mattingley commented in *The Defeat of the Spanish Armada*, 'Every man who was to sail with it [the Armada]—had confessed and communicated. They had all been warned severely against blasphemous swearing and other sins that soldiers and sailors are prone to. The ships had all been searched to make sure that no women had been secreted aboard. . . .'

Despite his initial unwillingness to accept Philip's commission, Medina Sidonia had achieved a near-miracle in getting the Armada ready for sea. The prestige of his name had ensured that everything possible had been done to expedite and make ready the sailing of the fleet. By the time that the Armada sailed, Medina Sidonia had 20 galleons, four large armed merchantships, and four galleasses, to make up his first line-of-battle. The galleass was a composite type of vessel, both oar-and-sail, heavily armed, and was expected to prove very

N

formidable in any naval engagement. However, like battle-cruisers, those other hybrids of a later era, they seem to have combined the defects of both types of vessel, while possessing few of the virtues. Forty armed merchantmen formed the second line, none of them quite as heavily gunned as their English equivalents, but all of them considerably larger in tonnage. By the time that the Armada was sent on its dedicated mission, it numbered nearly 130 ships. The organisation of such a fleet at sea presented almost as difficult a problem as did its victualling and supplying when in harbour. Both the English and the Spanish suffered from the primitive logistics of their day, but because their force was so much the greater, the Spanish suffered even more than did Howard and Drake.

On the 20th May, 1588, the largest fleet that the world had ever seen was under sail off Lisbon. The bad weather which only infuriated the English far north in the mouth of the Channel proved even more distressing for Medina Sidonia. Drake and his Admiral had only to guard the approaches to a comparatively narrow strip of water, with ships that had been built for working in those awkward, tumbled seas. But the unfortunate Duke—'Always seasick and always prone to colds', as he had written to Philip II—had to bring a vast and heterogeneous fleet across the Bay of Biscay, one of the most treacherous areas in the world. It took 13 days from Lisbon for the Armada even to reach Finisterre, not much more than 250 miles by sea—as the crow flies. But, as Medina Sidonia and his King were to realise, distances at sea cannot be calculated in so simple a way. The ships had to tack and tack again, lie idle in calms, and run back before bad weather. It was not until early June that the Spaniards made this north-westernmost point of the Spanish peninsula. Like all large mixed fleets they suffered from the disadvantage of being tied to the speed of their slowest vessel, and restrained to the manoeuvrability of their most awkward merchantman. Ahead of them lay the Bay of Biscay with all its unpredictable storms, its seas that surge in over the continental shelf from the long open spaces of the Atlantic, and its craggy coasts to leeward.

While the Spaniards were vainly endeavouring to beat up towards the Channel, their enemies were also suffering from the storms of that ill-omened year. The English fleet had finally sailed on the 19th June, only to be driven back after two days by strong south-westerlies. A few days later, Howard and Drake had again tried to get out into the ocean to meet their adversaries, and yet again had run into head-winds. It was not until the 7th July that the English fleet managed to get down near the Spanish coast. At this point, the onset of gale-force southerly winds scattered the ships, and drove them all the way back to Plymouth.

One thing Howard and Drake had learned in the course of their fruitless expedition was that the Armada had suffered far more severely than they had. In theory, of course, the southerlies and south-westerlies that gave the English such concern, either keeping them bottled up in the Channel or hurling them back once they had got out, should have boosted Medina Sidonia's fleet happily northward. In fact, any strong winds were too much for a fleet of that period, especially when it was composed of galleons, oared galleasses, awkward freighters and supply ships, and large merchantmen designed for the Mediterranean trade. The galleys which were to accompany the fleet had already suffered so severely from the weather that none of them ever sailed on the Enterprise of England.

The Duke's troubles were not confined to wind and weather. The slow progress of the fleet had inevitably meant that victualling problems had grown acute. Many of the casks in which food and water were stored proved to have been made of green wood, so that their contents became tainted or the wood warped and they were lost. Some of this may have been due to dishonesty on the part of Spanish contractors, but very largely it was the unlooked-for result of Drake's activities during the previous year. When his inshore squadron had been snapping up the Spanish coastal trade, they had captured and burnt nearly all the seasoned barrel-staves destined for the Armada.

A severe gale struck the Armada when the bulk of it was lying in Corunna, where it had put in to re-water and take on more provisions. Some of the ships, however, were still at sea. These were broadcast over the ocean, while in Corunna itself ships dragged anchor, collided with one another, and two days passed before Medina Sidonia got news of his scattered force. Most of them had taken shelter in other small ports along the coast, but nearly 30 of them were still unaccounted for. It was in this disastrous situation that the Duke sat down to write to Philip II. He pointed out that sickness was growing throughout the fleet, that many of the ships were badly strained from the weather—so unusual for that time of the year—and, in short, he implored His Most Catholic Majesty either to defer the invasion for a year, or to come to terms with England. Philip's reply was terse. Even if his force had been reduced in strength, the Duke was to take the Armada against England as soon as was humanly possible.

It was on the 12th July that the English fleet, after its second abortive foray into the Bay of Biscay, finally reached Plymouth with the southerly still strong in their sails. Merchantmen spoken to at sea, and reports reaching England from Europe, all told the same tale—the Armada had been hit by the same bad weather, but the winds that had merely driven the English home, had damaged, demoralised, and shattered Philip's fleet. Some confidence was now felt that the Spaniards would not try again that year. For the first time in many months the English, as they re-watered, reprovisioned, and made good their storm-damage, felt that their island was not destined to be attempted by the ships of Spain. It was on this very day, the 12th July, as Drake and Howard put back into harbour, that Medina Sidonia accepted the inevitable. 'The most happy Armada', now renamed 'the Invincible' once more put to sea.

During the following days, while the Armada swaggered towards England under a quiet and favourable southerly, Howard and Drake were debating how best to hurt the enemy. Thinking it unlikely that an invasion would now take place, they decided to divide their forces. One squadron would sail to intercept the Spanish ships coming from the Indies, thus cutting Philip's vulnerable supply-line, while the rest of the English fleet would head for Corunna and attempt to destroy the Armada in its base. It was an excellent plan, but the report of the Armada's devastation that prompted it had been far too optimistic.

Medina Sidonia, his sea captains and other officers, had done marvels in maintaining their fleet as well as they had, and in managing to get to sea again so quickly. The old idea, sometimes promulgated by English historians, that the Spaniards were totally incompetent at sea has no justification in fact. Both the Spaniards and Portuguese were natives of a hard coastline, had been the initiators of all trans-oceanic sailing and were brave men, inured to hardships. Medina Sidonia himself, too often dismissed as the buffoon in the tragic history of the Armada, showed himself to be an efficient organiser. He was probably better than his predecessor, Santa Cruz, and he was as resolute as any man could be in attempting to carry out almost impossible orders.

It was on the 17th July, five days after the Armada had left Corunna, that Howard wrote to Walsingham: 'Sir, I make all the haste I can possible out; and I and all my company that came from London will not stay for anything. Sir Francis Drake and some of those ships will be ready, within three or four days.' The ships to which he referred were some of the large galleons which the Queen had suggested might be paid off (now that the danger seemed to be over), but which Howard in his wisdom had insisted on keeping manned. Like their Spanish adversaries, both Howard and Drake were troubled by victualling problems and by the inevitable spread of disease among their troops. The admiral concluded by saying 'But there shall be neither sickness nor death, which shall make us yield, until this service be ended. I never saw nobler minds than we have here in our forces'.

As Sir Julian Corbett remarked of Lord Howard of Effingham, '. . . While the crisis lasted he bowed with fine humility to the subordinate, whom he recognised as the greater genius; and yet in giving way he never once lost dignity or forgot for a moment that it was he who was responsible for the tone of the fleet. From first to last he set an example of untiring labour, of loyal devotion, and of buoyant courage that is hardly to be surpassed and which entirely won the respect of his headstrong and self confident Vice Admiral.' Howard was a fine example of the *grand seigneur* at his best, and even Drake could take no exception to his senior officer. The two of them in many respects represent the full flower of the Elizabethan period: dignity, courtesy, and grandeur, on the one hand; on the other, fiery violence, and the self-confidence of vigorous maturity.

It was on the 19th July, 1588, that one of the screen of small English ships cruising off the mouth of the Channel sighted sails to the south of the Scilly Islands. Beyond the long, pale beaches of the islands, at the place where the horizon heaves into the Atlantic, there lifted the dark hulls, towering superstructures, and lofty masts of the enemy. Captain Thomas Fleming aboard his bark the *Golden Hind* (called appropriately enough after the most famous ship in English history), had sighted the Armada. Under full sail he hastened back to Plymouth, with the news that most of the ships he had seen had struck sail and were lying idle off the Scillies. They were clearly waiting for the bulk of the fleet to come up with them.

Behind these first fleet outriders of the Armada, the storeships and the troop carriers rolled leisurely towards the mouth of the Channel. Galleons of the India Guard, galleasses, frigates, caravels and coasters, they drew steadily northward under a fair south-wester. The wind that sat so favourably in their sails—a gift from God as it seemed—held the heretic English penned inside Plymouth harbour.

CHAPTER SEVENTEEN

The Narrow Seas

'THE southerly wind that brought us back from the coast of Spain, brought them out,' wrote Admiral Howard, 'God blessed us with turning us back.' It was, indeed, more than fortunate that the English Fleet had been driven home from the Bay of Biscay. If this had not happened, Howard and Drake might well have found themselves down off the Spanish coast, only to discover that the birds had flown from Corunna. The gale that at the time had seemed such an enemy to the English had proved their best friend.

As the rest of his fleet came up and joined him at the mouth of the Channel, the Duke of Medina Sidonia called a Council of War and reviewed his orders from King Philip. He was to make his way up-Channel—not entering any English port *en route*—until he reached the North Foreland off Margate. If he should encounter Drake, it was of course essential that he should defeat him. (What Philip II and his Admiral had not known when the Armada left was that almost the whole of the English fleet had been committed to the West Country and the Channel mouth.) Having reached the North Foreland in safety, and having also presumably defeated Admiral Howard—whom they expected to encounter in the Narrow Seas off Dover—Medina Sidonia was then to establish a beach-head at the mouth of the Thames. He would land his own troops, and convoy Parma's 20,000 men across from the Netherlands. The invasion point would be either in the Downs, or near Margate on the north Kent coast. This was left to the admiral's judgement, for it depended entirely upon the state of wind and weather. If a strong south-westerly blew up-Channel there would have been shelter for the fleet near Margate; while if the wind was in the north, they would have been able to find a lee in the Dover area.

It was during the afternoon of Friday, the 19th July, that Captain Thomas Fleming burst upon the Lord Admiral and the Vice-Admiral with his sighting report. Tradition has it that Drake and Howard were engaged in a game of bowls, and that Drake replied in the immortal

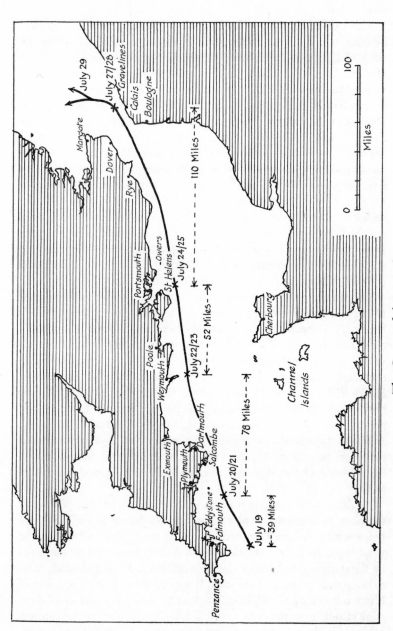

The Course of the Armada

words: 'There is time enough to finish the game, and beat the Spaniards too.'

This basis of the story is first found in a Spanish pamphlet published in 1624, which states that the Armada was successful in reaching the coast of England: 'while their commanders were at bowls upon the Hoe of Plymouth.' There must have been many men both in Spain and England alive at that time who had served in the rival fleets, so if it is only legend, it is at least living legend. The story has an authentic Drakeian ring about it. There was, in fact, no real reason why Drake and Howard should have immediately discontinued their game—although, no doubt, orders were immediately given for all men to report aboard, and for the ships to make ready for sea. On that Friday afternoon, not only was the south-westerly blowing into the mouth of Plymouth Sound, but the tide was also flooding up-Channel. Under such a combination of circumstances it would have been impossible to get the fleet to sea, and it was not until late that night that the ships began to warp out of the Sound. By this time the tide had turned, so that they had the ebb running in their favour, while the wind had most probably dropped a little—as it often does at sunset.

The one thing about the story which is probably a fiction—presented to popular imagination by painters of later centuries—is the picture of Drake and Howard with their attendant captains playing biased bowls on a smooth green. The modern type of bowls had indeed been invented by this time, but the bowling alley was far more common in the West Country. Technically, by a statute dating from the reign of Henry VIII and by an act passed in the time of Queen Mary, playing bowls was frowned upon, and even forbidden, as being likely to give rise to 'unlawful assemblies, conventicles, seditions, and conspiracies'. A bowl similar to the type which Drake may have used in this famous game can be seen in Buckland Abbey to this day. It is more like a large leather cheese than the comparatively small wooden bowl of today.

By dawn next morning the first galleons, which had warped out of the Sound overnight, were anchored in the lee of Rame Head, the point which shelters Plymouth from the west. Towards sunrise the wind began to freshen, and the English at once started to beat out to sea on the starboard tack, while the ships still left in Plymouth made haste to warp out on the next ebb tide. It appears that 54 ships got clear of Plymouth during the night of the 19th to 20th July, and all of them were standing out to sea by noon. When one remembers that this was achieved in the teeth of a foul wind, one can only admire the seamanship of the admirals and their commanders. Some further ten ships, which had missed the first tide, joined them later. This brought the total English force to 64 ships. Only 24 of them were fighting vessels of any size.

By three o'clock on the afternoon of Saturday 20th, the topmen in the English fleet were shouting down that they had the enemy in sight. The Armada was off Dodman Point, with a west-south-westerly giving them the weather-gauge over the English and boosting them gently up channel. Howard and Drake immediately started to work further out to sea, as the enemy came on in formidable order. They advanced with a military precision that was totally unlike the English fleet, who were spread out in a ragged line of sail, as they hauled themselves clear of the land.

The formation which the Armada adopted was rather like a crescent with a massive centre, the point where Medina Sidonia and his main battle fleet kept their stations. It was the heart of this bow which advanced first towards the English, while on both the extreme wings were heavily-armed fighting ships, including the galleasses. Behind the main battle-line came the storeships and auxiliaries, and these in their turn were protected on their rearward flanks by two smaller squadrons of warships.

The organisation was far from amateur. It is noticeable from all their accounts that the English were awed by the formation adopted by the Spaniards, as well as by their station-keeping efficiency. By having the tips of his crescent hardened by some of his best fighting ships, Medina Sidonia had ensured that if the English got the weather-gauge of him, off either flank, they would find nothing soft to bite on. If, on the other hand, any of the English were to work round and get to the rear of the crescent, and make for the 'soft' storeships and transports, they would soon find that the galleons on the wings had dropped back and cut them off. The English were also impressed by the discipline of this vast fleet, and by the way in which the ships maintained such accurate station; the galleases increasing or decreasing their oar-beat as necessary on the wings, while the sailing ships furled topsails or spread more canvas with a military precision. Medina Sidonia was bringing up Channel the largest fleet the world had ever seen, much as if he were conducting an army on manoeuvres. So long as the wind was favourable, this scientific precision could be maintained.

After the reports of its decimation by gales, the English were astounded at the size of the fleet which had reached their waters, — 'somewhat above a hundred sails, many great ships' as Drake wrote in his first despatch. Medina Sidonia was holding a Council of War aboard the *San Martin* at this time, and it is doubtful whether the Spaniards caught sight of their enemy before sunset. If any of them did, they must have been equally disturbed. The line of ships that tacked out athwart their course was far in excess of anything that they had expected to find at this end of the Channel. From behind Rame Head to the east of them, the land seemed to give birth to vessel after vessel—all of them quick on the wind and, although many of them were comparatively small, well-gunned and highly manœuvrable.

As the sun set, the wind brought up the rain. The English, having taken their first cautious glance, lost sight of the Armada as the typical Channel weather drew about their ears. The wind was still fair and astern for the advancing Armada as Howard and Drake, still close-hauled on the starboard tack, drew southward into the open Channel. During the thick night, while the remainder of the English ships were working their way out of Plymouth and then tacking along the coast between the Armada's northern wing and the shore, Howard and Drake continued to haul out to sea. In the small hours they came out on to the port tack, and stood back towards the coast.

At daybreak on the 21st July, the Duke of Medina Sidonia and his Vice-Admiral Juan Martinez de Recalde, who commanded the after-guard, were astonished to see the bulk of the English fleet to weather of them. In his flagship the 1,000-ton *San Martin*, the Admiral of the Ocean Sea now realised that his information about the disposition of the English forces had been totally incorrect. It seemed like magic that the English had managed to get out of Plymouth in the teeth of a foul wind, and round to weather of them unobserved. Howard merely commented laconically: 'The next morning being Sunday, all the English that were come out of Plymouth recovered the wind of the Spaniards two leagues to the Westward of the Eddystone.'

It was a masterly piece of seamanship, especially in view of the fact that it was carried out overnight. But the English commanders were in their home waters and knew the abilities of their ships to a nicety. Credit must also go to Hawkins whose building programme for the Navy had resulted in giving the sea officers ships that could do in two tacks what the more cumbersome Spanish-designed vessels could hardly have done in four or more.

Most Spanish ships of this period, whether warships or merchant-men, were designed for passages between Spain and America. This meant that on their outward passage from Spain they took the southerly trade-wind route while, coming back they had the Atlantic westerlies astern of them. Since they very rarely had any windward work to do, this had resulted in large ships which were great carriers, either of men or cargo, but which still preserved huge aftercastles and forecastles. The

English, while they still retained a fairly large aftercastle, had almost eliminated the forecastle. So much of their work was in the Channel, the North Sea, or the Atlantic approaches to England (all places where the sailor may expect to find head winds more often than not) that an ability to work to windward was essential. A high forecastle, with its immense windage, was clearly useless under these conditions, and all the latest English ships were, 'built very low at the head'. This, quite apart from their finer underwater hulls, gave them a distinct advantage in windward work over Spanish ships, designed largely for running free.

Recalde, the most experienced sea officer in the Armada, urged Medina Sidonia to seize the port of Plymouth. The Duke refused to do so, quoting the King's order that he was not to make any landing on the coast of England until he had reached the North Foreland and effected his junction with the Duke of Parma. Recalde's advice was sound, for if the Spaniards had captured the great west-country seaport they would have been in an excellent position to dominate the Channel mouth, and receive reinforcements from Spain. Both Drake and Howard assumed that this is what the Armada intended to do, and it was with this in mind that they initiated the first action.

As they passed in line ahead behind the seaward wing of the Spaniards, each ship discharged a broadside. Prior to this, following the mediaeval courtesies which were still observed even in these days of the Renaissance, Howard had 'denounced war' by sending his admiral's pinnace to fire her ordnance. In reply, Medina Sidonia had hoisted to his main top the consecrated banner from the Cathedral of Lisbon.

Making no attempt to attack the core of the Armada, the leading English ships crammed on all sail and made their way in line ahead towards the northern, or inshore, tip of the crescent. It is clear that Howard decided on this course of action because he thought the Armada was headed for Plymouth. The sensible course, therefore, was to engage the ships nearest to the coast. Howard in the *Ark Royal* at once attacked the rearmost ship, the *Rata Coronada* of Don Alonzo de Leiva. The great carrack, *Regazona*, fell back to render assistance as Howard's ships poured their broadsides into the port wing of the Armada. As Howard wrote, rather too optimistically, to Walsingham: 'We made some of them to bear room to stop their leaks. Notwithstanding we durst not adventure to put in amongst them, their fleet being so strong. . . .'

In the meantime, the thunder of guns on the seaward wing of the Armada showed that the Vice-Admiral and the ships following him were at work. Drake in the *Revenge*, Hawkins in the *Victory*, and

Frobisher in the *Triumph* were engaging Vice-Admiral Recalde in his large galleon the *San Juan*. It is some proof of the strength of her construction, as well as the determination of her commander and crew, that she withstood the fire of the English ships alone for over an hour. At this point, Medina Sidonia and some of the other larger warships dropped back to come to Recalde's rescue. Drake and the ships in company withdrew out of range, and worked round behind the Armada to join up with Admiral Howard.

In the first inconclusive action, the tactics of the English were clearly to harry their giant enemy without exposing themselves to close action. The Armada was the bull, while the elusive matador was the English fleet.

The wind had now veered and was coming west-north-west off the land. This put the Armada, for a large part of the engagement, to windward of the English and should have given them the advantage. But their sailing orders were such, that they were constrained to advance in convoy up Channel. Drake and Hawkins, on the other hand, were leading lines of independent ships—ships, moreover, which could tack and manœuvre better than their ponderous adversary.

At the close of the day's fighting neither side felt over-confident about the total issue. Even Drake had been surprised at the battering the *San Juan* had been able to sustain without any obvious damage, while Medina Sidonia, Recalde and the other senior officers were alarmed by the agility of the English ships. If Drake had expected to find the Spanish ships under-gunned, as he had done on previous occasions, he was disappointed. As the Armada continued its grand and stately way up Channel both Drake and Howard recognised that Philip II had sent a truly formidable adversary against them. In a despatch to Lord Henry Seymour, Drake wrote: 'The 21st we had them in chase; and so coming up unto them there hath passed some common shot between some of our fleet and some of theirs; and as far as we perceive they are determined to sell their lives with blows. . . .' Seymour was in command of the fleet stationed off the Downs and it was essential that he should know in advance how the battle fared, and what type of enemy was on its way to meet him.

The English could certainly congratulate themselves on one thing—by nightfall, the Armada was past Plymouth. They could forget about any threat to that area. Ahead of them now loomed the craggy shoulders of Bolt Head and Prawle Point, and beyond lay the great expanse of Lyme Bay where, immediately behind Berry Head, there were excellent landing places between Brixham and Torquay. Unaware that Medina Sidonia had no intention of landing anywhere on this part of the coast, the English commanders were naturally afraid that some attempt might be made in the area.

All the time, other ships—most of them small—were coming up to join the English fleet, and in Plymouth every available man was being conscripted to get aboard anything that could float and carry a cannon. From the moment that the Armada had first been reported off the English coast, the beacons had flared from headland to headland, while the militia had everywhere stood to arms in the fortified defence points. It did not take many hours for the news to reach London. The Queen realised at long last that her temporisings could no longer save her country. Everything depended on less than a hundred ships, and on the ability and resolution of a handful of commanders, and a few thousand illiterate sailors.

Like Churchill in a later day and age, the Queen sensed the mood of the people of England. She was to exemplify it in her speech to the troops at Tilbury, only a fortnight later:

'My loving people, we have been persuaded by some that are careful of our safety, to take heed how we commit ourselves to armed multitudes, for fear of treachery. But I assure you, I do not desire to live to distrust my faithful and loving people. Let tyrants fear. I have always so behaved myself that, under God, I have placed my chiefest strength and safeguard in the loyal hearts and good will of my subjects. And therefore I am come amongst you at this time, not as for my recreation or sport, but being resolved in the midst and heat of the battle, to live or die amongst you all; to lay down for my God, and for my kingdom and for my people, my honour and my blood even in the dust. I know I have the body of a weak and feeble woman, but I have the heart of a King, and of a King of England too, and think foul scorn that Parma or Spain, or any prince of Europe, should dare to invade the borders of my realms: to which, rather than any dishonour shall grow by me, I myself will take up arms. I myself will be your general, judge, and rewarder of every one of your virtues in the field. . . .'

No other ruler in the world at that time could have, or would have, gone among their people with such words. In her burned the same spirit that animated Drake and the other men at sea. This spirit, it must be confessed, stemmed to some degree from the English dislike of all foreigners, whether they came peaceably to trade or—as now—in armed vessels bent on conquest. As the Florentine historian, Petruccio Ubaldini wrote in his history of the Armada campaign: 'It is easier to find flocks of white crows than to find one Englishman (no matter what his religious beliefs) who loves a foreigner.'

It was late in the afternoon of the 21st, while the Spaniards were closing their ranks and taking up their station which, willy-nilly, had been somewhat disorganised by the harrying tactics of the two English attacks, that the first disaster occurred to the fleet. The *San Salvador*, on the starboard quarter of the Armada—a large galleon carrying the Paymaster-General—suddenly suffered an explosion which blew away a large part of her poop. This was most likely due to an accident, for in wooden ships with large quantities of gunpowder aboard, and little understanding of the stringent regulations necessary for fire-precaution, such accidents were not uncommon. (Rumour later had it that a dissident Englishman or Dutchman in the crew had deliberately sabotaged the ship). Medina Sidonia immediately turned back to help the *San Salvador*, signalling to the Armada by gunfire to reduce speed while the rescue operation was under way. Obediently the ships furled their topsails, the slaves in the galleasses lay to their oars, and the whole great fleet practically came to a standstill. The badly damaged ship was finally taken in tow and brought into the centre of the Armada.

The incident was typical of the problems that beset the unfortunate Duke in attempting to bring his vast fleet in war-order up the Channel towards the Narrow Seas. A collision, for instance, which occurred between two other ships necessitated a further delay. Medina Sidonia had been given an impossible task, one which he laboured to bring to a successful conclusion. But the Spaniards were attempting something for which there was no precedent in naval warfare, while the English, for their part, were totally unprepared for tackling a fleet of this size. The commanders on both sides were grappling with problems that were quite beyond them. The English, however, had the advantage of being in home waters, while their almost total lack of hard-and-fast sailing orders gave them a freedom of movement which was greatly to their advantage.

The wind began to get up as the night fell. Howard, concerned that the enemy was bent on making a landing in Torbay, put his greatest seaman in the van, while he followed in the *Ark Royal*, with the rest of the fleet behind him. Drake in the *Revenge* led the English up Channel hard on the heels of the Armada. He kept a stern light burning for Howard to follow. The sky was overcast, and the wind was still off the land on their port quarter, as they kept up their pursuit. A night action was unthinkable in those days, and the only tactical idea that can have been considered at all by Howard and Drake was to stay as close to the enemy as possible. They would engage them as soon as they could in daylight. Above all, they must prevent them from sailing into any port or anchorage.

It was during this night that Drake acted in a way which shows that his opportunist methods, so successful in the past, were already outmoded in this new age of fleet engagements. Seeing the outline of hulls and sails to seaward of him—there was a quarter-moon scudding through the overcast—he jumped to the conclusion that the Spaniards were attempting exactly the same stratagem that he and Howard had used the night before. He assumed that they were enemy men-of-war, bent on getting to windward of the English—and thus having the weather-gauge of them at daybreak. If this had indeed been the case, the English fleet would have found themselves crushed between the upper and lower millstones, with the bulk of the Armada ahead of them and, presumably, the finest fighting ships in their rear.

Acting on his suspicions, Drake, extinguished his stern light, hauled out to starboard and made sail after the mysterious ships. They turned out to be a group of harmless German merchantmen who had stumbled by sheer accident into the theatre of war. Drake's action might well have proved disastrous for his admiral and indeed for the whole fleet. Howard, informed that the stern light of the *Revenge* could no longer be seen, thought that she had possibly outpaced the *Ark Royal*. This was something that he must have been loath to believe, for—like all captains—he considered his own ship the fastest afloat. He pressed on with all the canvas he could, while the ships immediately astern of him did their best to keep up with him.

When dawn broke, the Lord Admiral of England found himself almost alone amongst the rearguard of the Spanish fleet. There were only two other ships of his own in close company, and the rest were straggling a long way astern. He was just off the blunt brow of Berry Head, and opening up before him was the long curve of Tor Bay. Howard was in a desperate position, for he assumed that the enemy might well have decided to make this their invasion point. At the same time, he was equally aware that some of the galleons or galleasses might decide to put back and snap up the *Ark Royal* and her attendants, before proceeding leisurely on their way. Even more disturbing, there was no sign of his Vice-Admiral in the *Revenge*.

Drake, meanwhile, in company with a private ship out of Plymouth and two small pinnaces, had stood back into the Channel—only to discover that the ships to seaward of him were harmless. Hastening up during the forenoon to rejoin the fleet (which he should by all right have been leading) he had a very pleasant surprise. Lolling awkwardly on the ocean, her foremast gone, lay *Nuestra Señora del Rosario*. This was the ship that had been involved in a collision on the previous evening, broken her bowsprit, and subsequently dropped astern of the main body.

The story of what happened next is best told by John Speed in his *History of Great Britain* (1611): 'Sir Francis Drake, espying this lagging galleon, sent forth a pinnace to command them to yield, otherwise his bullets should force them without further favour; but Valdez [Pedro de Valdez in command of the Andalucian squadron] to seem valorous, answered that they were four hundred and fifty strong; that he himself was Don Pedro, and stood on his honour, and thereupon propounded certain conditions. But the Knight [Drake] sent his reply, that he had no leisure to parley; if he would yield, then do it; if not, he should well prove that Drake was no dastard; whereupon Pedro, hearing that it was the fiery Drake (ever terrible to the Spaniards) who had him in chase, came on board Sir Francis's ship. . . . He protested that he and all his were resolved to die in defence, had they not fallen under his power, whose valour and felicity was so great that Mars and Neptune seemed to attend him in his attempts, and whose generous mind towards the vanquished had often been experienced, even of his greatest foes. Sir Francis, requiting his Spanish compliments with honourable English courtesies, placed him at his own table, and lodged him in his own cabin. The residue of that company [the officers etc. of the *Rosario*] were sent to Plymouth, where they remained eighteen months until their ransoms were paid; but Sir Francis and his soldiers had well paid themselves with the spoil of the ship, wherein were fifty-five thousand ducats in gold, which they shared merrily among them.'

Drake rejoined the fleet in the afternoon, and at once sent a despatch over to Howard explaining his actions. The Lord Admiral preserved his usual tact and courtesy. (He never at any time seems to have complained about his Vice-Admiral's behaviour.) Drake's conduct in turning aside only seems inexcusable because he never dropped back to tell his admiral what he was about to do, and why. Subsequent documentary evidence has proved that there were indeed German merchantmen in the Channel, and in that part of it, during the night concerned, so Drake's story is corroborated by fact.

Napoleon always used to require of his generals that, above all, they should be 'lucky' and this magic quality was something that Drake certainly possessed. Frobisher—who disliked Drake intensely—always maintained that he had deliberately slid off into the night to capture a fat prize, which he subsequently refused to share with the other commanders. This, one is led to suspect, was what really annoyed Frobisher. The only thing one can say about the incident four centuries later, is that Drake can certainly have had no idea that the *Rosario* was an important prize. One of the German merchant captains, Hans Buttber, confirmed when he got back to Hamburg that his ship had indeed been boarded by the English, and that he had himself been present when Drake captured the *Rosario*.

Martin Frobisher was a Yorkshireman, one of the greatest seamen of his time, and had been Vice-Admiral to Drake in the Indies expedition of 1585. A confirmed believer in the North-West Passage, Frobisher was in some respects a greater explorer (in the intentional sense) than Drake. He never had the latter's luck and good fortune. As a blunt Yorkshireman, in any case, he probably distrusted a wily 'soft-speaker' from the West Country.

Later that day the *San Salvador*, which had been slowly sinking ever since the explosion in her after-powder store, was abandoned and allowed to drift astern of the fleet. She was boarded by Lord Howard in person, but he did not stay long, for the stench of burnt corpses was more than he could stomach. She was then taken in tow by the same Captain Fleming who had first reported the Armada, and brought successfully into Weymouth. The news quickly spread throughout all the small towns and fishing ports along the coast that two great ships had already been captured. This was good for the morale of the lands-men, but only the men in the fleet knew that neither of these successes could be ascribed to English action.

In the late afternoon the wind fell away, and soon an oily calm spread over the Channel. The distance from Berry Head to the next main point on the coast, Portland Bill, is under 50 miles, and at nightfall on the 22nd July, the Armada was lying completely becalmed in the vicinity of the Bill. On the morning of Tuesday 23rd, a wind came up with the dawn. It was from the East, and gave the Spaniards the weather-gauge. Even so it can have been little to their liking, for Medina Sidonia's orders still constrained him to press on to the Narrows. Up to date he had lost two ships, but the Armada had suffered very little real damage. So far, the English had done no more than snap at his flanks and his course up Channel, slow though it was, had been unimpeded.

On this day, which was marked by many independent actions—all of them 'managed with confusion enough'—one basic pattern seems to emerge. Howard, worried perhaps that the enemy would try to weather Portland Bill and effect a landing in Weymouth, was deter-mined to drive the inshore wing of the Armada away from the land. The Spaniards were equally determined not to be outflanked, and Medina Sidonia brought down his galleons to intercept the English line as it stood in towards the Bill. Howard tacked, when very close inshore, and led his ships back in a south-west direction to try and weather the Armada's seaward wing. The Spanish rearguard at once

fell back towards the English line, and a running battle developed.
'The great guns,' wrote Camden, 'rattled like so many peals of thunder;
but the shot from the high-built Spanish ships flew for the most part
over the heads of the English without doing any execution, owing to
their high forecastles, and their inability to depress their guns. One
Mr. Cook was the only English man who died bravely in the midst of
his enemies, commanding his own ship. The reason was, that the
English ships were moved and managed with such agility, giving their
broadsides to the larger and more unwieldly of the enemy, and shearing
off again just as they pleased, while the Spanish heavy ships lay as so
many butts for the English to fire at.'

Again and again the English tried to weather the seaward wing of
the Armada, but the Spaniards always fell back to prevent them, and
tried at the same time to force their enemies into boarding-actions.
Drake and Howard were not to be tempted. They knew well enough
that at close quarters the superiority of the Spanish numbers, and the
greater weight of their small arms fire would have proved fatal. While
this main struggle was developing to seaward, Martin Frobisher in the
Triumph, in company with five other ships, had been cut off inshore.
Separated from the main body of the fleet, he was hotly engaged by the
strong Spanish wing. Four galleasses, as he later reported, 'took
courage and bare room with them and assaulted them sharply'.

As the day wore on, the wind had veered with the sun and was now
blowing gently from the south. Howard now disengaged from his
action on the southern wing of the Armada, and led a line of 16 ships to
rescue Frobisher. Vice-Admiral Recalde's flagship *San Juan* had been so
badly damaged during this engagement that she had been forced to
withdraw, and it was now the turn of the Duke himself in the great
San Martin. Medina Sidonia advanced with resolution to meet Howard
in the *Ark Royal* and his line of English ships, striking his topsails as an
invitation to the enemy, to come aboard and 'fight like gentlemen'.
Howard and the others disregarded this old-world gesture of courtesy,
and raked the *San Martin* with their broadsides. For a whole hour
Medina Sidonia endured the concentrated fire of the English, at the
end of which his great galleon was badly mauled. She was pierced
through and through with round-shot, her sails and rigging were in
tatters, and even the Holy Standard at her masthead was ripped in two.
As other Spanish galleons drew back to give assistance to their admiral,
Howard passed on to effect Frobisher's rescue.

At the end of the Battle of Portland Bill—as the English drew off,
and the great Armada re-formed its ranks—both sides had learned a
hard lesson. The English, who had left Plymouth with about 30 rounds

per gun and an equivalent amount of powder on board, found themselves almost completely out of ammunition. Spanish ships like the *San Martin* were so massively-built that, although hit time and time again, they refused to sink. Fast pinnaces were immediately despatched to all ports along the nearby coast to get fresh supplies. Both cannon shot and powder proved almost equally hard to come by, and after this day's action it is noticeable that the English fleet conserved their fire as much as possible. In some of the ships they were even reduced to firing improvised shot such as lengths of iron chain.

The Spaniards, for their part, had learned that this enemy had no intention of fighting a battle at sea in a traditional way by laying their ships alongside, and fighting it out hand-to-hand. They had been unable to cope with the manoeuvrability of an enemy who, on every point of the wind, could out-sail them, as well as get away before they could be brought to action at close quarters. Drake, for instance, and his ships in company—after he had so badly damaged Recalde's flagship as to compel her to withdraw from the battle—had had no difficulty in sliding off before the heavy ships which came to Recalde's rescue could get anywhere near them. Drake had then dashed down and engaged Medina Sidonia in the *San Martin*, thus permitting Howard's ships to draw off and rescue Frobisher.

Medina Sidonia had another cause for worry. Like the English, he realised that he could not afford such an immense expenditure of ammunition. The Armada had left Spain with approximately 50 rounds per gun, which had been considered more than adequate. (Santa Cruz in the earlier planning stages had calculated that 30 would be enough.) But whereas the English were able to get fresh ammunition, Medina Sidonia was on a hostile coast and knew that he had no chance of further supplies until he made contact with the Duke of Parma in the Netherlands. Even then it was problematical whether he would get what he wanted.

For the next 36 hours the Armada continued a slow and inexorable progress up Channel, for the English were busy obtaining what ammunition and supplies they could from the shore. At dawn on the 25th July, the two fleets were again becalmed—this time off the Isle of Wight, some 40 miles to the east of the scene of their last engagement. There was another confused battle in the course of this day, centring around a large Spanish galleon, the *Gran Grifon*, which had drifted astern of the main body of the fleet. Out of the smoke, one catches a glimpse of Drake in the *Revenge* leading an attack on the seaward wing of the Armada, while Howard and Hawkins were engaging the *Gran Grifon* and the other ships that dropped back to her rescue.

A breeze sprang up late in the day, which enabled Frobisher's inshore squadron to get into action. Drake made use of the wind to press home his attack on the seaward flank. Recalde's flagship, which had previously been the heart of the defence on this tip of the crescent, was no longer there, and the post of honour was held by a Portuguese galleon, the *San Mateo*. She fought valiantly and well, but was incapable of standing up against the English fire and retired, her place being taken by the *Florencia*, the great galleon which belonged to the Duke of Tuscany. The seaward end of the Armada began to crumple under the weight of Drake's attack, with the result that ship after ship began to edge over towards the land, as they strove to maintain their station-keeping. Some commentators have believed that all this action was totally haphazard. It is almost certain that Drake was deliberately trying to drive the Armada on to one of the major hazards of this awkward coast.

Ten miles east of the Isle of Wight lie the formidable Owers—a grim bank of shoal water, toothed here and there by rocks, and still fatal to any shipping that falls among them. If the gradual movement of the whole fleet could have been kept going in this direction—pressurised, as it were, by the weight of Drake's attack on the seaward wing—there would have been little left of Medina Sidonia's fleet. Drake, who had known all this area as a boy in a small coaster, knew only too well the dangers of the Owers. It can hardly have been pure chance that he launched his attack just at a moment when the enemy fleet might have been forced to collapse on to a deadly hazard. The wind, however, veered to the south-west, coming over the Armada's starboard quarter. Medina Sidonia—whose pilot had already reported the shoaling water to port of the fleet—was just given time to extricate his ships. A hasty signal was made by gunfire, and the Armada went over to the port tack, and drew offshore in a south-easterly direction.

In the course of the action, one of the Spanish galleons had been so badly damaged that she was forced to detach from the Armada and make over to the friendly coast of France. The English, because they had suffered some casualties during the day, were in no position to press home their attack. Once more they were almost out of powder and shot. Medina Sidonia, for his part, as he led his fleet away from the treacherous Owers, was in no happier a mood, for his supply of cannon balls was nearly exhausted. An immediate despatch was sent to the Duke of Parma, begging him for ammunition, as well as asking him to send 40 small ships to join the Armada. Parma could do nothing. The fact was that the handy, shallow-draught ships of Justin of Nassau, Admiral of Zeeland, dominated the whole of the Dutch coast. Despite

Parma's previous confidence that he could take a fleet of invasion
barges across the Narrow Seas without even having to call on the
Spanish fleet, not a single one of his ships could move on the coastline.
English and Dutch troops still held Walcheren and Flushing, thus
denying the use of either of these ports to the Spaniards. As the
Admiral phrased it: 'the heaviness of our ships, compared with the
lightness of theirs, rendered it impossible in any manner to bring them
to close action. . . .'

'It was,' Hawkins wrote, 'a hot fray, wherein some store of powder
was spent, and after all, little done.' The English felt that they could
claim it as a victory. On the following day, as the two fleets lay becalmed yet again, Admiral Howard knighted Frobisher and several
others on the deck of his flagship. All the same, both he and Drake must
have realised that they had little cause for self-congratulation. The
Invincible Armada plodded gently on its way, and all the English
attacks had done little more than inflict a few flesh wounds.

The total impossibility of the orders which he had been given by his
master, far away in the Escorial, must by now have begun to dawn on
the unfortunate Duke of Medina Sidonia. His only thought seems to
have been to effect his junction with the Duke of Parma as soon as
possible, as well as to replenish his stores and amunition. After the
engagement off the Owers, the Armada made use of the southerly
winds and steered across the Strait of Dover in the direction of Calais.
Howard and Drake, who until now had been mainly concerned that
the enemy intended to capture a port on the Channel coast, must have
been relieved to see them heading eastward for France.

It was on the afternoon of the 27th July, that Medina Sidonia brought
his great fleet to anchor in the roads off Calais. As Dr. J. A. Williamson
wrote: 'The vision of "the Cape of Margate" had vanished into thin
air, for to go thither would mean for ever getting out of touch with
Parma. The unlucky Medina Sidonia could only send word by land to
Parma and ask him what he meant to do, to which the answer could
only be, nothing. . . .' Drake, who had probably conjectured that the
enemy were only swinging across the Channel before coming back
on the starboard tack to head for Dover, the Downs, or the North
Foreland, was surprised when the Armada dropped anchor. In the
casual independence of their command, he and Howard can hardly
have realised how a bureaucratic European army or fleet was tied
hand-and-foot by its written orders.

The English came to anchor about a mile to windward of the Spanish
fleet, and began to consider what they should do next. While they
looked and pondered, the Spaniards were also in council. Medina

Sidonia was growing hourly more uneasy. Astern of him he could see
the English wolves on his flanks, behind him was the narrow-womb-
neck of the Channel, and ahead lay the desolate and uninviting North
Sea—with not a single friendly anchorage in sight. Howard meanwhile
had sent an urgent despatch to Dover for fireships and Henry Seymour,
who had been guarding the Downs, now crossed the Narrow Seas to
join the fleet. Unwilling to wait for the arrival of the hulks from Dover,
Drake proposed one of his own vessels, the *Thomas*, as a fireship. His
energy and enthusiasm prompted others to sacrifice their vessels, and
soon he had raised a further seven ships out of the fleet.

Loaded with pitch, gunpowder, resin, and anything else inflammable,
and with all their guns fully-primed, fireships were the terror of any
fleet caught in harbour. 'Hell-burners' they were called, and the Duke
of Medina Sidonia had good reason to fear that now he was on a lee-
shore, with the English anchored to windward of him, the heretics
would certainly use this weapon. (Fireships were considered as unethical
as was the use of gas in the First World War.) The whole thing was as
'ungentlemanly' as had been the English refusal to come alongside and
fight. But what else could you expect of a man like Drake, who was
not a gentleman in any case? At midnight on the 28th July, at the
moment when the flood-tide was making into Calais, the English sent
down their fireships on the crowded ranks of the Armada.

So it was that in the dark night, as they lay uneasily at anchor, the
Spaniards suddenly saw to windward of them the sinister bright
shapes of the 'Hell-burners', driving in towards them. With a flood-
tide behind, and the wind easy in their sails, the flames began to lick
up the rigging, the canvas to catch alight, and the loaded guns to
explode, as the fireships drove in among the anchored bulk of the
Armada. Some ships began to cut their cables, others to get up anchor,
while the confused herd of smaller vessels cowered together like cattle
in a thunder storm. Not a single Spanish ship, as far as the records show,
was sunk by the fireships, but their effect was disastrous. A complete
panic ensued, and the morale of captains, soldiers and sailors alike was
destroyed. From the moment that they swept down on the tide, the
formidable order of the Armada was broken. Nothing that the
English had managed to do in their predatory prowling off the flanks
of the fleet on its passage up Channel, had managed to break the
magnificent order of the Spaniards. The 'Hell-burners' did it.

From this moment on, the Armada was a dying animal. It had
entered the Channel like a bull coming into the arena—self-confident,
tossing its horns, and eyeing the matador with disdain. It had been
harassed, picadors had lanced its shoulders, and banderilleros had

planted their darts in its humped muscles. Now the bull had found its *querencia*—a corner of the ring where it felt secure—only to be driven out of it by 'firecrackers'.

Medina Sidonia, almost alone, seems to have kept his head. His flagship made a short tack out to sea, and then dropped anchor. Had the rest of the fleet followed his example, they would have come to little or no harm. But too many horrific legends had been spread about fire-ships, and for too many of the Spanish captains the knowledge that the legendary 'Dragon' was to windward of them had resulted in a total loss of self-confidence. The great galleas *San Lorenzo* made for the shore-line, and ran aground. Most of the other ships stood out to sea independently, and all order was lost. The Armada had survived so far largely because of its bulk, and this had been held together only by iron discipline.

When the dawn came, the English moved in to the attack. Rein-forced by Seymour's fleet from the Downs, they numbered about 150 sail, and they were driving in on an enemy who had lost his greatest asset—his close-order formation. The wind was still in the south-west. There was little the Spaniards could do but take it over their sterns, and run before it into the unwelcoming North Sea. Drake, Howard, Hawkins and Frobisher, having driven the wounded animal out of its *querencia*, made ready for the kill.

CHAPTER EIGHTEEN

The Winds of God

THE running battle up Channel had been almost as desultory as the Armada's progress had been slow. Sighted off the Scillies on the 19th, the first action had occurred west of Plymouth on the 21st. It had taken seven days for the two fleets to cover the 240 miles between Plymouth and Calais, and it was now Monday the 29th. The last engagement was about to take place.

Weighing anchor, the Duke of Medina Sidonia stood out to sea, gathering round him his Vice-Admiral Recalde in the *San Juan*, and three other galleons. It was his duty as admiral, to provide a rallying point for his scattered fleet, alone if need be. Meanwhile his pinnaces were despatched to round up the stragglers, and order them back to take up their station and reform. This was the moment when the whole English fleet should have made a concerted attack on the dispersed enemy. But unfortunately their fluidity of command, and their habit of independence—so often the English strength—lost them this one great opportunity. Howard drew off with his squadron, and concentrated on the great galleass, *San Lorenzo*, which had drifted rudderless towards the shore where her slaves were striving desperately to get her clear under oars. Three other squadrons were despatched to deal with whatever Spanish galleons they might find to the north-east beyond Calais, while Drake chose to head the attack on Medina Sidonia.

The wind was south-south-west, driving the dispersed Spanish fleet up the coast towards the grim banks and shoals off Gravelines. Already the ships furthest away were luffing up desperately to try and clear the off-shore dangers. This was the one moment in the whole Armada Campaign when the English, with their more manœuvrable ships, and in waters that were completely familiar to them, should have been able to destroy the enemy. Howard's inability to resist the lure of the *San Lorenzo* is regrettable, and it is the only time that he seems to have acted without a proper realisation of what his duties should have been. When the *San Lorenzo* finally grounded, Howard and the English galleons with him—compelled to lay off because of the shoal water—

despatched their ships's crews in boats to take her by storm. She yielded only after her commander, Don Hugo de Moncada, had been shot dead and the Great Galleon was then looted by the English sailors.

Meantime, Drake's *Revenge* had closed the Spanish flagship, *San Martin*. Both ships held their fire until the last moment, the English determined to make their shots tell, and the Spaniards conserving what little ammunition they had left. Medina Sidonia took the wind on his beam and presented his full broadside to the *Revenge*, who closed to within about 100 yards before opening fire with her bowchasers. A second later the *Revenge*'s helm was put down, and she gave the great Spanish vessel her full broadside as she rolled past—receiving in return an immense weight of fire, so that she was 'pierced through by cannon balls of all sizes'. Thomas Fenner in the *Nonpareil* followed the example of the Vice-Admiral, as did the rest of Drake's squadron. It was proof of the sturdiness of Spanish ship construction that the *San Martin* did not suffer any major damage from the weight of this attack, although the casualties among her men were very heavy.

Drake drew away to the north-east, with his squadron in line astern of him, and engaged the other ships near the *San Martin* as he passed. At about this point Martin Frobisher came up in the *Triumph* and, instead of following on after Drake once he had fired his broadside, elected to stay and fight a ship-to-ship battle with Medina Sidonia in the hard-hit *San Martin*. The *Triumph* was as big as the flagship of Spain, and Frobisher would hardly have been human if he had resisted the impulse to try and defeat the Admiral of the Ocean Sea. Frobisher seems to have assumed that Drake and his ships in company were unwilling to stay and engage because the enemy was so dangerous. As he later remarked: 'He [Drake] came bragging up at the first indeed, and gave them his prow and his broadside; and then kept his luff, and was glad that he was gone again like a cowardly knave or traitor—I rest doubtful, but the one I will swear.'

Drake, with a better seaman's instinct than the blunt Yorkshireman, had seen that the wind was beginning to veer into the north-west, and that the galleons trying to reform further north were having a hard time getting clear of the coast. If the wind did get into the north-west and stay there, now was the moment to attack that straggling line, and drive them to destruction on the shoals.

It was not to be. Hawkins in the *Victory* came up to join Frobisher around the embattled Spanish admiral, who was soon ringed by English ships. The fact that so much of the fleet had hauled off to join in this one action meant that Drake was unable to accomplish what was clearly in his mind. Gradually the bulk of the Armada's fighting ships were able to claw back towards the *San Martin* to support their admiral —instead of being engaged severally, which would almost certainly have resulted in them never being able to reform. While the bulk of the storeships and light craft were scattered along the Flemish coast, the main weight of his fighting ships slowly gathered around Medina Sidonia. Once more that hard crescent began to take shape. As Winter's account describes it: 'They went into the proportion of a half moon, their Admiral and Vice Admiral in the midst and the greatest numbers of them; and there went on each side, in the wings, their galleasses, galleons of Portugal and other good ships, in the whole to the number of sixteen in a wing, which did seem to be their principal shipping.' Vice-Admiral Recalde was there along with Leiva, and something like 50 ships—the hard core of the Armada—managed to get back into formation. It was a remarkable feat of seamanship, and a triumph of discipline. It could have been prevented if the other English commanders had followed Drake's lead.

In the confused action that followed—which began shortly after dawn and carried on to four o'clock that afternoon—the commanders of the other Spanish ships showed the same resilience as their admiral. They can have had no doubt by now that the object of their whole mission was lost; that no landing would be made on the English coast; and that no help could be expected from the Duke of Parma. Nevertheless, confronted by the full weight of the English battle fleet (most of whom had had an opportunity to reammunition), the Spaniards refused to accept defeat.

From the moment that Howard and his ships in company came up and joined the main battle, the endurance of the enemy began to crack up. They had suffered immense casualties, hulls were leaking, and many of the ships were broken-winged from damage to rigging and sails. The wind was still in the north-west and, as evening drew on, it began to look as if what Drake had hoped for during the forenoon would actually happen. Throughout the day, the whole battle had been drifting eastwards, and the banks off the Flemish coast were boiling under the Armada's lee. Suddenly a hard squall hit both fleets. In the drenching rain, tattered fringes of nimbus cloud and blown spume, the English lost contact with the enemy. They were fully occupied in handling their own ships.

When the visibility cleared, Howard and Drake saw that the Spanish Armada were running up the coast beyond Dunkirk. Almost miraculously they were still in the tight formation. With night coming down, the English held off, suffering as usual from shortage of ammunition, but moderately confident that if the wind stayed in the same quarter

nothing but disaster could befall the 'Invincible Armada'. Yet Howard
was still under no illusions about the potential threat from this great
fleet. In a despatch written that night to Walsingham, begging for more
ammunition, he described the day's events: 'We have chased them in
fight until this evening late and distressed them much; but their fleet
consisteth of mighty ships and great strength.' He went on: 'Their
force is wonderful great and strong; and yet we pluck their feathers
little by little.'

Although it can hardly ever have been conceived as a deliberate
policy, this 'plucking of feathers little by little' had been more damaging to the Armada than if the English had attempted a major, and
conventional, sea-battle of the type for which the Spaniards had been
prepared. In the day's action off Gravelines one galleon had been sunk
by gunfire. Two went ashore that night on the banks near Ostend,
where they were seized by the shallow-draught vessels of the Dutch.

At the conclusion of the Armada campaign, some of the English
complained how little help they had received from their allies in
the Netherlands. Howard wrote: 'There is not a Hollander or Zee-
lander at sea.' The fact was that Medina Sidonia had never received
the light vessels he had asked for from the Duke of Parma, nor indeed
any assistance from that quarter whatsoever. This was because the
Dutch had been so busy strangling the Spanish shipping off their coast
that none of it could effectively get to sea. Any English indignation felt
in this quarter was due to ignorance of what was happening. It can be
compared to the resentment felt by sailors in the Royal Navy against
the Royal Air Force during the withdrawal from Dunkirk in the
Second World War. The Air Force they maintained, had not been in
action over the Channel while they themselves were being heavily
attacked by the Luftwaffe. Their situation was very like that of the
English fleet in the battle of Gravelines. The reason that the English
fleet, on both occasions, did not have to endure worse, was that large
sections of the enemy were being 'tied down' on the continent.

Throughout a night of driving rain while the wind stayed in the same
quarter, the English kept on the heels of the Armada, as it was borne
relentlessly towards the Zeeland shoals. Because of their windage and
hull shapes, the Spanish ships made more leeway than their enemies and,
when dawn came, the whole Armada was in shoal water off those
treacherous sands. Aboard the great *San Martin*—as the leadsman stood
in the chains and called out the shallowing fathoms beneath her keel—
there was little doubt that they were certain to strike and, along with
them, the rest of the large ships who were still in company. Most of the
fleet was well to leeward of the *San Martin*, but Medina Sidonia and

his sailing master had done better than them by clawing to windward. This meant that, at first light, she was—as on the previous day—the nearest ship to the enemy-pack who hung off her flanks.

It was during the grey hours after dawn, when disaster seemed inevitable to the whole Armada, that the prayers of all the faithful appeared to have been answered. As the light came back into the sky, spreading over those toppled, bitter seas, the wind suddenly backed. The sun rose, and the wind went round to the south-west. According to the Spanish account: 'It pleased God to change the wind and the Armada was enabled to set course to the north.' Drake commented about this switch of wind and weather that the reason for it was 'best known to God'. In terms of weather the Armada had been lucky throughout; had held a fair south-westerly most of the way up Channel; and had been spared at the last by this sudden shift of wind.

It was the end of their luck. The English, who watched them bitterly as they headed into the North Sea, hardly realised at the time that the action was over—and that Philip II's attempt on England had failed. Still frantically sending despatches back begging for powder and shot, they kept after Medina Sidonia, whose fleet still maintained at least a semblance of its formidable order. But, once they had been driven clear of the Channel, the Spanish failure was assured.

Although few of the English realised it at the time, they had gained a great victory. They felt that they had only prevented the Armada from landing on the southern coast of England (which was not true). But, by the fireships at Calais and the action off Gravelines, they had ensured that the whole of the Spanish plan of campaign was ruined. Drake wrote cheerfully, '. . . There was never anything please me better than the seeing the enemy flying with a southerly wind to the north-wards. . . . With the Grace of God, if we live, I doubt not but ere it be long, so to handle the matter with the Duke of Sidonia as he shall wish himself at St. Mary Port among his orange trees.'

The wind stayed in the south-west. While ships were detached from the English fleet to re-water, provision, and collect further ammunition, the bulk of the fleet kept hard after the Spaniards. They could not be sure that there was not some alternative plan in Medina Sidonia's mind: perhaps to land in the Firth of Forth and then, with the assistance of the Scots, invade England from the north. If such had been the Spanish plan from the beginning, it might, given propitious weather, have been successful. Had Medina Sidonia been able to draw off the bulk of the English fleet to Scotland, while the Duke of Parma crossed the Narrow Seas to land near the Thames mouth, a thoroughly efficient pincer movement might have been effected. But there was no such intention in the Duke's mind. All he hoped for was to bring back to Spain as much as he could salvage from the wreck of the Enterprise of England.

Once it was clear that the Firth of Forth was not the Spanish objective, but that they were clearly headed for the very North of Scotland, Drake and Howard discontinued the action. They were short of food, water, and—as always—ammunition. There seemed no point in pursuing what was obviously a beaten enemy. Drake sent two fast light ships to keep the remnants of the Armada in sight, instructing them to report back at once if there was any sign that the Spaniards were attempting a landing anywhere.

It was on the 2nd August that, as the Spanish *Narrative* records: '[The English fleet] turned towards the coast of England, and we lost sight of them.' As Drake and Howard ran southward towards the North Foreland, to collect all the stores they so badly needed, the wind steadily increased. Their ships were scattered from one port to another, southward from Norfolk to the Downs. Yet, even after all the hard fighting, they had suffered only slight damage. In the whole of the campaign the English had not lost a single ship, and only about 100 men.

'God breathed and they were scattered'—so runs the legend on one of the Armada medals. For two weeks and more, the remnant of the Spanish fleet split up into small groups, or single ships sailing alone, ran round the treacherous north coast of Scotland—past the roaring waters off Cape Wrath, and down the west coast of Ireland. Some sank from battle damage, others were wrecked on those iron-bound shores, and others just 'disappeared' in the wild nights. The coast of Ireland claimed more victims than anywhere else—a bitter irony, for this was the country that the Spaniards had so long preserved as a thorn in the flesh of England.

The story that the Latin-type features to be found in parts of the Irish west coast are a legacy from shipwrecked Spaniards, is almost certainly as incorrect as the one that the Irish tribesmen massacred the Spaniards when they crawled ashore from their wrecked ships. All the evidence goes to show that almost all the shipwrecked Spaniards were carefully returned to Spain. The physical appearance of so many Irish can hardly be ascribed to the activities of a few 'Don Juans' who stayed behind, but to Celtic-Iberian blood. No one has suggested that shipwrecked Spanish sailors were active in Wales, and yet one finds there similar types of features and physical characteristics.

A Portuguese prisoner, when being interrogated, said that 'It is commonly said among the soldiers, that if they once can get home, they will never again meddle with the English.' Medina Sidonia and his fellow officers did, in fact, manage to get nearly half the Armada back to Spain. But the morale of the Spanish soldiers and sailors was shattered. They had seen the hostile Channel: they had gazed on the white headlands of the heretic island; and they had felt the power of that Lutheran Navy which never called itself 'Invincible'. The English, for their part, felt that they had missed a great victory, but were soberly relieved at the outcome.

The defeat of the Spanish Armada, although no one really understood it at the time, was one of the decisive battles of the world. It helped to ensure that the Counter-Reformation did not triumph in Europe. From 1588 onwards, the ebb-tide had set in. Hawkins who had been responsible for the ships, Howard who had ably commanded the fleet (with the one exception of Gravelines) and Drake who had taught Englishmen how to fight at sea had achieved a signal victory. They did not realise it.

While Drake was writing to Walsingham that, 'We are ready to set sail to prevent the Duke of Parma,' Howard was soberly assessing the narrowness of England's escape. 'I do warrant you,' he wrote, 'all the world never saw such a force as theirs was.'

CHAPTER NINETEEN

Failure of an Expedition

THE astrologers had been right when they had predicted that the year 1588 would be momentous. It was true that no empires collapsed, but that vast empire of the soul, the Roman Catholic Faith, had suffered a damaging blow. After the survivors from the Armada had limped back into the ports of Spain and Portugal to be paid off, the crusading spirit deserted the Spanish people. Not only Philip II, but almost all his officers and men, had felt confident that God would bless their cause. Yet it was an act of God more than anything else that had defeated them. The Devil seemed to walk flagrantly on the earth, and he was incarnate in the figure of Sir Francis Drake.

As ever on these occasions, when a large military force had been kept aboard ships for a length of time, disease and pestilence spread like couch-grass among the despondent survivors of the great fleet. The same was equally true in England, where thousands of sailors and soldiers (rapidly paid off from their vessels) died in the streets of London and in the east coast ports, as well as in Plymouth. Victory though it had been, such service was of little or no value to working-men in those days, whose official pay was little more than a pittance. Only the officers and men aboard Drake's flagship, the *Revenge*, could congratulate themselves on the outcome, for they were the only ones to have captured a considerable prize.

Drake was now at the peak of his achievement, and his vainglorious manner did not endear him to conservative circles. Frobisher even went so far as to say that he was prepared to fight Drake, and that he was determined to have 'the best blood in his belly'. Whatever effect his bearing may have had upon his equals and his superiors, Drake, as ever, did not forget the poor seamen who had fought the ships in the hour of England's distress. It was now that, in collaboration with Hawkins, he founded the famous 'Chatham Chest', a fund designed for the relief of poor seamen. In those days, any conception that common working-men like sailors should be looked after (once their usefulness was at an end) was almost inconceivable. It was to Drake's great credit that he was largely responsible for the first of such welfare trusts ever to be started in England—thus fathering innumerable other organisations which flourish to the present day.

Philip II did not join in the general abuse of his unfortunate admiral, Medina Sidonia, but accepted the failure of the Armada as the Will of God. He never indulged in any recriminations against the Duke. To the people of Spain, however, Medina Sidonia became the whipping boy, and even in his retirement—surrounded by those orange groves which Drake had said he would make him 'wish he was back among'— the Admiral of the Ocean Sea was not spared the taunts of urchins, who would shout out whenever he passed: 'Look out, Drake is coming!'

However much the English may have felt that they had missed a decisive victory, the defeat of the Armada was seen by Protestants throughout the continent as a harbinger of hope. Petruccio Ubaldini wrote: 'The Spanish Armada in its passage through the Channel made from July 19, when it arrived off the Cape of Cornwall, till the 30th or 31st, when it was deprived of all possibility of joining its forces in Flanders, had lost about eleven good ships, and some 8,000 men of all sorts, and a large sum of public money; while of the English ships not one had perished, and of their men (marvellous to relate) little more than 100 in all the actions that took place.'

Ubaldini accurately saw the significance of the victory. It was the triumph of naval forces over a vast land empire—and it marked the beginning of a new era. '. . . all the weight of defending the coast of England from the hostile invasion, and all the work of impeaching the Spanish Armada from joining hands with the Duke of Parma, and finally of not permitting it to take a moment's rest at anchor in any part of these seas, rested upon the sagacity and technical grasp of the naval art possessed by the English officers, who had command in the Royal Navy according to their ranks, and by those who under them commanded their particular vessels. These men making good use of the trustworthy quality of their excellent and fast sailing vessels, which were not encumbered with useless soldiers but free for the guns, so that at any moment they could play without fail upon the enemy, knew ever from moment to moment what was best for them to do.'

It was now, when the value of naval power had been so successfully proven, that Drake and his colleagues clamoured for its worth to be demonstrated yet again—this time in an offensive campaign. Even Queen Elizabeth found it difficult to resist their entreaties, and especially when the tide of success appeared to flow so clearly in their favour. But the cost of mobilising the whole fleet of England against the Armada had almost broken the exchequer, and it was clear that any major expedition must be fitted out on the old system of a Joint Stock Company. The Queen, as usual, was the principal shareholder, contributing £20,000 in cash, as well as six naval galleons. Drake invested a similar amount of money himself, as did Sir John Norreys, the famous soldier who was to be in charge of the military side of the expedition.

Although there was some initial argument about the objects of this great counter-stroke against Spain, it was finally decided that the capture of Lisbon and the Azores should be the principal target. At the same time, so as to provide a political objective, Don Antonio, the Portuguese pretender to the throne, was to be reinstated. In return for all this, Don Antonio agreed to give the English full rights to trade with the East Indies. Like all exiles, the Portuguese prince was convinced that it was only necessary for him to set foot in his own country for all the people of Portugal to rise in his support. An interesting parallel to the Portuguese expedition of 1589 can be found in the history of the Second World War, when the English made their unsuccessful attempt on Dakar, capital of what was then French West Africa. On this occasion they had been led to believe by General de Gaulle that the whole of this territory would rise in support. Just as with Don Antonio in 1589, the magic of the General's name proved an insufficient lure.

The expedition was confounded from its very inception by the Queen's determination—as usual—to try to kill two birds with one stone. Not only was the fleet under Drake and the army under Norreys to capture Lisbon and reinstate Don Antonio, but they were also instructed to make sure that the remnant of the Armada was destroyed. This meant an attack on Santander, where it was known that about 40 of the principal ships were either laid up or refitting. Drake seems to have been determined, from the very beginning, to have nothing to do with his second objective. He was undoubtedly right in his feeling that an expedition with two quite separate aims would almost certainly come to grief, and in his conviction that nothing need be feared from the Spanish Navy for many a month to come. Nevertheless, he had to pretend to accede to the Queen's demands.

When the fleet finally sailed from Plymouth on the 18th April, 1589, they numbered more than 150 sail, including the transports which carried over 10,000 soldiers. It was the largest naval and military expedition that England had ever launched, and it was troubled by all the same problems of logistics that had harassed the Armada. There were victuals for only a month, and most of the soldiers were either inexperienced or completely untrained. They were stiffened by only

P

1,000 veterans from the Netherlands, while a number of impressed
Dutch ships—which Drake had casually seized in the Channel—
deserted before the fleet even got through the Bay of Biscay.

Although Norreys and Drake, who were men of somewhat similar
temperaments, seem to have got on well enough, there were the almost
inevitable rivalries between the military and sea officers. The military
had a contempt for what they liked to call 'The Idolatry of Neptune',
and were determined to prove that, while men like Drake might well
have defeated the Armada, it was only they who could successfully
carry the war into enemy territory.

As on a previous occasion, when Sir Philip Sidney had run away
from the Queen to join an expedition commanded by Drake, so now
the Queen's current favourite, Essex, emulated him and escaped from
the demanding be-jewelled hands. He was aboard the Queen's ship
Swiftsure under Captain Goring, and away before the inevitable royal
messengers could reach Plymouth and demand his return. Drake seems
to have connived at his escape. In itself, this was an ill omen, for
success had attended him previously when he had made sure that Sidney
was returned to the court. The *Swiftsure* made a lone passage through
the Bay, and joined up with Drake and his fleet after they had left
Corunna. For it was to Corunna that Drake directed his force, maintaining that the wind was foul for an attack on Santander—something
that does not seem to be corroborated by other evidence.

This was the first major mistake in the campaign, for Corunna
was unimportant compared to Lisbon and, whatever the English
successes there, it gave time for Lisbon to be put into a state of readiness.
Had Drake made straight for the Portuguese capital, it seems very
likely that the attack might have been successful and Don Antonio
restored to the throne. Even so, as with all major expeditions, the
intentions of the English had long been known by Philip II, and a
Portuguese friend of Don Antonio had been in communication with
Spain ever since the project had first been mooted. Drake was most
probably misled by information reaching him that Corunna, and not
Santander, was the main concentration-point of the Spanish naval
forces. They found there only one ship of any value. The English
landed successfully and captured the lower town, but the main citadel
which was built on higher ground resisted all their assaults—despite
the gallantry and dash shown by Norreys and his troops. Yet again, it
was a failure in planning and supply which invalidated the English
efforts. They had been promised a train of siege guns for the expedition,
but this had never materialised, so ships' guns had to be hauled up to
attempt to breach the walls of the upper city. These did not prove

heavy enough for, by the mid-16th century, all towns of any importance were defended by curtain-walls so thick that only the incessant
battering of heavy siege guns could really damage them.

Not for the last time in history did the women of Spain prove
themselves as brave, or braver, than their men. We read of Maria
Pita, the wife of an army officer, who 'With a spirit which women
have more often displayed in Spain than in any other country, snatched
up sword and buckler, and took her stand among the foremost of the
defendants; and so much was ascribed by the people to the effect of her
example, that she was rewarded for this service with the full pay of an
ensign for life, and the half-pay was settled upon her descendants in
perpetuity.' Southey quoting the Spanish poet Gongora in this
anecdote refers rather unchivalrously to the lady as 'this virago', but
he does not fail to do her honour by saying that she 'lost none of her
courage at seeing her husband killed before her eyes, and that she
wounded an English standard bearer mortally with a lance.' Byron
commemorated her, and the English failure before the citadel of
Corunna, by describing his countrymen as, 'foil'd by a woman's hand,
before a batter'd wall'.

Although Norreys was successful by land, driving off a Spanish
force of 9,000 men who had come up to try and relieve the city, the
attack on Corunna was a failure—and in more ways than one. The
worst thing that befell the English was that, in the lower city, among
the insignificant loot that came the way of the troops, were hundreds
of gallons of Spanish wine. The soldiers fell upon it—and there is
nothing more disastrous for a nation of beer drinkers than to swallow
down quarts of rough wine, as if it was their native brew. It would
hardly be an exaggeration to say that from now on, a high percentage
of Norreys's men were permanently drunk. This—coupled with the
inevitable typhus—rapidly reduced their fighting abilities.

As he led the fleet southward from Corunna, past Cape Finisterre
and down to Lisbon, Drake still felt confident as to the outcome of the
campaign: 'We have done the King of Spain,' he wrote blithely to
Walsingham, 'many pretty services at this place. And yet I believe he
will not thank us.' It was on the 16th May that the troops again disembarked, this time at Peniche—about 50 miles by land from Lisbon.
It has been said, though on no good authority, that Drake was opposed
to this plan, and was in favour of landing the troops at Cascais at the
mouth of the Tagus. This is doubtful, for the whole scheme is remi-
niscent of Drake's previous attacks on San Domingo and Cartagena in
1585. The idea was that the troops would land at some distance from
the main objective and, while the fleet engaged the attention of the

enemy, they would march swiftly overland and strike the city from the
rear. Despite the heavy sea that was running, the landing was carried
out successfully—Essex and Sir Roger Williams leading their troops in
to the assault, wading waist-high through the surf at the head of their
men.

At long last Don Antonio was on the soil of his native land. It was
now that, if his conjectures had proved correct, all the Portuguese
should have risen to support him. They had no love towards the
Spaniards, and Lisbon was only held by a comparatively small garrison
of Philip II's troops. Unfortunately, Philip's nephew, the Archduke
Albert, (who was both a Cardinal and a General) was in command of
Lisbon, and knew the best way to cow the populace. Within hours of
hearing of Drake's attack on Corunna, he and his soldiers, and his
police spies, had begun to round up all the independent spirits in the
Portuguese capital—hanging the most dangerous, and putting the
others safely in gaol. The peasantry—whom Don Antonio had
ingenuously expected to rise in his favour could hardly have cared, in
their lives of back-breaking toil, whether they were ruled by a Spaniard
or a Portuguese. Although Norreys and Essex managed to reach the
walls of Lisbon without being challenged, they did not find the country
falling in behind them, nor was there any general rising in Lisbon itself.
Weakened by disease, debilitated by lack of adequate provisions, and
sodden with Spanish wine, the English troops took five days to march
the 50 miles to the city.

Drake meanwhile had anchored off the mouth of the Tagus. It is
noticeable that he had never liked the look of the approaches to the
city of Lisbon, and even in the glorious year of 1587 he had hesitated
and decided against attempting it. It was 12 miles from the bar up a
winding narrow channel to the city itself, and the approaches had been
well fortified for a over a hundred years by gun-emplacements and
strongly-held positions. The wind was onshore when he first arrived,
and the old Drake of Cadiz days would surely have seized the opportunity and gone boldly into the attack. He was hampered on this
occasion by having a prior arrangement with Norreys, that they
should make a concerted pincer movement on the city. Norreys had
not yet arrived and Drake, for the first time in his life, hung back.

It has often been maintained that he was failing in his powers. He was
a man in his late forties, and in those days few kings, even, ever reached
the age of sixty. Drake had had an almost unimaginably hard life, had
been at sea since he was about 12 years old, had suffered from the
diseases and climate of South America, had endured privation, had
been wounded by musket shot in leg and face, and had driven himself

relentlessly in the service of his own ambition and his country. It seems unlikely, though, that it was a failure of will or nerve that made him lie-to off the approaches to Lisbon. It was, rather, that for the first time in his life he was trying to co-operate with the military in what was, for those days, an incredibly ambitious combined operation. His old lightning-flash grasp of a situation had been superseded by a determination to act as a responsible and mature Commander-in-Chief. By missing the onshore wind and the favourable flood tide, he inadvertently destroyed all the English chances of capturing Lisbon and reinstating Don Antonio—even if this had been possible, or acceptable to the Portuguese people. The wind turned foul, and blew in his teeth off the land.

Having landed some troops, he managed to capture the small fishing port of Cascais, but failed to take its fortress. He then waited for news from Norreys. The latter had finally reached Lisbon with his weakened and demoralised force, but only to find that Drake had not yet arrived off the city. Captain William Fenner who described the whole expedition as 'a miserable action', gives a good explanation why the army under Norreys failed in its task: 'The want of a single piece to make a breach or shoot against the gates prevented the English from taking it. The want of match [slow-match to ignite their arquebuses] among the soldiers, and of powder for their muskets, forced them to retire, when the Spaniards would sally out, in the habits of Portuguese, crying *amigos*, and slay the sick in the rear of the army. . . .' Monson, for his part, accurately recognised that it was the lack of siege guns which prevented the capture of Lisbon, a city whose strength consisted in 'the castle, and we having only an army to countenance us, but no means for battery, we were the loss of the victory ourselves. For it was apparent, by the intelligence we received, if we had presented them with battery, they were resolved to parley, and so, by consequence, to yield, and this was the main and chief reason of the Portuguese excuse for not joining us.'

As soon as the wind blew favourable again, Drake gave orders for the fleet to stand up the Tagus. They were to go in at dawn, with the *Revenge* in the van. Despite everything that had gone wrong, there was still a chance even at this late hour that they might succeed. But at this very moment a messenger arrived from Norreys, saying that he saw nothing for it but to withdraw his troops. Norreys marched down to Cascais the following day, and all the soldiers and their commanders were successfully embarked. Among them was Essex, who had challenged Philip II's nephew to single combat outside the walls of Lisbon, and had had his offer tacitly refused.

Elizabeth herself laid the blame for the failure of the expedition more upon the shoulders of Drake than she did on Norreys. It has been the custom of historians ever since to say that Drake was failing, or that his known inefficiency as an organiser was proved only too well by the campaign of 1589. But Drake and the fleet can hardly be blamed for an unfortunate combination of circumstances—the lack of discipline among the English troops which led to their demoralisation; the fact that the siege guns had never been provided; and the failure of the Portuguese to rise in support of Don Antonio. The soldiers had been efficiently landed at Peniche, and they were once again efficiently withdrawn from Cascais after their failure at the walls of Lisbon. Drake has been blamed for his reluctance to enter the Tagus with that first favourable wind, but there would have been no point in him bringing the fleet up river unless the English army had been simultaneously attacking the city from the land. To have taken five days to march 50 miles was inexcusable. If only the army had moved at the same pace as Carleill's troops had done at San Domingo in 1585, Drake would undoubtedly have moved up river on the first occasion.

There were only about 2,000 soldiers fit for duty when the fleet hauled off from the mouth of the Tagus, and made its way up the coast to Vigo. They sacked and burned the city, and managed to get their hand on a certain amount of most necessary victuals and stores. Drake was still hoping, even at this late hour, to attempt the Azores—and thus by capturing Philip II's bases there, to cut his supply line from the Spanish colonies. It was not to be: foul weather scattered the fleet, and the *Revenge* herself very nearly sank in a gale. Warships, merchantmen, and private ships, they individually made their way home—sadly recognising that the expedition had been a failure. All the investors, including the Queen, lost a large amount of money, and the survivors among the troops had little enough plunder to add to their insufficient wages.

The Lisbon expedition of 1589 marked the end of Drake's great career. Unfortunately for England, it was seen as a proof that the Navy was not so effective for foreign operations as people had been led to expect. On the face of it, the only real successes had been enjoyed by the army, particularly at Corunna when they had routed the Spaniards. There were many among the gentlemen who were happy to see the Navy removed at last from its position of especial favour in the royal eye.

Drake and Norreys did not make recriminations against one another. Both accepted the blame for a failure that, in the light of dispassionate investigation, can only be ascribed to a combination of unfortunate circumstances, and to the inability of any large force in those days to remain in a state of health and discipline for a period of anything over six weeks. The counterstroke of the English after the Armada might be said to have failed, but it had achieved almost un-looked-for aims. They had landed on the shores of Spain and Portugal, had captured Corunna and Cascais, put Lisbon into a panic, burned Vigo, and sailed away again without losing a single ship to the enemy. In the course of the expedition they had totally disrupted the Spanish coastal trade, and they had caused Philip II to lose even more face in Europe. By Tudor standards it was a failure, but in the light of later wars it would have been accounted a signal success.

After her immense expediture on the fleet during the Armada campaign, the Queen found herself once more heavily out of pocket. A scapegoat had to be found, and she did not have the generosity of Philip II to absolve her chosen admiral. No doubt there were many at court who were only too eager to pour their venom into the royal ear against Drake. Centuries later, after the unsuccessful attack on Teneriffe, in the course of which Nelson lost his arm, Lord St. Vincent signalled him: 'Mortals cannot command success. . . .' It might well stand as the epitaph to Drake's Lisbon expedition.

CHAPTER TWENTY

Drake Ashore

DRAKE was not employed in any sea-going command for the next five years. It may seem strange that one failure, which cannot be laid entirely at his door, should have resulted in so complete a dismissal from sea service. But in the court of Elizabeth favour was something that either materialised like magic, or disappeared just as swiftly. Even when a man was in the Queen's good graces, he could not relax in confidence, for Elizabeth was true to her nature in this as in all else, that she would never entirely give herself to anyone. A fall from favour meant total eclipse, for the Queen could be ruthless like a woman bent on terminating a love-affair abruptly.

Drake was wise, and withdrew almost entirely from London and the Court. He scorned to join the one-time favourites who clung to the edge of the royal circle, hoping to win their way back into the Queen's regard. His friend Walsingham died in 1590, his most powerful friend, Leicester, was already dead, and he knew that men who distrusted him, or actively disliked him, now had the confidence of the Queen. Quite apart from this, the pattern of Europe had changed yet again. With the murder of Henry III of France, and with the Catholic League occupying Paris, Philip II had come to the conclusion that there was a better way of enlarging his empire than by invading England. A number of the most important French Atlantic ports were in his hands, and he saw that if he could secure the throne of France for the nominee of the Catholic League, his empire would stretch from the Mediterranean all the way to the English Channel, and northward to the Netherlands. Once this had been achieved, the rebels in the Netherlands and the heretic island of England would fall like ripe fruit into his hands.

The result was a change in English policy, and it was one that suited Elizabeth's threadbare exchequer. Soldiers were cheaper and easier to come by than ships, and she could employ them under the Huguenot Prince's flag in France, while keeping no more than two or three squadrons at sea in the Channel to harass the Duke of Parma. At the same time, small individual expeditions, financed largely by City merchants, sporadically raided Philip II's treasure route from the West Indies. These, in fact, did little damage to Philip's economy and, during the years of Drake's virtual retirement, the Spanish fleet was built up to a greater strength than ever before. The new construction had benefited from the lessons of the Armada, and the old days of galleons which were little more than floating castles for soldiers were over. At the same time a fast and efficient courier service was established across the Atlantic by means of light vessels that used both sails and oars, so that there was now a regular monthly mail service between Havana and the Atlantic ports of Spain. In the West Indies and on the Spanish Main, Philip and his Governors had absorbed the lessons taught them by Drake's earlier raids. Fortress engineers drew up new plans for the chief ports and cities, new guns were despatched across the Atlantic from the foundries of Italy, and the whole system of imperial defence was tightened up.

During these years of disgrace, Drake was far from idle, for it was not in his nature to 'rust unburnish'd, not to shine in use'. If the Queen would not make use of his abilities at sea, he would make use of them ashore. Five years before, in 1584, when Drake had been the Member of Parliament for Bossiney in Cornwall, the Plymouth Water Bill had appeared in Parliament. Drake had been a Member of the Select Committee which approved the Bill. Although it was passed in 1585, five years elapsed before anything was done to put it in operation, and Drake was the prime mover in getting the Bill translated into fact. No one knew better than he the importance of having a thoroughly efficient water supply for the city and harbour of Plymouth. In the past, whenever a large fleet was getting under way, it had meant transporting thousands of gallons of water in barrels by cart and wagon from the country. What was needed, was a really adequate supply running right to the quayside.

The Act stated that the water was required not only for the shipping in the harbour but also for the town's protection from fire—always a great hazard in the days of timbered houses—and 'as well by the enemy, for the same was once burned by the French in time of war'. One can see Drake's hand again in another paragraph of the Act which makes provision for dredging out the harbour, since it 'doth daily fill with the sand of the tin works and mines near adjoining to the same, and in short time will be utterly decayed if some redress and speedy remedy be not had'.

It was in the year of his fall from favour, that 'The composition was made between the town and Sir Francis Drake for the bringing of the River Meve to the town.' Drake was paid £200 for seeing that the work was carried out, and a further £100 for compensating land-owners through whose property the projected water course was to run. It was an astute move on the part of the Plymouth corporation to make Drake the principal figure, for there were few landowners or tenant farmers who could withstand the prestige of his name. The length of the leat or water course from its Dartmoor source to Plymouth was 17 miles, and Drake formally cut the first sod in December 1590. With his usual perspicuity he used local tin miners and engineers to deal with the technical problems involved, and it is proof of the efficiency with which the work was carried out that, with only a few modifications and improvements, it provided Plymouth's main water supply for 300 years. Drake's drive and initiative is seen here, as always in his life, by the fact that the whole undertaking was completed in four months—an astounding feat when one realises that near the head weir, and through Burrator Gorge, the water had to be carried in great wooden chutes because of the immense boulders which made it impracticable to continue with the main ditch. Spry's contemporary map of Plymouth shows the course of what came to be known as 'Drake's Leat', and carries the note by Burrator Gorge; 'Here the river is taken out of the old river and carried 448 paces through mightye rocks which was thought impossible to carry water through.'

Drake most probably made a direct profit on the whole transaction—for he was a man with 'gold fingers'—but his main economic advantage was a 67-year lease granting him the right to erect and work six mills upon the Leat. In those days a single mill used for grinding flour was a highly profitable investment in itself, and Drake now had six in operation immediately behind the city of Plymouth. Somewhat naturally the established millowners in the area protested against Sir Francis Drake coming into the corn business. A Bill was introduced in the House of Commons, demanding the removal of Drake's mills, as well as asking compensation for loss of trade already sustained by the local millers. It is hardly surprising that the Bill never got through its Committee stage in Parliament, for the Chairman of the Committee was none other than Sir Francis Drake.

Drake was ever fond of pomp and ceremony, and he could not resist a gesture when the water course was officially opened. On the 23rd April, 1591, all the guns of the city boomed out, and the cheering people of Plymouth followed the Mayor and corporation as, heralded by four trumpeters, they rode out of the city along the dry bed of the Leat. Francis Drake rode in to meet them at the head of the advancing water, as it flowed down from Dartmoor. It seemed like a miracle to simple people, and gave birth to the legend that Drake had merely

ridden to the head of the water on Dartmoor, commanded it to follow
him and, as his horses hooves struck the earth, so the land parted to
bring the river down to Plymouth. At the doorway of his town house
Drake dismounted, and dipped his scarlet cloak in the swirling water
'in exultation that he had obtained his desired end'.

At no time in his life had Drake spent so long ashore as he did
between 1589 and 1594. It is the custom of naval biographers to cry out
at the wastage of his abilities, and to paint Drake as ever pining to get
back to sea. To a certain degree this may have been true, but it is
pleasant to think that in his late middle age Drake was able to enjoy all
the things he had worked for and fought so hard to gain ever since he
was a youth. The fact that we know so little about his second wife
Elizabeth Sydenham, or his relations with her, would seem to indicate
that theirs was a quiet and successful marriage—for 'happy is the
country that has no history'. There can be no doubt that he enjoyed
acting the part of the country squire—more perhaps than most men
born to it. The records of Plymouth show innumerable payments
made to messengers sent out by the Mayor and other dignitaries to
Buckland, for there can have been little done in the City about which
Francis Drake was not first consulted. His well-bred wife seems to have
been extremely popular with all the other gentlewomen in that part of
Devon, and there was never an entertainment given by the Plymouth
corporation but that Sir Francis and Lady Drake were invited to
attend. Similarly, whevener important visitors came to Plymouth either
by land or sea, it was inevitable that they should be entertained at
Buckland. Years before, aboard the *Golden Hind*, Drake had shown
himself even more fond of music and ceremony than most Englishmen
of his time. During his years of retirement, the great hall of the Abbey
must often have resounded with the lilt of viols and citterns, lutes,
and hautboys. There can be no doubt that, whatever he did while
the Armada was coming up Channel, he passed many a summer
afternoon playing bowls with friends on the green lawn outside the
Abbey.

He enjoyed all the other recreations of the country, fishing on the
Tavy, where he built a weir that—typical of Drake—not only improved
the fishing, but operated a small mill which ground all the corn needed
on his estate. He went stag hunting and, in those days when the deer
roamed wild over many parts of Devon, he enjoyed stalking them on
foot. In 1929 a great oak that grew near the Abbey was blown down in
a gale, and it was this oak in which, according to the story, Drake was
once forced to take refuge when charged by a stag. Getting down from
the tree, he went for his gun, and a set of antlers which still hang in the

kitchen of Buckland are said to have come from this stag that once drove 'The Dragon' up an oak tree.

Sheltered though Buckland Abbey is from the sea, at the end of the long green valley Drake could see the small boats dropping down the Tavy with corn for Plymouth. A legend in his own country and in Europe, he was celebrated by local ballad-mongers in these years more for his peaceful activities as squire and first citizen of Plymouth:

> *Who with fresh streams refresht this that first*
> *Though kist with waters yet did pine with thirst,*
> *Who both a pilot and a magistrate*
> *Steered in his turne the ship of Plymouth state.*

He had his coat of arms carved above the great fireplace in the library on the first floor, as if to erase the memory of the Grenvilles. But there must have been times when he paused to look at that plaster frieze which Richard Grenville had had set on the west wall of the hall, where the soldier, his war horse turned loose, and his shield hung a upon tree, contemplates the skull and hour-glass.

When the news reached Plymouth in the autumn of 1591 of the death of Sir Richard Grenville in the action off Flores in the Azores, it was carried by messenger to Drake at Buckland. He must have been sick at heart, for, whatever his personal feelings about Grenville, Drake cannot have been indifferent to his fate or happy to be sitting comfortably ashore while the Spaniards were still active on the high seas. Grenville in Drake's old flagship the *Revenge* had fought the whole Spanish fleet of over 50 ships for more than 12 hours. The *Revenge* had been boarded fifteen times; Grenville had been wounded twice, shot in the head, and the surgeon who was attending him had been killed at his side. He had asked the gunner to blow up the ship, rather than let the famous *Revenge* fall into Spanish hands, but at this point the crew had mutinied. Before she surrendered, the *Revenge* had beaten off 15 ships, sunk two outright, and left two others so disabled that they sank later. Taken aboard the *San Paolo*, the Spanish flagship, Grenville had been treated with the utmost courtesy by his enemies, who were unable to repress their admiration for the way in which he had fought his ship. 'Feeling the hour of death to approach he spake these words in Spanish and said: "Here I, Richard Grenville, die with a joyful and quiet mind; for that I have ended my life as a true soldier ought to do, fighting for his country, Queen, religion, and honour; my soul most willingly departs from this body, leaving behind the lasting fame of having behaved as every true soldier is in his duty bound to do."' It was an end such as Drake himself would have sought. The pleasant prospect

down the valley from Buckland must have been obscured to his eyes
by an image of the long Atlantic rollers, the craggy heads of the Azores
lifting out of the ocean haze, and the thunder of battle:,

> . . . *When each gun*
> *From its adamantine lips*
> *Spread a death-shade round the ships*
> *Like a hurricane eclipse*
> *Of the sun.*

In the winter of the following year, 1592, Drake was up in London
again, proposing to Hawkins and all who would listen that they should
once more send out a major expedition to the West Indies. He was
active in Parliament, recommending that strong measures should be
taken by sea and land before Philip grew too powerful for England to
be able to contest him. When Parliament was summoned in February
1593 it was asked for a grant of £200,000 to be voted to the Queen
with the obvious indication that she would then use it to send Drake
to sea again. Raleigh spoke in favour of the Bill, but many others
opposed it, and it was only after an 11-day debate that it was finally
passed, and the full amount voted to the Queen. Drake, who was now
the member for Tintagel, was active in the lobbies, seeking out friends
and supporters. Nothing came of all his efforts that year, and it was
not until the summer of 1594 that a fleet, under the command of
Martin Frobisher, was despatched to relieve Brest.

During the years of Drake's retirement at Buckland, it is noticeable
that Frobisher had become the Queen's favourite Admiral. Bearing in
mind the Yorkshireman's dislike of Drake, one must surely trace
something of the latter's eclipse from favour to Frobisher's hand. In
the campaign of 1594 Norreys and his two brothers, the 'Chickens of
Mars' as they were called, led the military forces. Brest was finally
stormed and taken, despite heavy losses, but in the course of the action
Frobisher himself was shot through the thigh, dying shortly after his
return to Plymouth.

The ranks of the great Elizabethan soldiers and sailors were steadily
thinning. It was natural that, when the Queen finally came to contem-
plate a major stroke against her Spanish enemy, she should turn to Sir
Francis Drake—in the hope that his magic touch would be able, as it
had done in the past, to restore her fortunes and reduce the ever-
growing power of Spain. In the winter of 1594, Drake reopened his
London house by the Dowgate, and he and Hawkins were constantly
to be seen together discussing their plan of campaign. Drake was now
in his early fifties, a little more thick-set and slower in his movements,

his beard now pepper-and-salt, and his hands a little softer, grown more used to the pen than the sword-hilt or the rope. His years of playing the country gentleman, the Devon squire, and the weighty Member of Parliament were behind him. Without any sign of regret, he seems to have turned his back upon his comfortable life, the lands at Yarcombe and Sherford, and the lush green coombes of Devon that he would never see again. Like many other man, he felt perhaps that if only he could return to the seas and countries he had known when young, he would find youth itself awaiting him.

CHAPTER TWENTY-ONE

The End of a Voyage

ON the evening of the 14th November, 1595, the English fleet came to anchor in a small bay to the east of the city of San Juan in Puerto Rico. Hawkins lay dead aboard the *Garland*. His last words 'that he saw no other but danger of ruin likely to ensue of the whole voyage' seemed to set a seal of ill-omen upon the expedition. That same night, as Drake was at dinner, a shot from one of the Spanish shore-guns crashed through his cabin and knocked from under him the stool on which he was sitting. It killed two of his guests, Sir Nicholas Clifford, and a young officer called Brute Brown, who was a great favourite of Drake. Several others in the cabin were wounded and Henry Drake, one of the admiral's brothers, later remembered Sir Francis's words: 'Ah, dear Brute, I could grieve for thee, but now is no time for me to let down my spirits.'

San Juan was a foretaste of all that was to come, and Drake quickly realised that he must move his fleet out of range. These were not like the old Spanish shore-guns, weak and inaccurate, but they fired a heavy weight of metal and their gun-laying was excellent. Next morning he brought the fleet round, and stood in from sea to the west of the harbour entrance, at a point where three small islands clustered together. He had despatched boats to make soundings the previous day, and had discovered a small channel between these islands and the coast. It was not deep enough to allow the passage of his fleet, but quite adequate for small boats and pinnaces. From where he dropped anchor he could see the frigates, that had been sent to collect the treasure, lying in the harbour, and he determined to make one of those small-boat attacks which had been so successful in the past.

While the flotilla of light craft was being organised, Drake made a diversion to the west, thus forcing the Spaniards to send some of their troops to follow him, in case he intended to make a landing in that direction. At nightfall he came back again to his anchorage in the lee of the islands, and the attack was launched on San Juan. There was no question of the Spanish defenders being demoralised by the night-action that followed. Losses were heavy on both sides and, at the end of it, only one of the treasure frigates had been taken and burned. The treasure itself was secure ashore, and the Spanish troops poured a devastating fire on the English boats as they came into the harbour. At daybreak, forced to withdraw, Drake realised that the action had been a total failure.

As the land breeze began to blow, he worked the fleet out to windward from the port, possibly with the intention of making a Cadiz-like attack on the main harbour entrance. The Spanish Governor was prepared for this, and immediately scuttled two large merchantmen, cargoes and all, so as to block the passage. Drake was worsted and, recognising that it was impossible to take San Juan from the sea, moved on up the coast. It seems that he had it in mind to land troops at the western end of the island, march them overland, and take San Juan from the rear. This was clearly impossible unless the fleet could, at the same time, make an efficient diversion off the port itself. But now that there could be no element of surprise, nor expectation of success by sea, a military expedition was unfeasible. Baskerville and the senior military officers were against the attempt, as was Drake himself, and when some of the younger officers protested that they were eager to try it, he said to them: 'I will bring you to twenty places far more wealthy and easier to be gotten.' A few days later the whole English fleet was under way southwards across the Caribbean, bound for the Spanish Main. After their failure at the Canaries, the death of Hawkins, and their repulse at San Juan, morale was ebbing. 'Here,' wrote Thomas Maynard, 'I left all hope of success.'

Drake knew that if he returned to England without having made the voyage a financial success, his career and reputation would be irretrievably ruined. It seems that he was still haunted by his youthful dream—the capture of Panama. He heard again the mule bells on the dusty road, and saw the Golden City rise like a mirage out of the flat pampas-land, with the Pacific shimmering behind it. But he was ageing and the old fire and dash that might still have saved the expedition had left him. Unable to resist a passing blow at Rio de la Hacha, he anchored off the harbour on the 1st December, 1595, and landed the troops. The capture of the small city and port was a fruitless victory, for all the inhabitants had left, and the small amount of treasure could not justify the time wasted. Baskerville and his men spent nearly a fortnight laying waste the countryside around, burning unimportant villages—and bringing back practically nothing of value. The fleet moved on again and captured the pearl-fishing centre of Rancheria. But the ransom offered for it by the Governor proved insufficient, and Drake had the empty pleasure of destroying a deserted and valueless village. To the last he retained his old quality of compassion, refusing to allow the church to be destroyed, and sparing the house of a Spanish lady who had begged for his clemency.

Passing by Cartagena, the scene of his early triumph, he made for Nombre de Dios, which he and Baskerville captured with hardly any opposition. This was to be his base for the attack on Panama, and Baskerville and all the soldiers disembarked and made ready for their march. But everywhere the conditions were different from ten years before, and it was Drake himself who had indirectly brought about all the improvements in the Spanish administration of their empire. There were many more troops on the mainland, the Cimaroons were no longer capable of being active allies, for their resistance had been crushed, and everywhere that Drake went the inhabitants had been long forewarned of his coming. All the Spanish coastal shipping had ceased and, from the moment that they appeared in the Caribbean, the English had hardly seen the sails of even a coastal trader, let alone any ships of value. The towns and harbours which Drake had taken so gaily in his youth, with only a handful of young Devonians in one or two small sailing boats, yielded nothing now. They had been abandoned before ever his fleet came in sight of them. There is an old observation that one should never go back in later years to places where one has been happy when young, and Drake was proving the truth of it. The Spanish Main, where he had made his fame and fortune, was turning to dust in his hands.

Baskerville, taking 750 soldiers with him, set off on the inland route from Nombre de Dios across the Isthmus to Panama. There seems little doubt that Drake's intention was to hold the harbour at his main base, while sending boats up the Chagres river to Venta Cruz to embark the returning soldiers and whatever treasure they had captured. Baskerville discovered, however, that the main pack-route that had formerly led to Nombre de Dios had reverted to jungle, for the Spaniards had made a new base at Puerto Bello 20 miles westward along the coast, where the new road started. The English soldiers found that they not only had to hack their way through the green arms of jungle, but that they were expected. Snipers from the surrounding woods, blinding rain storms, sickness, and the inevitable fever atracked their force. Finally, as they came up towards the watershed where Drake in his youth had climbed the high tree and seen the Pacific, they found that their passage was barred by a new Spanish fort. Their attack on it was repulsed with heavy losses, much of their ammunition and stores were ruined by the relentless tropical rain, and Baskerville decided that there was nothing for it but to return.

Q

Only four days after leaving Nombre de Dios he and his men were back again. It was on the 31st December, 1595 that Drake saw the remnants of his land force limping back into the smouldering ruins of the sacked town. Thomas Maynard, who had been on the expedition, reported that: 'Since our return from Panama, he never carried mirth nor joy in his face.' Yet still Drake would not admit himself defeated. He showed Baskerville a map and pointed out to him Trujillo, the port of Honduras, the lake of Nicaragua, and the other cities in that rich area. There, he said, they would find the success that had so far eluded them. Baskerville, to his credit, never seems to have doubted that Drake still had the magic touch that would redeem the expedition, and bring them all to fame and fortune. Unfortunately the wind turned foul and, after beating against it for several days, the fleet was forced to anchor under the lee of a small island, some distance from Puerto Bello. The place proved fever-infested and although Drake, in the manner of his youth, immediately put the men to work cleaning and careening the ships, sickness flared through their ranks. He, who had remembered the Caribbean and the Spanish Main as 'a delicious and pleasant arbour', was forced to confess that it had become no more than a 'vast and desert wilderness'.

Despite all his triumphs and successes Drake, like Hawkins, had had a life of almost unendurable hardship, and he was to be tested to the very end. The golden touch had gone, and he was not to be spared the anguish of total failure. His spirit, though, would never desert him. As Maynard recorded: 'In the greatness of his mind he would in the end conclude in these words, "It matters not, man! God hath many things in store for us, and I know many means to do Her Majesty good service and to make us rich, for we must have gold before we see England".'

At last, even his indomitable frame began to crack, and Drake fell ill with the dysentery that was ravaging his fleet. On the 23rd January, 1596, for the first time in his life, he was too ill to keep the deck but took to his cabin. Even then he did not relinquish his command, for his last order was that the fleet should weigh and sail out of the fever-ridden place and make back towards Puerto Bello. He would, as he said, 'Take the wind as God sent it,' but the wind blew from the west, which meant that his last enterprise against Honduras and Nicaragua was impossible. The 'Mosquito Gulf', as it later came to be called, had taken its greatest toll, and Drake was unable to shake off the dysentery and fever. He knew that he was dying and, indeed, as if always aware that this voyage was to be his last, he had brought his will with him. On the 27th January, 1596, he had it witnessed by six of his friends aboard the *Defiance*. In default of any issue and 'heirs of his body', he left all his estates and property in England to his brother, Thomas Drake, and to his brother's children. Elizabeth Drake was already provided for, and she would sit for many years to come, as lady of the manor, in the tranquil house at Buckland. During the night of the 27th, Drake grew delirious, struggled up from his bed, and insisted that he should don his armour so as to 'die like a soldier'. His old rough tongue came back to him again, and he 'raved in words that no one cared to record'. It was four o'clock in the morning, as the light stole back into the sea beyond Puerto Bello, that as Hakluyt records it, 'Our General, Sir Francis Drake, departed this life.'

The next day, enclosed in a coffin of lead, his body was borne out to sea and there, to the thunder of guns and the brazen lament of trumpets, Sir Francis Drake was laid to rest. With him—as if to mark his whole lifetime of war against the Spaniards—the English sank two prizes that they had recently taken. Behind him, like a funeral pyre, the whole of the new city of Puerto Bello went up in smoke.

> *Sir Drake, whome well the world's end knewe,*
> *Which thou didst compasse rounde:*
> *And whome both poles of Heavon once saw,*
> *Which North and South do bounde:*
> *The starrs above will make thee known,*
> *If men here silent were:*
> *The Sunn himself cannot forgett*
> *His fellow Traveller.*

So they laid him to rest in the sea that he had known as a youth, under the blue-glass waves of the Caribbean, with a funeral fit for the Viking that he was. One man alone—as it had seemed in those long-ago days—he had challenged the greatest monarch and empire on earth. He had inflicted more damage on Philip II and the Roman Catholic counter-Reformation than any army 'terrible with banners'. He had put heart into all the oppressed of Europe, and had shown to the Negroes and Indians of the new World that, in the view of a humane man, one human being was as good as another. His furious life was ended.

Select Bibliography

Barrow, J., *Life of Drake* (1843)

Benson, E. F., *Sir Francis Drake* (1927)

Bradford, E., *Southward the Caravels:* A biography of Henry the Navigator (1961)

British Museum, *Sir Francis Drake's voyage round the world* (1927)

Campbell, J., *The Life of Sir Francis Drake* (1828)

Christy, M., *The Silver map of the world:* A medallion of Drake's voyage (1900)

California Historical Society, *Drake's Plate of Brass:* Evidence of his visit to California in 1579 (1937)

California Historical Society, *Drake's Plate of Brass authenticated* (1938)

California Press, University of, *Francis Drake and the California Indians* (1947)

Corbett, Sir J., *Sir Francis Drake* (1890)

Corbett, Sir J., *Drake and the Tudor Navy* (1898)

Drake, Sir Francis, *The World Encompassed* (Hakluyt Society) (1854)

Drake, Sir Francis, *The World Encompassed:* Edited by Sir R. C. Temple (1926)

Elliott-Drake, Lady E. F., *Family and heirs of Sir Francis Drake*, 2 vols. (1911)

Gill, G., *Buckland Abbey* (1956)

Hakluyt, R., *Principal navigations, voyages, traffics and discoveries of the English nation*, 12 vols. (1905)

Hakluyt Society, *Documents concerning English voyages to the Spanish Main 1569-80* (1932)

Klarwill, V. (Ed.), *Fugger news-letters:* 2nd series, 1568-1605 (1926)

Laughton, J. (Ed.), *State papers relating to the defeat of the Spanish Armada*, 2 vols. (1894)

Mason, A. E. W., *Sir Francis Drake* (1941)

Mattingley, G., *The Defeat of the Spanish Armada* (1959)

Maynarde, T., *Sir Francis Drake, his voyage 1595 . . . with the Spanish account of Drake's attack on Puerto Rico* (1849)

Mettall, Z., *New Light on Drake:* documents relating to his voyage of circumnavigation (1914)

Monson, Sir W., *Naval tracts*, Vol. 1. (Navy Records Society)

Neale, J. E., *Queen Elizabeth* (1934)

Rowse, A. L., *The Expansion of Elizabethan England* (1955)

Unwin, Rayner, *The Defeat of John Hawkins* (1960)

Wagner, H. R., *Sir Francis Drake's voyage around the World* (1926)

Walling, R. A. J., *The Story of Plymouth* (1950)

Williamson, J. A., *The Age of Drake* (1938)

Williamson, J. A., *Hawkins of Plymouth* (1949)

Williamson, J. A., *Sir Francis Drake* (1951)

Index

Adventure, 18
Aid, 156
Albert, Cardinal Archduke, 228
Algarve tunny fisheries, 181
Almirante (Spanish), 57
Alva, Duke of, 63
Angel, 45, 57
Anton, San Juan de, 128, 130, 131
Antonio, Don, pretender to Portuguese throne, 189, 225, 226, 228, 229
Ark Royal, 203, 206, 207, 210
Armada, Spanish (the Great Enterprise), 176, 189, 192-222; aftermath of, 223-5
Azores, 230, 236

Baber, Sultan, 141
Babington plot, 176
Balboa, Vasco Nunez de, 85
Barnett, Robert, 56
Barrow, John, 63, 73, 121
Baskerville, Sir Thomas, 18, 20, 21, 24, 240, 241, 242
Bedford, Earl of, see Russell, Lord
Bellingham, Henry, 176
Benedict, 101, 103
Benson, E. F., 48, 69
Berthold of Regensburg, 171
Biggs, Walter, 166, 168
Bingham, 153
Bonaventure, see Elizabeth Bonaventure
Borough, William, 176, 177, 178, 180, 181, 182, 183, 186-7
Brewer, trumpeter, 103, 104, 108
Bright, Edward, 112
Brown, Brute, 239
Buckland Abbey, 150-1, 152, 172, 200, 235, 236, 237, 243
Burghley, Lord, 18, 97, 101-2, 112-13, 114, 148, 154, 156, 169, 186-7
Bustamente, Francisco de, 54
Buttber, Hans, 208
Byron, Lord, 227

Cabot, Sebastian, 103
'Cacafuego' (Nuestra Señora de la Concepcion), 127-9, 131, 147, 184

Cadiz, 177-9, 186
California, 137
Camden, William, 28, 85, 210
Canaries, 21-2, 47
Cape Horn, 122
Cape St. Vincent, 180, 181, 182, 186
Carib Indians, 161
Carleill, Christopher, 156, 161, 162, 165-6, 168, 230
Cartagena, 51-2, 76, 81, 164-8, 227, 241
Castellanos, Miguel de, 50, 51
Cavendish, Thomas, 119, 120, 123
Cecil, Sir William, 42, 45
Chatham, 28
'Chatham Chest', the, 223
Chester, John, 101
Cimaroon Indians, 68, 71, 72, 80, 82, 84-90 passim, 92, 93, 130, 163, 167, 241
Clifford, Sir Nicholas, 239
Coligny, Admiral, 92
Columbus, Christopher, 36
Corbett, Sir Julian, 8, 51, 61, 63, 112, 142, 184, 186, 197
Cortes, Hernando, 36
Corunna, 226-7, 228, 230, 231
Cromwell, Thomas, 27

Darien, Gulf of, 80
Dee, John, 109
Defiance, 18, 21, 23, 242
Delight, 22
Diego, negro servant, 80, 123-4
Doughty, John, 102, 109, 149-50
Doughty, Thomas, 97-8, 99, 101-2, 103-4, 105, 108-10, 143, 147, 149, 187; trial of, 111-15, 116, 124
Dragon, 62, 65
Drake, Edmund (father), 25-30, 32, 36
Drake, Elizabeth (2nd wife, née Sydenham), 152, 235, 243
Drake, Sir Francis: last expedition, 1-24, 237, 239-43; qualities and characteristics, 7, 33-4, 62, 115, 223; M.P. for Tintagel, 17, 237; birth, 25;

Drake, Sir Francis—*cont.*
nicknamed 'Pirate', 'Terrible Dragon', 25; and religion, 29, 134; in
coastal trade, 30; physical appearance, 33, 132; childlessness, 34; en-
lists under John Hawkins, 37; first
contact with Spanish, 38; and slave
trade, 41, 163; first command under
Hawkins, 47; hatred of Spain, 59,
89; first working capital, 62; dis-
appearances, 62 (1569), 96 (1575);
three independent voyages (1570-3),
65-93; attack on Nombre de Dios,
70-5; wounded, 73; first sight of
Pacific, 85; capture of treasure train
and narrow escape at Venta Cruz,
90-1; service in Ireland (?), 97;
official commission to Magellan
Straits, 98; voyage round the world,
99, 139-45; first meeting with Q.
Elizabeth (1577), 100; crosses the
Equator, 105; sermon on discipline,
114; captures treasure ship '*Cacafuego*', 128; takes possession of 'New
Albion', 137; knighted (1581), 149;
acquires Buckland Abbey and other
properties, 150-1, 152; interest in
local politics of Plymouth, 152;
Royal commission to release impounded ships, 155; instructions to
'impeach the provisions of Spain'
(1586), 176; 'singes the King of
Spain's beard', 179; command of
Royal Naval vessels, 189; Vice-
Admiral of the fleet, 193; the game
of bowls, 198; foundation of the
'Chatham Chest', 223-4; retirement
(1589-94), 233-7; liking for music,
235; death, 242-3
Drake, Francis (nephew), 38
Drake, Henry (brother), 239
Drake, John (brother), 69, 72, 74, 78-9,
81, 82-3, 84
Drake, John (nephew), 102, 134
Drake, Joseph (brother), 83
Drake, Mary (1st wife, *née* Newman),
64, 68, 146, 150, 151, 152
Drake, Thomas (brother), 18, 102, 103,
104, 156, 243
Drakes of Asshe, 151
Dreadnought, 176
Dudley, Edward, 47

Edward VI, 27, 29, 30
El Greco, 170

Elizabeth, Queen, 8, 17, 18, 42, 45, 46,
63, 66, 95-6, 99, 113, 117, 141, 146,
147, 148, 149, 153, 155, 158, 175-6,
185, 186, 192, 225, 230, 231, 232,
237; Drake's first meeting with, 100;
state visit to the *Golden Hind*, 148;
gift of manor of Sherford, 151; contribution to expedition of 1581, 156;
Throckmorton Plot, 154; Babington
Plot, 176; speech to troops (1588),
205
Elizabeth, 101, 113, 116, 120, 121-2,
123, 125, 126, 130, 144, 146
Elizabeth Bonaventure, 18, 156, 176,
179, 183
Enriquez, Don Martin, 54, 55, 57,
58-9, 65, 132
Enterprise of England, the, *see* Armada
Essex, Earl of, 96-7, 226, 228, 229

Fenner, Thomas, 156, 176, 217
Fenner, William, 229
Fireships, 214, 220
Fitzwilliam, George, 47
Fleming, Thomas, 197, 198, 209
Fletcher, Francis, 102, 114, 115, 123,
125, 138, 142-3, 187
Foresight, 18
France, 148-9
Francis, 22, 156
Frobisher, Martin, 18, 61, 150, 153,
156, 168, 187, 204, 208-13 *passim*,
215, 217, 223, 237
Fuller, Thomas, 32

Galleon Leicester, 156
Garland, 18, 25, 239
Garret, John, 70
Golden Hind (Drake's), 36, 101, 117,
121, 122, 123, 125-9 *passim*, 130-9
passim, 140-5, 146, 235; Queen's
state visit to, 148; as a national monu-
ment, 149
Golden Hind (Fleming's), 197
Golden Lion, 176, 179, 183, 186
Gongora, Luis de, 188, 227
Gonson, Benjamin, 32
Goring, Captain, 226
Grace of God, The, 47
Gran Grifon (Spanish), 211
Gregory XIII, Pope, 89
Grenville, Sir Richard, 18, 61, 98, 150,
187, 236
Greville, Fulke, 153
Guatulco, 134, 135

Hakluyt, Richard, 24, 36, 111, 243
Harris, Christopher, 151
Hartop, Job, 49, 50
Hatton, Sir Christopher, 98, 117
Hawkins, John, 17-24 passim, 26, 37,
    38-9, 41, 96, 101, 115, 132, 133, 237;
    death of, 24, 65, 239; marriage, 32;
    expedition to West Indies and defeat
    at San Juan de Ulua, 42-60, 61, 63,
    65, 187; Treasurer of the Navy, 98,
    153-4; system of double-sheathing,
    143; attacked at Santiago, 160-1;
    part against Armada, 202, 203, 213,
    215, 217, 222; foundation of the
    'Chatham Chest', 223
Hawkins, Richard, 119
Hawkins, William, snr., 26, 32
Hawkins, William, jnr., 26, 32, 102
Heizer, Robert F., 136
Hele, John, 151
Henry III of France, 232
Henry the Navigator, 36, 40, 41, 48,
    173, 181
Henry VIII, 26, 29
Herrara, Antonio de, 61
Holinshed, Raphael, 149
Hondius's map, 122
Hope, 18
Howard of Effingham, Lord, 189, 192-
    204 passim, 206-11, 213-15 passim,
    218-19, 221, 222

Indians, see Cimaroons, Carib Indians,
    Miwok Indians
Isle of Pines, 71, 77, 79

Jesus of Lubeck, 32, 45, 46, 49, 52, 53,
    55, 56, 57, 59, 61
Johnson, Samuel, 31, 36, 82, 149
Jonson, Ben, 149
Judith, 45, 47, 48, 50, 57, 58, 59, 61, 62

Knollys, Sir Francis, 156

Lane, Ralph, 168
Leicester, Earl of, 97, 98, 232
Leiva, Alonzo de, 203, 218
Leo X, Pope, 174
Lepanto, battle of, 147
Le Testu, Guillaume, 89-90, 92, 94
Lincoln, Admiral, 98
Lisbon, 225-31
Lovell, John, 37, 38-9, 42, 50, 65

Machiavelli, Nicholas, 66
Magellan, Ferdinand, 103, 110-11, 117,
    119, 140
Magellan Strait, 98-9, 100, 102-3, 107
    (map), 118-20, 124, 147
Marchant, Captain, 183
Marigold, 101, 116, 117, 120, 125, 126,
    144
Mary, 103, 104, 108, 109
Mary, Queen, 30
Mary Stuart, 185
Mattingley, Garrett, 190, 193
Maynard, Thomas, 21, 240, 242
Medina Sidonia, Duke of, 182-3, 190-1,
    193-6 passim, 201-4, 206, 209-15
    passim, 216, 218-20, 222, 224
Mendoza, Spanish Ambassador, 25,
    147, 154
Minion, 45, 46, 57, 58, 59, 61
Miwok Indians, 136
Moluccas, 141
Moncada, Hugo de, 217
Monson, Sir William, 18, 103, 229
Moone, Thomas, 78, 101, 124, 134,
    156, 167

Nassau, Justin of, Admiral of Zeeland,
    212
New Albion (California), 137, 141
Newman, Harry, 64
Newman, Mary, see Drake, Mary
Nombre de Dios, 66-9, 70-5, 84, 88, 89,
    90, 132, 135, 241, 242
Nonpareil, 217
Norreys, Sir John, 225-30 passim
Nuestra Señora del Rosario, 207, 208

Oliver, Isaac, 33
Oxenham, John, 72, 74, 84, 85, 88, 92
    130, 131

Palau Islands, 140
Panama, 19, 35, 66, 77, 85, 87, 126,
    135, 167, 240, 241
Parma, Duke of, 175, 186, 187, 198,
    203, 212-13, 218, 220, 222, 224, 232
Pascha, 69, 77, 78, 79, 82, 84, 88, 92,
    94, 102, 160
Pedro, Cimaroon leader, 84, 87, 89, 92
Pelican, 101, 104, 108, 109, 111, 112;
    renamed Golden Hind, 117
Philip II of Spain, 8, 19, 20, 22, 25, 26,
    30, 38, 39, 45, 51, 63, 66, 95, 147,
    161, 165, 167, 169, 176, 179, 182,
    183, 185, 220, 226, 231, 232, 233,

Philip II of Spain—*cont.*
243; seizure of English merchant ships, 154-5, 158; his place in history, 170-4; and building of Escorial, 173; and the Armada or Grand Enterprise, 187, 190, 192, 195, 198, 223, 224
Philips, Miles, 59
Pike, Robert, 86, 87
Pita, Maria, 227
Plymouth, 17, 44, 61, 93, 94, 143, 146, 155, 169, 187, 189, 197, 198, 204-5, 225; local politics of, 152, 233-4
Port Pheasant, 67, 70, 80
Port St. Julian, 110-11
Portugal, 146
Potosi mines, 127
Primrose, 154, 156
Prince, *Worthies of Devon*, 69

Rainbow, 176
Raleigh, Sir Walter, 8, 18, 138, 187, 237
Rance, James, 70, 71, 76, 96
Rata Coronada (Spanish), 203
Recalde, Juan Martinez de, 202, 203, 204, 210, 211, 212, 216, 218
Regazona (Spanish), 203
Regiomontanus, 189
Revenge, 192, 203, 206, 207, 211, 217, 223, 229, 230, 236
Rio de la Hacha, 38-9, 50-1, 65, 164, 240
Russell, Francis, 26
Russell, Lord, 25, 27, 29, 98

Sagres, 180-1, 182, 185
St. Bartholomew's Day, 89
Sampford Spinney, 152
San Domingo in Hispaniola, 161-4, 165, 227, 230
San Felipe (Spanish), 183-4
San Juan (Spanish), 204, 210, 216
San Juan de Ulua, 19, 41, 53-60, 62-4, 65, 76, 96, 115, 122, 132, 187
San Juan in Puerto Rico, 20, 23, 25, 50, 239-40
San Lorenzo (Spanish), 215, 216
San Martin (Spanish), 201, 202, 210, 211, 217, 218, 219
San Mateo (Portuguese), 212
San Salvador (Spanish), 206, 209
Santa Cruz, Alvaro de Bazan, 1st Marquis of, 175, 179, 182, 187-91, 196, 211

Santander, 225
Santiago, 160
Sao Paolo (Spanish), 236
Seymour, Lord Henry, 204, 214, 215
Shakespeare, William, 109, 124
Sherford, manor of, 151, 152, 238
Sidney, Sir Philip, 158, 226
Sierra Leone, 144
Silva, Diego Guzman de, 42, 44
Silva, Nuño da, 103, 109, 112, 132, 134
Sitwell, Sir Osbert, 49
Sixtus V, Pope, 100
Slave trade, 32, 38-41, 48-9, 163
Southey, Robert, 227
Spain, English relations with, 42-5, 63-4, 95, 99, 113, 146, 150, 153-5, 156, 176, 185, 232; *see also* Armada
Spanish colonialism, 35, 36, 38
Speed, John, 208
Spice Islands, 141
Stow, John, 7, 25, 33, 96
Swallow, 45, 57
Swan, 62, 65, 66, 69, 77-8, 94, 101, 102, 108, 109, 110, 160
Swiftsure, 226
Sydenham, Elizabeth, *see* Drake, Elizabeth
Sydenham, Sir George, 152

Teresa, St., 170-1
Terra Australis, 99, 101, 120, 121
Thomas, 214
Thomas, John, 101, 116, 120
Throckmorton Plot, 154
Tristão, Nuno, 47
Triumph, 204, 210, 217
Tuscany, Duke of, 212

Ubaldini, Petruccio, 192, 205, 224
Unwin, Rayner, 56

Valdez, Pedro de, 208
Valparaiso, 124-5
Venta Cruz, 86-8, 89, 241
Vespucci, Amerigo, 103
Vicary, Leonard, 112
Victory, 203, 217
Villanueva, Agustin de, 56
Virginia, 162, 168

Wachen, Admiral de, 45
Walsingham, Sir Francis, 98, 99, 100, 101, 150, 182, 184, 192, 203, 219, 222, 227, 232
William, Prince of Orange, 154

William and John, 45, 57
Williams, Sir Roger, 228
Williamson, J. A., 39, 96, 156, 213
Winter, Edward, 156
Winter, George, 98
Winter, John, 101, 113, 116, 120-2, 130, 146, 152, 218
Winter, Robert, 111

Winter, William, 98
Wyatt, Sir Thomas, 30

Yarcombe estate, 151, 152, 238
Yellow fever, 83

Zarate, Francisco de, 36, 132, 133, 134

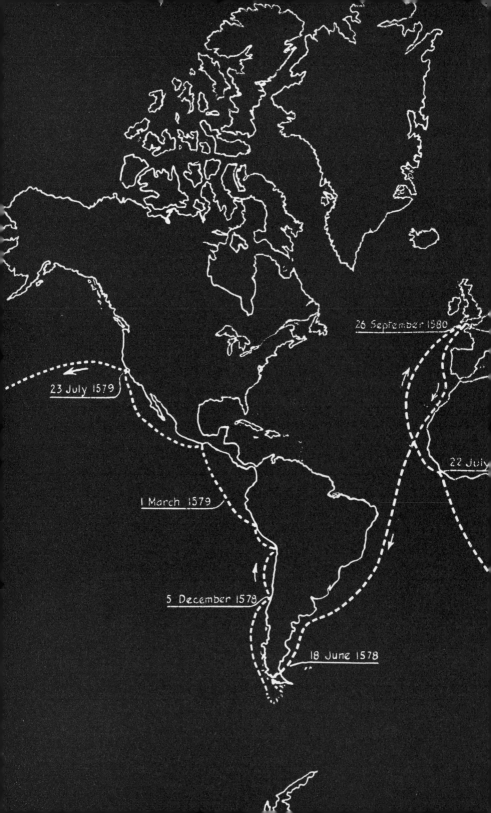

26 September 1580

23 July 1579

22 July

1 March 1579

5 December 1578

18 June 1578